SRI AUROBINDO

OR

THE ADVENTURE OF CONSCIOUSNESS

Sri Aurobindo

or
The
Adventure
of
Consciousness

Satprem

Translated from the French by Tehmi

First Indian Edition: 1968
Reprinted: 1970, 1973, 1975, 1977, 1982, 1987, 1991, 1995

ISBN 81-7058-081-1

© Sri Aurobindo Ashram Trust 1968
Published by Sri Aurobindo Ashram Publication Department
Printed at Sri Aurobindo Ashram Press, Pondicherry
PRINTED IN INDIA

DEDICATED

TO

THE MOTHER

In this our century, so hurried, incoherent, full of riches which dominate us more than they serve, we have need of a true mastery, of that joy which comes of this mastery. But our psychology knows yet only the surfaces of being and our imported orientalisms illumine some obscure depths which may perhaps be all right for the cross-legged sage, but not for the beleagured men we are.

This book has been written from a Western point of view and for those who yearn for a truth of Life and not only a truth with eyes closed. It presents just one aspect of Sri Aurobindo, the most practical one. We only hope it will lead the reader to explore for himself Sri Aurobindo and perhaps, with him, to find the perfect harmony of East and West, of inner freedom and outer mastery.

PREFACE

TO

THE THIRD EDITION

The age of adventures is over. Even if we go to the seventh galaxy we shall go there masked and mechanized, and we shall find ourselves once again such as we are: children in front of death, living beings who do not know very well how they live or why or where they are going. And on earth, we know quite well that the times of Cortez and Pizarro are gone: the same Machine locks us in, the rat-trap snaps shut. But, as always, it is found that our gloomiest adversities are our best opportunities and that the dark passage is a passage only, leading us to a greater light. We are hence pushed to the wall before the last ground that remains for us to explore, the final adventure: ourselves.

And the signs abound, they are simple and evident. The most important phenomenon of this decade is not the trip to the moon but the "trips" of the drug and the great transhumance of the hippies and the effervescence of the students across the world — and where are they to go? There is no longer any space on the swarming beaches, no space on the crushing roads, no space in the growing termitaries of our cities. We must open out elsewhere.

But there are all kinds of "elsewheres". Those of drugs are uncertain and sown with danger, and above all they *depend* upon outer means — an experience ought to be obtainable at will and no matter where, in the middle of the market-place as in the solitude of our room, else it is not an experience but an anomaly or a bondage. Those of psychoanalysis are limited, for the moment, to some ill-lit cellars, and chiefly they lack that lever of consciousness which allows one to go where one wants, as master and not as impotent witness or sickly victim. Those of religion are more illumined, but they too depend on a god or a dogma, and above all, they shut us up in *one* type of experience, for one can as well, and more so, be a prisoner of other worlds as of this one. And finally, the value of an experience is gauged by its power of transforming life, else we are before a vain dream or a hallucination.

Now, Sri Aurobindo shows us how to make a double discovery of which we are in urgent need if we want not only to give an outlet to our stifling chaos but to transform our world. For, following step by step with him his prodigious exploration — his technique of inner spaces, if one may venture to put it thus — we are led to the greatest discovery of all times, to the door of the Great Secret which must change the face of the world, namely, that *consciousness is a power*. Befogged as we are by the "inevitable" scientific condition wherein we are born, it would seem that the only hope man has is in an ever larger proliferation of his machines, which will see better than he can, hear better than he, calculate better than he, heal better than he — and finally perhaps live better than he. It is a matter of knowing that we can do better than our machines and that this enormous Mechanism which stifles us can collapse as fast as it was born, if only we would touch the lever of the true power and descend into our own heart as methodical, rigorous and clear-sighted explorers.

Then we shall discover, perhaps, that our splendid 20th century was still at the Stone Age of psychology, and that with all our science we had not yet entered into the true Science of Living or the mastery of the world and of ourselves, and that before us are opening horizons of perfection and harmony and beauty, beside which our superb inventions are like the rough sketches of a novice.

SATPREM

Pondicherry, January 27, 1970

TABLE OF CONTENTS

*I become what I see in myself. All
that thought suggests to me, I can do ;
all that thought reveals in me, I can
become. This should be man's unshakable faith in himself, because
God dwells in him.*[1]

INTRODUCTION

There was once a wicked Maharaja who could not bear
to think that anyone was his superior. So he summoned
all the pandits of the realm as was the practice on momen-
tous occasions and put to them this question: "Which of
us two is the greater, I or God?" And the pandits shook
with fear. Being wise by profession they asked for time,
and then through old habit they clung to their position
and their lives. But they were worthy men who would
not displease God; they were therefore deep in grief,
when the oldest pandit reassured them: "Leave it to me,
tomorrow I shall speak with the Prince." The next day
the whole court was gathered in a solemn *durbar* when
the old man quietly arrived, his hands humbly joined
together, his forehead smeared with white ashes; he
bowed low and pronounced these words: "O Lord, undoubtedly, thou art the greater," — the Prince twirled
thrice his moustaches which he wore long and tossed
high his head — "Thou art the greater, King, for thou
canst banish us from thy kingdom whilst God cannot:
for verily, all is His kingdom and there is nowhere to go
outside Him."

This Indian tale which comes from Bengal where
Sri Aurobindo was born, was surely not unknown to him
who said that all is He: gods, devils, men, the earth and
not the heavens alone, — and whose entire experience
leads to a divine rehabilitation of Matter. For the last
fifty years psychology has been ceaselessly trying to rein-
state the demons in man; it is possible, as André Malraux
believed, that the task of the next half century will be
"to reintegrate in him the gods", or rather, as Sri
Aurobindo wanted, to reintegrate the Spirit in man and in
Matter — a spiritual squarefield — and to create "the
life divine on the earth": *The heavens beyond are great and
wonderful, but greater yet and more wonderful are the heavens
within you. It is these Edens that await the divine worker.*[2]

There is many a way of setting to work; in fact each
one of us has his particular opening: for one it may be a
well-wrought piece of metal, a duty well done, for another
a beautiful idea, a harmonious philosophical system; for
others still it may be a page of music, a river, a shaft of
sunlight on the sea — and all are ways of breathing in the
Infinite. But these are brief moments and we want permanence. These are elusive minutes subject to imperceptible conditions and we would have something that is
lasting, something which does not depend on condition or
circumstance — a window within us which shall never
close again.

And as these conditions are quite difficult to obtain
on earth, we speak of "God", of "Spirituality", of Christ
and of Buddha and all the lineage of those who have
founded the great religions; and all these are ways of
finding permanence. But we perhaps are not religious
men nor spiritual men, we are just men, we believe in
the earth; we are suspicious of big words, we are tired

of dogmas; we are perhaps weary also of too much fine thinking — we want only our own little river that flows into the Infinite. There was a great saint in India who, for years and years, before he had found true peace, used to ask whomever he met: "Have you seen God?... Have you seen God?" and he would go away disappointed and angry because people told him fantastic stories. He wanted to see. He was not wrong, considering the amount of falsehood men have piled behind this word as behind so many others. When we have seen, we shall speak about it, or probably we shall be silent. No, we do not want to dupe ourselves with words, we want to start with what we have, just here where we are, with our wooden shoes and the clay which sticks to them and also with our little sunbeam in the knapsack of fair days, because this is our simple faith. And then, we see that the earth as it is is not too wonderful, we would have it change, but we have become sceptical also of universal panaceas and of movements, of parties, of theories. We take our road at zero point, that is, begin with ourselves; it is not much, but this is all we have, and it is this little bit of the world we are going to try to change before attempting to save the other. And perhaps this is not so foolish after all, for who knows whether to change the one is not the most efficacious means of changing the other?

What can Sri Aurobindo do for us at this low altitude?

There is Sri Aurobindo the philosopher, Sri Aurobindo the poet, the visionary of evolution, but everybody is not a philosopher nor a poet and much less a seer. But if he should give us a means of believing in our own possibilities, not only in our human but in our superhuman and divine possibilities, and not only of believing in them but of discovering them ourselves, step by step, and of *seeing*,

and of becoming wide, wide as the earth which we love and
as all the lands and all the seas which are within us, perhaps we would be satisfied? For there is Sri Aurobindo the
explorer — who was also a yogi, but has he not said
Yoga is the art of conscious self-finding?[3] It is this exploration of consciousness we are going to undertake with him
and, if we proceed calmly, patiently, with sincerity, facing
bravely all the difficulties of the ground — and God
knows it is rocky enough — there is no reason why one
day a window should not open irradiating us for ever.
Truly speaking it is not one but several windows which
open turn by turn, each time on a wider vista, a new
dimension of our kingdom, and each time it is a change of
consciousness, as radical as can be, for instance, the passage from sleep to waking. We are going to follow now
the principal stages of these changes of consciousness as
Sri Aurobindo has experienced them and described them
to his disciples in his *integral yoga* — right up to the point
where they lead us to the threshold of a new, still unknown
experience which perhaps will have the power of changing
life itself.

For Sri Aurobindo is not only the explorer of consciousness, he is the builder of a new world. And what is the
good of changing one's own consciousness if the world
around remains what it is? We are in danger of imitating
Anderson's Emperor who walked naked through the
streets of his city. So, after having gone over the last
frontiers of worlds not unknown to ancient wisdom,
Sri Aurobindo discovered another world not found on
any map, which he called the *Supermind* and which he
wanted to draw down to the earth. He invites us to pull a
little with him and to take our part in this beautiful
story if, however, we like stories. For the Supermind,

Sri Aurobindo tells us, brings a decisive change in the evolution of the earth-consciousness which will have the power to transform our material world and to transform it as thoroughly and as lastingly, and for the better, as the mind did when it appeared for the first time in Matter. We shall see then how the integral yoga opens on a *supramental yoga* or the yoga of terrestrial transformation which we shall try to sketch briefly — sketch only, for the story is still in the making, it is quite new and difficult and we do not yet know very well where it will lead us or even if it will succeed.

Actually, this depends a little on us all.

CHAPTER ONE

AN ACCOMPLISHED WESTERNER

As a man Sri Aurobindo is close to us, for after all, when we have respectfully bowed before the "wisdom of Asia" and the queer ascetics who seem to make light of our good laws, we find that our curiosity has been touched, but not our life and that we still need a practical truth which would hold out under our harassing winters. Now, Sri Aurobindo knew well our winters, he had lived through them all his formative years, from the age of seven till he was twenty. He had moved from one lodging-house to another at the sweet will of more or less benevolent landladies, satisfied with one meal a day and not having even an overcoat to throw on his back, but always loaded with books: the French symbolists, Mallarmé, Rimbaud whom he read in the original long before reading the Bhagavad-Gita in translation. Sri Aurobindo represents for us a unique synthesis.

He was born in Calcutta on the 15th August, 1872, the year of Rimbaud's *Illuminations*; already, modern physics had been born with Max Planck; Einstein was a few years younger and Jules Verne was probing the future. Queen Victoria was getting ready to proclaim herself empress of India, the conquest of Africa was not over — we are at the hinge of two worlds. We have often the impression in history that periods of trial and of destruction precede the birth of a new world, but this is perhaps a mistake, perhaps it is because the new seeds are already sown that the forces of subversion (or of clearance?) are infuriated. Whatever it be, Europe was at the peak of its glory; the game was being played in the West. This was how the situation struck Sri Aurobindo's father, Dr. Krishnadhan Ghose, who had studied medicine in England and had come back completely anglicized. He did not intend his sons — he had three, of whom Sri Aurobindo was the youngest — to be in the least contaminated by the "smoky and retrograde" mysticism in which his country was running to waste. He did not even want them to know anything of the traditions and the languages of India. Sri Aurobindo was therefore provided not only with an English first name, Akroyd, but also with an English governess, Miss Pagett, then sent off hastily at the age of five to an Irish nun's school in Darjeeling, with the sons of the British administrators. Two years later the three Ghose boys left for England. Sri Aurobindo was seven. He had to wait till he was twenty to learn his mother-tongue, Bengali; he did not see his father again for he died just before his son's return to India, and he hardly met his mother, who in her illness did not recognise him. We are in the presence of a child who grew up altogether independent of every influence of family, nation and tradition — a free genius. The first lesson that Sri Aurobindo gives us is perhaps just this lesson of liberty.

Sri Aurobindo and his two brothers were placed in the care of an Anglican clergyman of Manchester, *with strict instructions that they should not be allowed to make the acquaintance of any Indian or undergo any Indian influence.*[1] Surely this Dr. Ghose must have been a very strange man. He also ordered Pastor Drewett not to give his sons any religious instruction so that they could choose for themselves their religion if they wanted one when they came of age. Then he left them to their fate for thirteen years. One would think that Dr. Ghose had a hard heart; nothing of the kind; he gave not only his medical care but his money to the poor Bengali villagers (whilst his sons had hardly anything to eat or to wear in London) and he died of shock when he heard the false news that his favourite son, Aurobindo, had been drowned. But he believed that his children should be men of character.

The first few years at Manchester were of some importance for Sri Aurobindo, for he learnt there French (*English was of course his "mother-tongue"*) and discovered by it a spontaneous affinity for France; at the end of his long years in England he was to say: *There was an attachment to English and European thought and literature, but not to England as a country; I had no ties there.... If there was attachment to a European land as a second country, it was intellectually and emotionally to one not seen or lived in in this life, not England, but France.*[2] And then the poet was awake in him; he was listening already to *the footsteps of invisible things* of which he speaks in one of his earliest poems; already his inner window was open, although religion had hardly touched him if one were to judge from the account he gives of his "conversion". The mother of clergyman Drewett had in fact undertaken to save the soul of these heretics or at least of the youngest one, whom she dragged along with her one day to a meeting of non-conformist ministers. *After the prayers were over*, says Sri Aurobindo, *all nearly dispersed but devout people remained a little longer and it was at that time that conversions were made. I was feeling completely bored. Then a minister approached me and asked me some questions. (I was about ten at that time). I did not give any reply. Then they all shouted, 'He is saved, he is saved', and began to pray for me and offer thanks to God.*[3] Sri Aurobindo, the seer, was never a religious man — not any more in India than in the West — and he has very often taken care to point out that religion and spirituality are not necessarily synonymous: *True theocracy,* he was to write later, *is the kingdom of God in man and not the kingdom of a Pope, a priesthood or a sacerdotal class.*[4]

When he went to London Sri Aurobindo was twelve; he was already well-grounded in Latin and French. The headmaster of St. Paul's School which he joined was so surprised at the ability of his student that he himself coached him in Greek. In the last three years Sri Aurobindo could almost skip half the school course and spend most of his spare time in his favourite occupation, reading. Nothing seemed to escape this voracious adolescent (except perhaps games which decidedly interested him as little as Sunday School); but Shelley and "Prometheus Unbound", the French poets, Homer, Aristophanes and soon the whole of European thought — for he quickly came to know enough German and Italian to read Dante and Goethe in the original — peopled a solitude of which he has told us nothing. He never bothered to make acquaintances, whilst Manmohan, the second brother, roamed through London in the company of Oscar Wilde and was to distinguish himself in English poetry. In fact the three brothers lived each one in his own way. Sri Aurobindo, however, had nothing of the austere young man about him, still less of the puritan (*the prurient*[5] as he said), it was just that he was "elsewhere" and his world was full. He had even a way of jesting with a serious face which never left him: *Sense of humour? It is the salt of existence. Without it the world would have got utterly out of balance — it is unbalanced enough already — and rushed to blazes long ago.*[6] For there is Sri Aurobindo, the humorist, and this Sri Aurobindo is perhaps more important than the philosopher of whom the Western universities speak so

solemnly; philosophy for Sri Aurobindo was only one
means of explaining things to a certain class of men who
understand nothing without an explanation; it was but
one language, as poetry for him was another language,
more clear, more true; but humour was the very essence
of his being; not the frivolous banter of the so-called wit,
but a sort of joy which cannot help dancing wherever it
goes. Sometimes we intuit, like a flash of lightning which
leaves us a little bedazzled, behind the most tragic, the
most pitiful human conditions, a laughter almost mocking,
as of a child who plays a tragedy and suddenly makes a
face to himself because it is his vocation to laugh, and
because ultimately nothing in the world, nobody, can
touch this hidden corner where one is king for ever. Perhaps this is the true quality of the Aurobindonian humour,
a refusal of drama, but much more the feeling of an inde-
feasible royalty.

Whether St. Paul's School appreciated his humour
or not we do not know, but it certainly valued his astonishing learning; he was granted a scholarship which
enabled him to go on to Cambridge (since long the family
remittances had practically disappeared) but this was too
little to relieve him from cold and hunger, for the older
brothers partook solidly of the windfall. What was he
going to do then in this nursery of gentlemen? He was
now eighteen. Undoubtedly he obeyed the wishes of his
father. But not for long. In his first year at King's College
he took away all the prizes for Greek and Latin verse, but
his heart was no longer there. It was Joan of Arc, the
American Revolution, Mazzini, that haunted him, —
in fact, the liberation of his country, the independence of
India of which he was to be one of the pioneers. This
unforeseen political calling was to hold him for almost

twenty years, and yet then he did not even know exactly who an Indian was, much less a Hindu! But he was to make up this lack quickly; of Hinduism as of occidentalism he knew how to take double mouthfuls and digest them; for the rest, he would be truly Sri Aurobindo only when he had digested both and found the point where the two worlds meet in something which is neither of them nor even a synthesis, but what we may call with the Mother, the continuer of Sri Aurobindo's work, a *third position*, a "something else" which we acutely need, we who are neither narrow materialists nor exclusive spiritualists.

He became the secretary of the "Indian Majlis", an association of Indian students at Cambridge, delivered many revolutionary speeches, cast off his English first name, joined a secret society, the "Lotus and Dagger" if you please! (but romanticism can also lead to the gallows!) and finally became a marked man and was put on the black list of Whitehall. This did not prevent him from taking the First Part of the Classical Tripos, then, the examination once passed, from rejecting the graduation degree as though this was quite enough. In the same casual way he appeared for the famous I.C.S. which would have opened to him the doors of the government of India and drawn him close to the British administrators; he did brilliantly, then neglected to present himself for the Riding Test — he went for a walk that day instead of trotting at Woolwich — and got himself disqualified. This time the Senior Tutor of Cambridge was moved and wrote to the authorities, "That a man of this calibre should be lost to the Indian government merely because he failed in sitting on a horse or did not keep an appointment appears to me, I confess, a piece of official shortsightedness which it would be hard to beat.... He has had a very hard and anxious time of it for the last two years. Supplies from home have almost entirely failed, and he has had to keep his two brothers as well as himself.... I have several times written to his father on his behalf, but for the most part unsuccessfully. It is only lately that I managed to extract from him enough to pay some trades-men who would otherwise have put his son into the County Court..."[7] The pleading of the Tutor had no effect. The Colonial Office had made up its mind, Sri Aurobindo was a dangerous proposition. They were not wrong.

When he sailed for India Sri Aurobindo was twenty. His father had just died. He had no position, no quali-fications. What had remained with him of those fourteen years in the West? We are tempted to recall the felicitous definition of Édouard Herriot, for, if it is true that culture is what remains when everything is forgotten, what re-mains of the West after one has left it is not its books or its museums or its theatres but a need to translate into living acts what one has conceived. In this, undoubtedly, lies the true strength of the West. Unfortunately, we are too intellectual to have much of a vision to translate into out-ward action, while India, too full within, has not enough urgency to match what she sees with what she lives. This lesson was not to be lost upon Sri Aurobindo.

CHAPTER TWO

THE ETERNAL LAW

The proletariat among us is sunk in ignorance and overwhelmed with distress![1] exclaimed Sri Aurobindo soon after landing in India. It was not metaphysical problems which troubled him but a problem of action. To act, we are in the world to act; what action should be ours and, above all, what its most efficacious method still remain to be known. This practical point of view was to be Sri Aurobindo's from his very first days in India right up to his highest yogic realisations. I remember, pardon me the digression, going to the Himalayas and living there for a few privileged days in the company of a wise man, among the pines and oleanders, with all around the sparkling snows between the sky and the valley. All this was very well and I said to myself that it was easy to have divine thoughts, perhaps even visions, at this height of the world, but down below? I was not quite wrong, though I learnt later that one can *act* and do much for the world in the silence and stillness of the body—a clinging illusion makes us identify agitation with action — but still, what remains of those divine moments once we are stripped of our solitude and drawn down to the plains? Here is a mirage which the enthusiasts of Hinduism in the West would do well to consider, for, after all, if it is escape from the world which attracts us, a little corner in the Alps or of the moors can do the job as well or even a tiny cell with white-washed walls—the "pilgrimage to the source"* cares little for the Ganges or the Brahmaputra. What

* Note: Title of a French book on Hinduism by Lanza del Vasto.

was India to give to Sri Aurobindo? and does she hold
any secret which is valuable for action in life?

To go by the books which speak of Hinduism would
be a sort of spiritual palaeontology interspersed with
Sanskrit polysyllables, as though the Indian were an
enigmatic philosopher plus an impenitent idolater. But if
we look at India clearly, from within, without the pre-
tension of cutting it up into paragraphs of Hinduism (always false, for we risk being like the traveller who went
round Delhi in May and found India violently hot, but
who, if he had gone to the south or east in November or
in March and in all directions, would have seen that India
is at once cold, boiling, sodden, desert-like, Mediterranean
and lovely; that she is a world as indefinable as her
"Hinduism", which in fact does not exist, for Hinduism
is not a belief or a spiritual longitude, one cannot take the
bearings there; it has all possible bearings) we discover
that India is a country of a vast spiritual liberty. The
so-called "Hinduism" is an invention of the West; the
Indian speaks only of "the eternal law", *sanatana dharma*,
which he knows is not an Indian monopoly but is also for
the Musulman, the Negro, the Christian and even the
Anabaptist. That which seems to be the most important
part of a religion for the Westerner, the structure which
distinguishes it from all other religions and which says that
man is not a Catholic or a Protestant unless he thinks in
this way or in this other and subscribes to such and such
an article of faith, is the least important part for the
Indian, who instinctively seeks to remove all outward
differences in order to find the whole world at a central
point where all things communicate.

This largeness is something very different from "tole-
rance" which is only the negative inverse of intolerance;

this is the positive understanding that every man has an inner need, which he may call "God" or by any other name, and that every man must needs love what he *understands* of God, at his own level and the particular stage of his inner development, and that the way of Paul is not that of John — that all the world could love a crucified God, for example, seems unnatural to the average Indian, who will bow reverently before Christ (with as much spontaneous respect as before his own image of God) but who will understand that the face of God is also in the laughter of *Krishna*, the terror of *Kali*, the sweetness of *Saraswati*, and in the thousands and thousands of others who dance, multi-coloured and moustached and gay and redoubtable, illumined, compassionate, on the deliriously carved temple-towers — *A God who cannot smile could not have created this humorous universe*,[2] said Sri Aurobindo, — and that all is His face, all is His play, terrible and beautiful, baroque like our world itself. For, this country so teeming with gods is also and at the same time the country of a monolithic faith in Oneness: "One, He presides over all wombs and natures; Himself the womb of all" (Swetaswatara Upanishad V.5). But everybody cannot jump at once into the Absolute, there are many degrees in the scale of Ascension and one who is ready to understand a little *Lalita* with the face of a child and to bring to her his incense and his flowers, would not perhaps be able to speak to the Eternal Mother in the silence of his heart; and another will throw aside all forms to plunge into the contemplation of That which is formless. "Even as men come to Me, so I accept them. It is my path that men follow from all sides," says the Gita* (IV, 11). As we see, there

---

* All quotations from the Upanishads, the Vedas, the Gita in this book are from Sri Aurobindo's translations.

are so many ways of knowing God, in three persons or in a thousand, that it would be well not to dogmatise, for fear of chopping and chopping and finally leaving nothing behind but a Cartesian God, one and universal by the very force of his narrowness. Perhaps we still confuse unity with uniformity. It was in the spirit of this tradition that Sri Aurobindo was soon to write: *The perfection of the integral Yoga will come when each man is able to follow his own path of Yoga, pursuing the development of his own nature in its upsurging towards that which transcends the nature. For freedom is the final law and the last consummation.*[3]

The Indian too never says "Do you believe in God?" The question seems to him as puerile as to ask "Do you believe in CO_2?" He says simply *"Make the experiment;* if you do this, you will have this result, and if you do that other, you will have another." All the ingenuity, the skill, the precision that we have expended for the last century or two in the study of physical phenomena, the Indian has brought, with an equal exactitude, for four or five millenniums, to the examination of inner phenomena — for a "dreaming" people, they have many a surprise in store for us. And if we have a little honesty, we are quickly made to see that our "inner" studies, that is to say, our psychology, our psychoanalysis, our knowledge of man are yet like the babbling of an infant, for the simple reason that self-knowledge demands an askesis, as methodical, as patient and sometimes as fastidious as the long years of introduction to nuclear physics; if one wants to go further on this path, it is not sufficient to read books nor even to collect clinical cards and all the neuroses of a decentred century, it is necessary *to give oneself completely.* Truly speaking, if we bring as much sincerity, minute application and perseverance to the study of our inner self as we do to our books, we shall go fast and far — the West also has surprises for us. Yet it must get rid of its preconceived ideas — Columbus did not make the map of America before leaving Palos! These childish truths perhaps bear repetition, for we seem to be caught between two falsehoods: the too serious falsehood of the spiritualists who have already settled the affair of God in a certain number of infallible paragraphs and the not serious enough falsehood of the rudimentary occultists and clairvoyants who have reduced the invisible to a sort of imaginative profligacy. India wisely sends us back to the direct experience and to the methods of experience. Sri Aurobindo was soon to put into practice this fundamental lesson of experimental spirituality.

But what kind of men, what human material was he going to find in this India which he did not know? When we have put aside the exotic colourfulness and (for us) the bizarre customs which amuse and disconcert the tourist, there remains, in spite of everything, something strange, and if we say that they are a gentle, dreamy, fatalistic people, detached from the world, we shall have described the effect, not the cause. "Strange" is the word, for spontaneously, in his very physical substance, unaffected by the faintest "idea" or even the least "faith", the Indian plunges his roots into other worlds; he does not altogether belong here. And these other worlds crop up constantly in him — *at the least touch the veil is rent*, remarks Sri Aurobindo — to such an extent that this physical world, for us so absolute, so real, so unique, seems for him but one way of living among many other ways, one modality of the total existence among many others; in short, a little frontier, chaotic, agitated, painful, on *the margin of immense continents which lie behind unexplored.*[4] This difference of

texture between the Indian and the other peoples appears
most strikingly in his art, as it does also in Egyptian art
(and, we suppose without knowing it, in the art of Central
America); for if we leave behind our cathedrals, light,
open, soaring like a triumph of the divine thought of man,
and if brusquely, in the silence of Abydos on the Nile, we
find ourselves in the presence of *Sekmeth,* or behind the peri-
style of Dakshineshwar, face to face with *Kali,* we feel
clearly something — we stand gaping suddenly before an
unknown dimension, a "something" which leaves us a
little stunned and which is absolutely not there in all our
Western art. There are no secrets in our cathedrals! everything is there, neat and proper, open to the four winds for
whoever has outer eyes — yet, there are many secrets....
There is no question here of comparison — it would be
quite absurd! — but of saying simply that we have *forgotten* something. How is it that it has not struck us, in
spite of everything, that if so many civilisations, which
were as glorious and refined as ours — let us have the
modesty to admit it — and whose élite was not less
"intelligent" than that of our Sorbonnes, have had the
vision and the experience of hierarchies invisible (for us)
and of great psychic rhythms which exceed the brief
pulsation of a single human life, it was not perhaps a mental aberration — strange aberration which is found thousands of leagues apart in civilisations utterly unknown
to one another — nor a superstition of fanciful old ladies.
We have swept away the age of the Mysteries, that is
understood, everything is admirably Cartesian, but
something is missing. The first sign of the new man is
probably that he awakens to a terrible lack of something
which neither his science nor his Churches nor his flashy
pleasures can give him. One cannot amputate with

impunity man from his secrets. Here too is a living testimony that India brought to Sri Aurobindo, unless he knew it already in his own being.

However, if we suppose that India where ancient Mysteries presumably survive, will give us the practical solution we seek, we risk being disappointed. Sri Aurobindo, who quickly learnt to appreciate the liberty, the spiritual amplitude and the immense experimental endeavour which India reveals to the seeker, was not to let himself be won over in everything, far from it; not that there is anything to reject, there is nothing to reject anywhere, neither in the so-called Hinduism any more than in Christianity or in any other aspiration of man, but there is everything to widen, to widen endlessly. What we take to be the ultimate Truth is very often only a partial experience of the Truth — and undoubtedly the totality of the Experience does not exist anywhere in time or space, in no place, in no being however luminous, for the Truth is infinite, it always goes ahead. *But always man takes upon his shoulders an interminable burden,* said the Mother one day in a talk on Buddhism. *He does not want to drop anything of the past and he stoops more and more under the weight of a useless accumulation. You have a guide for a part of the way, but when you have travelled this bit, leave the road and the guide and go farther. This is a thing men do with difficulty; when they get hold of something which helps them, they cling to it, they do not want to budge from there. Those who have progressed with the help of Christianity do not want to give it up and they carry it upon their shoulders, those who have progressed with the help of Buddhism do not want to leave it and they carry it upon their shoulders, and the journey is clogged and you are indefinitely delayed. Once you have passed the stage let it drop, let it go! Go farther!* The eternal law, yes, but eternally young and

eternally progressive. Now India, which could also understand the eternal Iconoclast that God is in his cosmic
march, did not always have the strength to support her
own wisdom; the *immense invisible* which pervades this
country took from it a double ransom, both human and
spiritual: human, because these men saturated with the
beyond, aware of the great cosmic Game and the inner
dimensions where our little surface life is reduced to a point
periodically flowering and swiftly swallowed up, ended by
neglecting the world — inertia, indifference to progress,
resignation quite often put on there the mask of wisdom;
spiritual also (this one much more serious), because in
this immensity too great for our little present consciousness,
the destiny of the earth, our earth, ended by losing itself
somewhere on the confines of the nebulae, or nowhere,
reabsorbed in Brahman, from whom after all it had perhaps never emerged except in our dreams — the illusionism, the trances, the closed eyes of the yogi, there also put
on quite often the mask of God. It would be well therefore to define a little clearly the general goal which religious India has in view and we shall see better what she
can or cannot do for us who seek an integral truth.

Let us admit straightaway that we find ourselves
before a very surprising contradiction. Here is a country,
in fact, which has brought a great revelation: "All is
Brahman", it says, all is the Spirit, this world also is the
Spirit, this earth, this life, these men — nothing is outside Him. "All this is Brahman immortal, naught else;
Brahman is in front of us, Brahman behind us, and to the
south of us and to the north of us and below us and above
us; It stretches everywhere. All this is Brahman alone, all
this magnificent universe" (Mundaka Upanishad II, 12);
the dichotomy is then healed, at last, which tugs this poor

world to God and to the Devil, as though it were always necessary to choose between the heavens and the earth and never be saved except when mutilated. And yet, *in practice*, for three millenniums, the entire religious history of India has conducted itself as though there were a true Brahman, transcendent, immobile, for ever beyond this bedlam, and a false Brahman or at least (it is here that the schools are divided) a minor Brahman with an intermediate reality more or less debatable — that is, life, the earth, our poor scullion of an earth. "Abandon this world of illusion," cried out the great Shankara.* "Brahman is real, the world is a lie," says the Nirlamba Upanishad: *brahmasatyam jaganmithya.* In spite of all our good will, we confess the inability to understand by what deformation or what forgetfulness the "all is Brahman" became "all, except the world, is Brahman".

If we put aside the Scriptures, for the human mind is so sagacious that it can easily see sheep graze on an obelisk, and if we examine the practical disciplines of India, the contradiction becomes yet more flagrant. Indian psychology, in fact, is founded upon a very shrewd observation, that all things in the universe, from mineral to man, are constituted of three elements or qualities (*gunas*) which are found everywhere, although they may be qualified a little differently according to the order of reality considered: *tamas*, inertia, obscurity, inconscience; *rajas*, movement, struggle, effort, passion, action; *sattva*, light, harmony, joy. Nowhere do these three elements exist in a pure state; we are always caught between inertia, passion and light; sometimes sattvo-tamasic, good but a bit dull, well-meaning but sufficiently inconscient; or sattvo-raja-

* Shankara (788-820), mystic and poet, theorist of *Mayavada* or the doctrine of illusionism which supplanted Buddhism in India.

sic impassioned upwards; or tamaso-rajasic, impassioned downwards; and most often an excellent mixture of the three. In the darkest *tamas* the light also shines—but unhappily the inverse is equally true. Indeed we are always in an unstable equilibrium; the warrior, the ascetic and the brute share comfortably our home in varying proportions. The several Indian disciplines seek therefore to re-establish the balance: to come out of the play of the three *gunas* which toss us endlessly from light to darkness, from enthusiasm to exhaustion and from a grey indifference to our fugitive joys and our repeated sufferings, and to take a stand above, that is, to find the divine consciousness (*yoga*) which is the state of perfect equilibrium. To this end they all direct their effort, to bring us out of the state of dispersion and wastage in which we live and to create in us a concentration sufficiently powerful to break ordinary limits and in time to tip us over into another state. This work of concentration can be carried out at any level of our being — physical, vital, mental. According to the level chosen, then, we practise such or such a yoga: *hatha-yoga, raja-yoga, mantra-yoga*, and many more, innumerably more, which land-mark the story of our effort. It is not necessary to discuss here the excellence of these methods or the very interesting intermediate results to which they can lead, we are preoccupied only with their goal, their final destination. Now, this "standing above" seems to have no connection with life, first of all because these disciplines, extremely binding, exact hours of work every day, if not complete solitude; then because the criterion of success is a state of trance or of yogic ecstasy, *samadhi*, perfect equilibrium, ineffable beatitude, in which the consciousness of the world is swept away, engulfed — Brahman, the

Spirit, decidedly has no contact with our ordinary waking consciousness; He is outside all that we know, He is not of this world. Others have said this, who were not Indians.

In fact, all the religions of the world have said it. And whether one speaks here of "salvation" or down there of "liberation", *mukti*, whether one speaks of "paradise" or the cessation of the round of rebirths makes no difference, if finally it is a question of coming out of it. However, it was not always thus. Between the end of the age of the Mysteries all over the world and the appearance of the great religions, a chasm has been dug; a knowledge existed before which did not make this formidable distinction between God and the world — all the traditions, all the legends testify to it. The conflict between Matter and Spirit is a modern creation; the so-called materialists are actually the children, legitimate or not, of the spiritualists, as prodigal sons are the issue of miserly fathers. Between the first Upanishads of about three or four thousand years ago, themselves heirs of the Vedas which saw God everywhere in this "marvellous universe", and the last Upanishads, a Secret has been lost — it has been lost not only in India; it has been lost in Mesopotamia, in Egypt, in Greece, in Central America. It is this Secret which Sri Aurobindo was to rediscover, perhaps just because in his flesh were reunited the purest Western tradition and the profound spiritual urgency of Asia. *East and West,* he says, *have two ways of looking at life which are opposite sides of one reality. Between the pragmatic truth on which the vital thought of modern Europe enamoured of the vigour of life, all the dance of God in Nature, puts so vehement and exclusive a stress and the eternal immutable Truth to which the Indian mind enamoured of calm and poise loves to turn with an equal passion for an exclusive finding, there is no such divorce and quarrel as is*

now declared by the partisan mind, the separating reason, the ab-
sorbing passion of an exclusive will of realisation. The one eternal
immutable Truth is the Spirit and without the Spirit the pragmatic
truth of a self-creating universe would have no origin or founda-
tion; it would be barren of significance, empty of inner guidance,
lost in its end, a fire-work display shooting up into the void only
to fall away and perish in mid-air. But neither is the pragmatic
truth a dream of the non-existent, an illusion or a long lapse into
some futile delirium of creative imagination; that would be to
make the eternal Spirit a drunkard or a dreamer, the fool of his
own gigantic self-hallucinations. The truths of universal exis-
tence are of two kinds, truths of the spirit which are themselves
eternal and immutable, and these are the great things that cast
themselves out into becoming and there constantly realise their
powers and significances, and the play of the consciousness with
them, the discords, the musical variations, soundings of possibility,
progressive notations, reversions, perversions, mounting conversions
into a greater figure of harmony; and of all these things the Spirit
has made, makes always his universe. But it is himself that he
makes in it, himself that is the creator and the energy of creation
and the cause and the method and the result of the working, the
mechanist and the machine, the music and the musician, the poet
and the poem, supermind, mind, and life and matter, the soul and
Nature.[5]

But it was not enough for Sri Aurobindo to reconcile
on paper Spirit and Matter. That the Spirit is or is not of
this world does not make much difference, after all, if the
knowledge of the Spirit in life is not accompanied by a
power over life:

For truth and knowledge are an idle gleam,
If Knowledge brings not power to change the world....[6]

The lost Secret was not a theoretical truth, it was a real power of the Spirit over Matter. It is this pragmatic Secret which Sri Aurobindo was to find again, step by step, experimentally, having the courage to leap both beyond his occidental culture and beyond the Hindu religious tradition; so true is it that the real thing emerges when everything is forgotten.

CHAPTER THREE

THE LAST OF THE INTELLECT

It had taken Sri Aurobindo fourteen years to cover the road of the West; it was to take him almost as much time to cover the path of India and to attain the "summit" of the traditional yogic realisations, that is, the starting-point of his own work. But what is interesting for us is that even this traditional road, which we must look upon as a preparation, Sri Aurobindo traversed outside all customary rules, as a freelance or rather as an explorer who cares little for precautions and for maps and thus avoids many useless windings because he has simply the courage to go straight ahead. It was then not in solitude nor with legs crossed nor under the guidance of an enlightened Master that Sri Aurobindo was to begin the journey but as we might do ourselves, without knowing anything about it, right in the midst of life — a life as tumultuous and disturbed as ours may be — and all alone. The first secret of Sri Aurobindo is undoubtedly to have always refused to cut life into two — action, meditation, inner, outer, and all the gamut of our false separations; from the day he thought of yoga he put everything into it: high and low, within, without, all was good enough for him, and he started off without a look behind. Sri Aurobindo has not come to give us a demonstration of exceptional qualities in an exceptional milieu, he has come to show us what is possible for man and that the exceptional is only a normality not yet mastered, even as *the supernatural*, he said, *is that the nature of which we have not attained or do not yet know, or the means of which we have not yet conquered.*[1] Fundamentally, everything in this world is a question of right concentration; there is nothing which will not finally yield up to a well-directed concentration.

When he landed at the Apollo Bunder in Bombay a spontaneous spiritual experience seized him, *a vast calm* took possession of him; but he had other problems: food, living. Sri Aurobindo was twenty. He found a job with the Maharaja of Baroda as professor first of French, then of English, at the State College of which he soon became Vice-Principal. He also worked as the private secretary of the Prince. Between the Court and the College his hands were already full, but it was the destiny of India which preoccupied him. He went several times to Calcutta, acquainted himself with the political situation, wrote articles which created a sensation, for he was not satisfied with calling the queen-empress of India *an old lady so called by way of courtesy*,[2] he invited his compatriots to shake off the British yoke and attacked the *mendicant policy* of the Indian Congress: *no reforms, no collaboration*. His aim was to organise all the energies of the nation for a revolutionary action. This must have required some courage in 1893 when the British hegemony extended over three-fourths of the globe. But Sri Aurobindo had a special way of attacking the problem; he did not lay the blame upon the English but upon the Indians themselves: *Our actual enemy is not any force exterior to ourselves, but our own crying weaknesses, our cowardice, our purblind sentimentalism*.[3] Here is already a dominant note of Sri Aurobindo who, in the political battle as in the spiritual and in all circumstances, asks us to search within ourselves and not outside or elsewhere for the causes of our misfortunes and of the calamities of the world; *outer circumstances are merely the unfolding of what we are*, said later she who shared his work. Sri Aurobindo soon realised that newspaper articles did not suffice to awaken a country; he began underground work which was to lead him to the threshold of the gallows. For thirteen years Sri Aurobindo was to play with fire.

However, this young man was neither agitated nor fanatical: "His smile was simple like that of a child, as limpid and as sweet," wrote his Bengali teacher who lived with him for two years (Sri Aurobindo had naturally begun to study his mother-tongue), and with a touching naïvety his teacher adds: "Before meeting Sri Aurobindo I had imagined him as a stalwart figure dressed like a European from head to foot, immaculate, with a stern look behind his spectacles, a distorted accent (of Cambridge, evidently!) and a temper exceedingly rough.... Who could have thought that this bronzed young man with the soft and dreamy eyes and long wavy hair parted in the middle and falling to the neck, clad in a common coarse Ahmedabad *dhoti* and a close-fitting Indian jacket, on his feet old-fashioned slippers with upturned toes, and the face slightly marked with small-pox, was no other than Mister Aurobindo Ghose, a living well of French, Latin and Greek?"

For the rest, Sri Aurobindo was not yet through with books, the occidental momentum was still there; by huge cases he devoured books ordered from Bombay and Calcutta: "Aurobindo would sit at his work-table," continues his Bengali teacher, "and read in the light of an oil lamp till one in the morning, oblivious of the intolerable mosquito-bites. I would see him seated there in the same posture, for hours on end, his eyes fixed on the book, like a yogi plunged in the contemplation of the Divine, lost to all that went on around. Even if the house had caught fire, it would not have broken this concentration." Novels,

English, Russian, German, French, filed past him thus and also in ever larger numbers the sacred books of India, the Upanishads, the Gita, the Ramayana, without his having ever stepped into a temple save through curiosity. "Once having returned from College," narrates one of his friends, "Sri Aurobindo sat down, picked up a book at random and began to read it whilst Z and some friends began a noisy game of chess. After half an hour he put down his book and took a cup of tea. We had already seen him do this many a time and were waiting eagerly for a chance to verify whether he read the books from cover to cover or whether he only skimmed through a few pages here and there. The test began immediately. Z opened the book, read a line aloud and asked Sri Aurobindo to repeat the sequel. Sri Aurobindo concentrated for a moment and repeated the entire page without a single mistake. If he could read a hundred pages in half an hour, no wonder he could read a caseful of books in so incredibly short a time." But Sri Aurobindo did not stop at the translations of the sacred texts, he began to study Sanskrit which he learnt by himself — a fact typical of him: indeed a thing had but to be considered difficult or impossible, and he refused to take anyone's word for it, be he grammarian, pandit or clergyman, and wished to make the experiment himself, directly. This method possibly had advantages, for not only did he learn Sanskrit but discovered a few years later the lost meaning of the Vedas.*

The day came, however, when Sri Aurobindo had had enough of these intellectual gymnastics. Probably he had seen that one can continue indefinitely to amass knowledge and to read and read and to learn the languages,

* The Vedic Age, prior to that of the Upanishads, which was its heir, may be placed before 4000 B.C.

even all the languages in the world and all the books in the world, and yet not advance an inch. For the mind does not seek to know truly, though it seems to — it seeks to grind. Its need of knowledge is primarily a need of something to grind. And if perchance the machine were to come to a stop because the knowledge was found, it would quickly rise in revolt and find something new to grind, to have the pleasure of grinding and grinding. This is its function. That within us which seeks to know and to progress is not the mind but something behind it which makes use of it: *The capital period of my intellectual development,* confided Sri Aurobindo to a disciple, *was when I could see clearly that what the intellect said might be correct and not correct, that what the intellect justified was true and its opposite also was true. I never admitted a truth in the mind without simultaneously keeping it open to the contrary of it.... And the first result was that the prestige of the intellect was gone!*[4]

Sri Aurobindo had come to a turning-point; the temples did not interest him and the books were empty. A friend advised him to practise yoga, Sri Aurobindo refused: *A yoga which requires me to give up the world is not for me;*[5] he even added, *a solitary salvation leaving the world to its fate was felt as almost distasteful.*[6] But one day Sri Aurobindo witnessed a curious scene, though one quite common in India; yet banality is often the best pretext for an inner starting-point. His brother Barin had fallen ill having caught a dangerous hill-fever (Barin was born when Sri Aurobindo was in England; it was he who served as Sri Aurobindo's secret messenger for the organisation of the Indian resistance in Bengal), when there arrived one of those half-naked wandering monks, smeared with ashes, who are called *naga-sannyasins.* He was perhaps on his way begging food from door to door as is their custom, when he saw Barin rolled up in his bed-sheets, shivering with fever. Without a word he asked for a glass of water, cut it through cross-wise with a knife while he chanted a *mantra*, and gave it to the sick man to drink. Five minutes later Barin was cured and the monk had disappeared. Sri Aurobindo had heard much about the strange powers of these ascetics but this time he had seen with his own eyes. He felt then that yoga could serve other ends than mere escape. Now, he had need of *power* to liberate India: *The agnostic was in me, the atheist was in me, the sceptic was in me and I was not absolutely sure that there was a God at all.... I felt there must be a mighty truth somewhere in this yoga.... So when I turned to the yoga and resolved to practise it and find out if my idea was right, I did it in this spirit and with this prayer to Him, "If Thou art, then Thou knowest my heart. Thou knowest that I do not ask for Mukti (liberation), I do not ask for anything which others ask for. I ask only for strength to uplift this nation, I ask only to be allowed to live and work for this people whom I love...."*[7] It was thus that Sri Aurobindo set out.

CHAPTER FOUR

THE SILENT MIND

Mental Constructions

The first stage in Sri Aurobindo's yoga and the fundamental task which gives the key to many realisations is
the silence of the mind. One may ask, why silence the
mind? but it is quite obvious that if we want to discover
a new world within us, we must first leave the old — all
depends on the resolve with which we take this step.
Sometimes just a flash suffices; something in us cries out,
"Enough of this twaddle!" and we cling on once and for
all, and we go ahead without a look behind us. Others say
yes-no and sway endlessly between two worlds. But clearly
it is not a question of lopping off a possession painfully
acquired, in the name of heaven knows what Wisdom-
Peace-Serenity (on this side also we are not going to be
taken in by fine words), we are not in quest of holiness
but of youth — the eternal youth of a being who grows,
— not in quest of lesser being but of better being and above
all of vaster being: *Has it not occurred to you that if they really
sought for something cold, dark and gloomy as the supreme good,
they would not be sages but asse?*[1] Sri Aurobindo once humorously remarked.

All kinds of discoveries are made, in truth, when the
mental machinery stops, and the first is that if the power
to think is a remarkable gift, *the power not to think*[2] is even
more so; let the seeker try it for just five minutes and he
will see what stuff he is made of! He will find that he lives
in a clandestine turmoil, an exhausting whirlwind, but

never exhausted, where there is room only for his thoughts, his feelings, his impulsions, his reactions — himself, always himself, enormous gnome who obtrudes everywhere, veils everything, hears only himself, sees only himself, knows only himself (if that) and whose perpetual themes, more or less alternating, can give him the illusion of novelty. *In a certain sense we are nothing but a complex mass of mental, nervous and physical habits held together by a few ruling ideas, desires and associations — an amalgam of many small self-repeating forces with a few major vibrations.*[3] At the age of eighteen we seem to be set, our major vibrations established, and around them indefinitely will come to be coiled in thicker and thicker, more polished, more refined layers, the sediments of a sempiternal same thing with a thousand faces which we call culture or "ourselves" — in fact, we are shut up in a *construction*, which may be of lead and without a skylight, or graceful like a minaret, but always shut up, buzzing, repetitive, men in a skin of granite or in a statue of glass. The first work of yoga is to breathe freely. And naturally, to break this *mental screen* which allows only a single type of vibration to filter through and to know the multi-coloured infinitude of vibrations, that is, the world at last and all beings such as they really are and another "ourself" worth much more than we think.

Active Meditation

When one sits down with eyes closed to silence the mind, one is at first submerged by a torrent of thoughts — they crop up from everywhere like frightened, nay, aggressive rats. There is but one way of stopping this commotion:

34 THE ADVENTURE OF CONSCIOUSNESS

to try and try again, patiently, persistently. And above all not to commit the mistake of struggling mentally with the mind; one must shift the centre. We have all of us, above the mind or somewhere deeper, an *aspiration*, the very one which has put us on the way, a need of our being, like a password which has an efficacy for us alone; if one clings to it the work is more easy, for we pass from a negative to a positive attitude — the oftener we repeat our password, the more it will gather strength. We may also take the help of an image like that of a vast ocean, without a ripple, on which one lies floating — one floats along, one becomes that tranquil vastness; at the same time we get to know not only silence but a widening of consciousness. In fact, each one must find his way, and the less taut he is the quicker he will succeed: *One may start a process of one kind or another for the purpose which would normally mean a long labour and be seized, even at the outset, by a rapid intervention or manifestation of Silence with an effect out of all proportion to the means used at the beginning. One commences with a method, but the work is taken up by a Grace from above, from That to which one aspires or an irruption of the infinitudes of the Spirit. It was in this last way that I myself came by the mind's absolute silence, unimaginable to me before I had its actual experience.*[4] This is a very important point, for we are tempted to think that these yogic experiences are beautiful and quite interesting, but, after all, they are far beyond our ordinary humanity; how shall we, such as we are, be able ever to reach there? Our mistake is to judge by our present self the possibilities of another self. Now, precisely, yoga awakens *automatically*, by the simple fact that one has started on the way, a whole gamut of latent faculties and invisible forces which considerably surpass the possibilities of our surface being and which can do for us that of which we are normally incapable: *One has to have the passage clear between the outer mind and something in the inner being... for they (the Yogic consciousness and its powers) are already there within you,*[5] and the best way of "clearing" is to make the mind silent. We do not know who we are and still less what we are capable of.

But the practice of meditation is not the true solution of the problem (though it be quite necessary at the beginning to give the push) because we shall attain perhaps a relative silence, but the very moment we put our foot outside our room or our retreat, we shall fall back into the habitual clamour and this will mean again the eternal separation of the within and the without, the inner life and life in the world. We need a complete life, we need to live the truth of our being, every day, at every moment, not only on holidays or in solitude, and for this, blissful arcadian meditations are not the solution: *We may get incrusted in our spiritual seclusion and find it difficult later on to pour ourselves triumphantly outwards and apply to life our gains in the higher Nature. When we turn to add this external kingdom also to our inner conquests, we shall find ourselves too much accustomed to an activity purely subjective and ineffective on the material plane. There will be an immense difficulty in transforming the outer life and the body. Or we shall find that our action does not correspond with the inner light: it still follows the old accustomed mistaken paths, still obeys the old normal imperfect influences; the Truth within us continues to be separated by a painful gulf from the ignorant mechanism of our external nature.... It is as if we were living in another, a larger and subtler world and had no divine hold, perhaps little hold of any kind, upon the material and terrestrial existence.*[6] The only solution then is to practise silencing the mind there where it is *apparently* most difficult, that is, in the street, in the tube, in work and everywhere. Instead of going down the Boulevard Saint Michel four times a day like a harassed man who is ever in a hurry, one can go down consciously four times, like a seeker. Instead of living haphazardly, dispersed in a multitude of thoughts which not only are quite uninteresting but are exhausting like an obsessive tune, one gathers together the scattered threads of his consciousness and works — works on himself — at every moment; and life begins to acquire quite an unusual interest, because the least little circumstance becomes the occasion for a victory — we are *orientated*, we are going somewhere instead of going nowhere.

For yoga is not a way of doing, but a way of being.

Transition

We are then in quest of another country but, it would be well to say, between the one we leave behind and the one which is not yet found there is a fairly painful no man's land. It is a period of trial, more or less long according to our determination; but at all times, as we know, from the Asiatic, Egyptian or Orphic initiations to the quest of the Holy Grail, the story of man's ascent has been attended by trials. In the past they were romantic, and, good God, there was nothing very difficult in getting oneself enclosed in a sarcophagus to the accompaniment of fifes or in celebrating one's own funeral rites around the pyre; now we know of public sarcophagi and of lives which are a kind of burial. It is therefore worth while to make some effort to come out of it. And besides, when one takes a good look at it, there is not much to lose.

The main ordeal of this transition is the inner void.
After having lived in a mental feverishness, one suddenly
finds oneself like a convalescent, a bit lost, with strange
hummings in the head, as though this world were terribly
noisy, tiring, and an acute sensibility which gives the impression of being knocked about everywhere, against opaque and aggressive men, heavy objects, brutal events —
the world seems enormously absurd. This is a sure sign
of the beginning of interiorisation. However, if one tries
to descend consciously inside, by meditation, one finds
a similar void, a sort of dark well or an amorphous neutrality; if one persists in descending, it even happens that one
glides suddenly into sleep, for two seconds, ten seconds,
two minutes, sometimes longer — in fact, it is not an ordinary sleep; we have only passed into another consciousness, but there is no *link* yet between the two and one
comes out of it not more advanced apparently than one
had entered. This transitional position would lead easily
to a sort of absurd nihilism — nothing outside but nothing
within either. Neither this side nor that. And it is here
that we must be very careful, after demolishing our outer
mental constructions, not to become enclosed again in a
false profundity, under another construction, absurd,
illusionist, or sceptical, perhaps even rebellious. We must
go farther. When we have begun the yoga we must go *to
the very end*, whatever it may cost, for if we let go the thread
we risk never finding it again. Here indeed is the trial.
Only, the seeker must understand that he is being born to
another life and that his new eyes, his new senses are not
yet formed, like those of the new-born child who alights
in the world. It is not a diminution of consciousness
but a passage to a new consciousness: *The cup [has to be]
left clean and empty for the divine liquor to be poured into it.*[7]

Our only resource in these circumstances is to stick to our aspiration and to make it grow and grow, exactly through this terrible lack of everything, as a fire into which we throw all our old things, our old life, our old ideas, our feelings — simply, we have the unshakable faith that behind this passage there is a door which opens. And our faith is not senseless; it is not the stupidity of the credulous but a *fore*knowledge, something in us which knows before us, sees before we do and which sends its vision to the surface in the form of a need, a seeking, an inexplicable faith. *Faith*, says Sri Aurobindo, *is an intuition not only waiting for experience to justify it, but leading towards experience.*[8]

Descent of the Force

And little by little the void is filled. There follows then a series of observations and experiences of a considerable importance, which it would be wrong to present as a logical sequence, for from the moment one leaves the old world one finds that everything is possible and, above all, that there are no two identical cases — whence the mistake of all spiritual dogmatisms. We can only trace a few general lines of experience.

To begin with, when peace is relatively established in the mind, failing absolute silence, and when our aspiration or our need has grown, has become constant, piercing, like a hole within, we observe a first phenomenon which has incalculable consequences for all the rest of our yoga. We feel around the head and more particularly in the nape of the neck, an unusual pressure which may give the sensation of a false headache. At the beginning we can scarcely endure it for long and shake it off, we seek distraction, we "think of something else". Gradually this pressure takes a more distinct form and we feel a veritable current which *descends* — a current of force not like an unpleasant electric current but rather like a fluid mass. We find then that the "pressure" or the false headache at the start was caused simply by our resistance to the descent of the Force, and that the only thing to do is not to obstruct the passage (that is, block the current in the head) but to let it descend into all the strata of our being from top to bottom. This current at first is quite spasmodic, irregular, and a slight conscious effort is necessary to get reconnected with it when it is blurred; then it becomes continuous, natural, automatic, and it gives the very pleasant sensation of a fresh energy, like another breath more ample than that of our lungs, which envelops us, bathes us, lightens us and at the same time fills us with solidity. The physical effect is almost exactly that of walking in the breeze. Actually we do not notice the real effect (for it settles in very gradually, by little doses) till, for one reason or another, distraction, error, excess, we are cut off from the current; then we find ourselves abruptly empty, shrunken as though we lacked oxygen all of a sudden, with the very disagreeable sensation of a physical shrivelling; we are like an old apple squeezed of its sunshine and its sap. And we ask ourselves truly how we have been able to live before without this. This is a first transmutation of our energies. Instead of going to the common source, below and around us in the universal life, we draw from above. And this is an energy much more clear and much more sustained, without breaks, and above all much more alive. In our daily life, in the midst of our work and the thousand other occupations, the current of force is, to begin

with, quite diluted, but as soon as we stop for a moment
and concentrate, it becomes a massive inrush. All comes
to a standstill. One is like a full jar; even the sensation
of the "current" disappears, as though the whole body
from head to foot were charged with a mass of energy
compact and crystalline at once (*a solid cool block of peace*,[9]
says Sri Aurobindo); and if our inner vision has begun
to open we find that all is bluish; one is like an aqua-
marine — and vast, vast. Tranquil, without a ripple.
And that indescribable coolness. Truly, one has plunged
into the Source. For this "descending force" is the very
Force of the Spirit — *Shakti*. Spiritual force is not a mere
word. Finally it will no longer be necessary to close the
eyes and to withdraw from the surface to feel it; every
minute it will be there, no matter what one is doing,
whether one eats or reads or speaks; and it will gather
a greater and greater intensity as the organism gets used
to it; in fact, it is a formidable mass of energy limited
only by the smallness of our receptivity or capacity.

When they speak of their experience of this descending Force, the disciples of Pondicherry call it "The Force
of Sri Aurobindo and the Mother"; they do not mean
by this that this *Shakti* is the personal property of Sri
Aurobindo and the Mother; they express in this way,
spontaneously, the fact that it has not its equivalent in
any other known yoga. Here we find experimentally
the fundamental difference between the integral yoga
of Sri Aurobindo (*purna yoga*) and the other yogas. If
one practises other methods of yoga before that of Sri
Aurobindo, one finds in fact an essential practical difference; after a time one experiences an *ascending* Force
(called *kundalini* in India), which awakens quite brutally
in our being at the base of the vertebral column and rises

from level to level till it reaches the top of the head where it seems to open into a sort of luminous, radiant pulsation, accompanied by a sensation of immensity (and often by a loss of consciousness which is called ecstasy) as though one had emerged eternally Elsewhere. All the yogic processes which could be called thermogenetic (the *asanas* of Hatha-yoga, concentrations of Raja-yoga, breathing exercises of *pranayama*, etc.) aim at the awakening of this ascending Force; they may bring much danger and profound disturbances and so they make the presence and the protection of an enlightened Master indispensable. We shall come back to this. This difference in the direction of the current, ascending or descending, is due to a difference of orientation which can never be overstressed. The traditional yogas and, we suppose, the religious disciplines of the West aim essentially at the liberation of the consciousness : the whole being is craned towards the heights in an ascending aspiration; it seeks to shatter the appearances and emerge above in the peace or the ecstasy. Hence the awakening of this ascending Force. But, as we have seen, the aim of Sri Aurobindo is not only to ascend but to descend, not only to whisk away into the eternal Peace but to transform Life and Matter, and first of all this little life and this spot of matter which we are. Hence the awakening or rather the response of this descending Force. Our experience of the descending current is the experience of the transforming Force. It is that which will replace our quickly-exhausted energies and our awkward efforts, which will begin where other yogas end, illumining at first the summit of our being, then descending from level to level, gently, peacefully, irresistibly (for it is never violent; its power is strangely measured out, as though it were guided directly by the Wisdom of the Spirit) and it is this which will universalise our entire being, right down to the lowest layer. This is the basic experience of the integral yoga. *When the Peace is established, this higher or Divine Force from above can descend and work in us. It descends usually first into the head and liberates the inner mind centres, then into the heart centre...then into the navel and other vital centres...then into the sacral region and below.... It works at the same time for perfection as well as liberation; it takes up the whole nature part by part and deals with it, rejecting what has to be rejected, sublimating what has to be sublimated, creating what has to be created. It integrates, harmonises, establishes a new rhythm in the nature.*[10]

Emergence of a New Mode of Knowledge

With the silence of the mind there comes another change, a very important one but more difficult to distinguish for sometimes it extends over a number of years and its signs are at first imperceptible; this is what may be called the emergence of a new mode of knowledge and therefore of a new mode of action.

One can understand that it is possible to keep the mind silent when walking in the crowd, when eating, when dressing or resting, but how is it possible when it is a question of working in the office, for example, or when having a discussion with friends? We are obliged to reflect, to remember things, to search, to bring in all kinds of mental mechanisms. Experience, however, teaches us that this necessity is not inevitable, that it is only the result of a long evolution in whose course we have grown accustomed to depend on the mind for knowledge and action, but this is only a *habit* and it can be changed. Fundamentally, yoga is not so much a way of learning as of unlearning a crowd of so-called imperative habits which we have inherited from our animal evolution.

If the seeker undertakes to silence the mind in work, for instance, he will pass through several stages. At the start, he will just manage to remember his aspiration from time to time, and to interrupt his work for a few minutes to switch himself on again to the right wave-length, then once again all will be engulfed in the daily routine. But as he develops the habit of making an effort elsewhere, in the street or at home and everywhere, the dynamism of this effort will tend to be perpetuated and to draw him suddenly in the midst of his other activities—he will remember more and more often. Then this remembrance will gradually change its nature; instead of a deliberate interruption to contact again the true rhythm, the seeker will feel something which *lives* in his depths, in the background of his being, like a little muffled vibration; a slight withdrawal into his consciousness will suffice for him to find again at any time, within a second, the vibration of silence. He will discover that it is there, always there, like a bluish depth behind, and that he can at will refresh himself there, relax himself in the very midst of all the tumult and the troubles, and that he carries in himself an inviolable and peaceful retreat.

But soon this vibration somewhere behind becomes more and more perceptible, continuous, and the seeker feels a separation taking place in his being: a silent depth which vibrates, vibrates in the background, and the fairly thin surface where activities, thoughts, gestures, words are unrolled. He will have discovered the *Witness* in himself and will let himself be captured less and less by the exterior play which ceaselessly, like an octopus, tries to swallow us alive; this is a discovery as old as the Rig Veda : "Two birds beautiful of wing, friends and comrades, cling to a common tree, and one eats the sweet fruit, the other regards him and eats not" (1.164.20). At this stage it becomes easier to intervene, intentionally at first, and substitute for the old superficial habits of mental reflection, of memory, planning, anticipation, a habit of referring silently to this vibrating depth. In practice this is a long period of transition with setbacks and with progress (the impression, however, is not so much of a setback or an advance as of something which veils and unveils itself in turn) in which the two workings encounter each other, the old mechanisms tending constantly to interfere and to recapture their old rights, wanting to convince us that it is not possible to do without them—and they gain by a sort of laziness which finds it more convenient to proceed "as usual". But this work of unhooking will be powerfully helped, on one side, by the experience of the descending Force which, automatically, untiringly, will set the house in order and exercise a quiet pressure on the rebellious mechanisms as though each wave of thought were gripped, frozen; and, on the other side, by the accumulation of thousands of small experiences, more and more perceptible, which will make us realise that we can do very well without the mind, and that in truth we are the better for it.

Gradually, in fact, we find that it is not necessary to think, that something behind or above does the work, with a precision and an infallibility growing ever greater as we get into the habit of referring to it; that it is not necessary to remember but at the required moment the exact indication comes up, not necessary to plan one's action but a secret spring sets it going without one's willing it or thinking about it and makes us do exactly what is needed with a wisdom and a foresight of which our mind, always short-sighted, is quite incapable. And we see that the more we obey these swift intimations, these lightning suggestions, the more they become frequent, clear, imperious, habitual, somewhat like an intuitive process but with this important difference that our intuitions are almost always blurred, deformed by the mind which, moreover, excels in imitating them and in making us take its whims for revelations, whilst here the transmission is clear, exact, for the good reason that the mind is dumb. But we all have the experience of those problems "mysteriously" solved in sleep, that is, precisely when the thinking machine is hushed. No doubt there will be errors and blunders before the new working is established with any surety, but the seeker must be ready to make mistakes in order to learn; in fact, he will find that the mistake comes always from an intrusion of the mind; each time the mind intervenes, it blurs everything, splits up everything, impedes everything. Then, one day, through the very mistakes and repeated experiences, we shall understand once and for all and see with our own eyes that *the mind is not an instrument of knowledge, but only an organizer of knowledge,* as the Mother says, and that knowledge comes from elsewhere.* In the silent mind words come, speech comes, action comes and everything comes, automatically, with an exactitude and a swiftness altogether surprising. It is indeed another way of living, light and free. For, in truth, *there is nothing mind can do that cannot be better done in the mind's immobility and thought-free stillness.*[11]

* This "elsewhere" will be discussed later in the study of the Super-conscient.

The Universal Mind

So far we have analysed the progress of the seeker in terms of his inner being but this progress translates itself equally on the outer plane; and besides, the inner-outer partition becomes thinner and thinner, it seems more and more like an artificial convention established by the adolescent mind, wrapped up in itself, seeing only itself. The seeker will feel this partition slowly losing its hardness, he will experience a kind of change in the texture of his being, as though he were becoming more light, more transparent, more porous, if one may venture to say so. This difference of texture makes itself felt at first through unpleasant symptoms, for the average man is generally protected by a thick hide, whilst the seeker will no longer have this protection: he will receive people's thoughts, their wishes, their desires in their true form and in all their nudity, as they really are — outrages. And here "bad thoughts" or "bad will" are not alone in sharing this virulence; nothing is more aggressive than the good will, the good feelings, the altruisms of men — on one side or the other it is the ego which feeds itself, with sweetness or with strength. We are civilised only on the surface; underneath, the cannibalism continues. The seeker, therefore, must needs be in possession of this Force we have spoken about — with It he can go everywhere; and besides, in the cosmic wisdom, this transparency would not come unaccompanied by a corresponding protection. Armed with "his" Force and with the silence of the mind the seeker will slowly find that he is permeable to outside impacts, that he receives, receives from everywhere, that distances are unreal barriers — no one is far, no one has gone away! all stands together, all is at the same time —

and that ten thousand miles away he can receive clearly the thoughts of a friend, someone's anger, a brother's suffering. It is enough that in the silence the seeker switches on a place, a person, to have a more or less exact perception of the situation — more or less exact according to his capacity for silence, for here too the mind jams everything, because it desires, because it fears, because it wants, and nothing reaches it which is not immediately falsified by this desire, this fear, this will (there are other constituents of this jamming also, we shall speak of them later). It seems then that with the silent mind comes a widening of the consciousness and it can turn at will towards any point of the universal reality to know there what it needs to know.

But in this silent transparency we make another discovery, very important in its implications. We find not only that the thoughts of others come to us from outside, but that our own thoughts also come to us in the same way, *from outside*. When we are sufficiently transparent we can feel, in the silent immobility of the mind, little swirling eddies which strike our atmosphere or certain light vibrations which draw our attention, and if we lean over a little to "see what it is", that is, if we let one of these swirls enter into us, we find ourselves suddenly thinking of something: what we had caught at the periphery of our being was a thought in its pure state or rather *a mental vibration* before it had the time to enter unperceived and to rise again to the surface with a personal form which would make us say triumphantly, "This is my thought." A good thought-reader can thus read what passes even in a person whose language he does not know, because it is not the "thoughts" which he catches but the vibrations to which he gives in himself the corresponding mental form. But it is the contrary which would be truly surprising, for if we were capable of creating a single thing ourselves, were it even a tiny thought, we would be the creators of the world! *Where is the I in you, which can create all that?* asked the Mother. Only, the mechanism is imperceptible to the common man, first because he lives in a constant turmoil, then because the mechanism for the appropriation of the vibrations works almost instantaneously, automatically; once and for all, by his education, his environment, man is accustomed to select from the universal Mind a certain type of vibrations, fairly narrow in range, with which he has an affinity, and to the end of his life he switches on the same wave-length, reproduces the same vibratory mode, with more or less sonorous words and more or less new turns — to put itotherwise, he turns round and round in the cage; only the more or less sparkling scope of our vocabulary can create the illusion that we are progressing. Certainly we change our ideas but to change one's ideas is not to progress, it is not to rise to a higher or more rapid vibratory mode, it is to spin round one more pirouette in the midst of the same environment. This is why Sri Aurobindo spoke of the *change of consciousness*.

Once he has seen that his thoughts come from outside and has repeated this experience hundreds of times, the seeker holds the key to the true mastery of the mind, for if it is difficult to get rid of a thought which we believe to be ours when it has entered inside, it is easy to reject the same thought when we see it coming from outside. And once we are masters of this silence, we are necessarily masters of the mental world, because, instead of being eternally clamped to the same wave-length, we can run through the whole gamut of waves and choose or reject what we please. But let Sri Aurobindo himself describe for us the experience as he first had it with another yogi, Bhaskar Lele, who spent three days with him: *All developed mental men, those who get beyond the average, have in one way or other, or at least at certain times and for certain purposes to separate the two parts of the mind, the active part, which is a factory of thoughts and the quiet masterful part which is at once a Witness and a Will, observing them, judging, rejecting, eliminating, accepting, ordering corrections and changes, the Master in the House of Mind, capable of self-empire, samrajya. The Yogi goes still further, — he is not only a master there but even while in mind in a way, he gets out of it as it were, and stands above or quite back from it and free. For him the image of the factory of thoughts is no longer quite valid; for he sees that thoughts come from outside, from the universal Mind, or universal Nature, sometimes formed and distinct, sometimes unformed and then they are given shape somewhere in us. The principal business of our mind is either a response of acceptance or a refusal to these thought waves (as also vital waves, subtle physical energy waves) or this giving a personal-mental form to thought-stuff (or vital movements) from the environing Nature-Force. It was my great debt to Lele that he showed me this. "Sit in meditation", he said, "but do not think, look only at your mind; you will see thoughts coming into it; before they can enter throw these away from your mind till your mind is capable of entire silence." I had never heard before of thoughts coming visibly into the mind from outside, but I did not think either of questioning the truth or the possibility, I simply sat down and did it. In a moment my mind became silent as a windless air on a high mountain summit and then I saw one thought and then another coming in a concrete way from outside; I flung them away before they could enter and take hold of the brain and in three days I was free. From that moment, in principle, the mental being in me became a free Intelligence, a universal· Mind, not limited to the narrow circle of personal thoughts as a labourer in a thought factory, but a receiver of knowledge from all the hundred realms of being and free to choose what it willed in this vast sight-empire and thought-empire.*[12]

Having started from a small mental construction wherein he believed himself quite at ease and very enlightened, the seeker looks behind him and asks himself how he has managed to live in such a prison. He is struck above all to see how for years and years he has lived amidst impossibilities, and how men live behind barriers: "One can't do this, one can't do that, this is against such and such a law, this against such another, this is illogical, this is not natural, this is impossible...." And he discovers that all is possible and that the true difficulty is to believe that it is difficult. After having lived for twenty, thirty years in his mental shell, like a sort of thinking periwinkle, he begins to breathe freely in the open air.

And he finds that the eternal inner-outer antinomy is resolved, that this also was a part of our mental calcifications. In truth the "without" is everywhere within! we are everywhere! the error is to believe that if we could bring together the admirable conditions of peace, beauty, solitary countryside, it would be much easier, for there will be *always something* to disturb us, everywhere, and it is better to resolve to break our constructions and to take in all this "without" — then we shall be at home everywhere. The same thing holds for the action-meditation antinomy; the seeker has attained inner silence and his action is a meditation (he will glimpse even that meditation can be an action); whether he be dressing or setting his affairs in order, the Force passes, passes in him, he is for ever tuned in elsewhere. And he will see at last that his action becomes more clear-sighted, more effective, more powerful, without in the least encroaching upon his peace: *The substance of the mental being...is still, so still that nothing disturbs it. If thoughts or activities come, they...cross the mind as a flight of birds crosses the sky in a windless air. It passes, disturbs nothing, leaving no trace. Even if a thousand images or the most violent events pass across it, the calm stillness remains as if the very texture of the mind were a substance of eternal and indestructible peace. A mind that has achieved this calmness can begin to act, even intensely and powerfully, but it will keep its fundamental stillness — originating nothing from itself but receiving from Above and giving it a mental form without adding anything of its own, calmly, dispassionately, though with the joy of the Truth and the happy power and light of its passage.*[13]

Must we recall that Sri Aurobindo was then directing a revolutionary movement and preparing guerrilla warfare in India?

CHAPTER FIVE

CHAPTER FIVE

CONSCIOUSNESS

A disciple of Sri Aurobindo, having one day to take a
serious decision, had written to ask for advice; now, he
was quite at a loss when he was told to take his decision
from the "summit of his consciousness". He was a Westerner and he asked himself what the dickens this could really
mean; whether this summit of the consciousness was a
powerful method of thinking or a sort of enthusiasm when
the brain was well warmed up, or what? because this is
the only way of consciousness we know in the West. That
is, for us the consciousness is always the mind: I think
therefore I am. This is one point of view, our own; we
put ourselves at the centre of the world and we grant the
benefit of being conscious to those who share our way of
living and feeling. However, if we want to understand
and discover what consciousness is and to manipulate
it, we must pass beyond this narrow point of view. Sri
Aurobindo, having attained a certain degree of mental
silence, observed: *Mental consciousness is only the human range
which no more exhausts all the possible ranges of consciousness
than human sight exhausts all the gradations of colour or human
hearing all the gradations of sound — for there is much above or
below that is to man invisible and inaudible. So there are ranges
of consciousness above and below the human range, with which
the normal human has no contact and they seem to it unconscious,
— supramental or overmental and submental ranges[1].... What
we call unconsciousness is simply other-consciousness.... We are
really no more unconscious when we are asleep or stunned or
drugged or "dead" or in any other state, than when we are plunged*

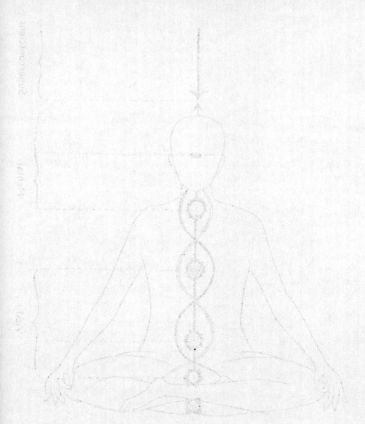

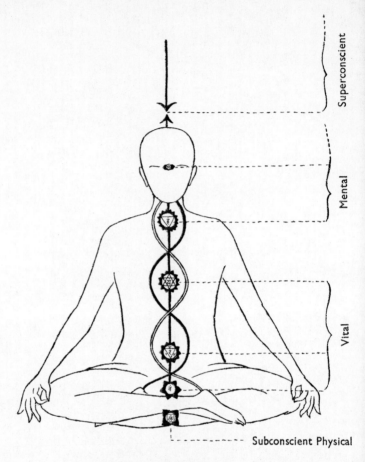

Superconscient

Mental

Vital

Subconscient Physical

The Centres of Consciousness
according to the Tantric tradition in India.

The canal at the centre and the two canals which intercross on both sides correspond to the medullary canal and, probably, to the sympathetic nervous system ; they represent the paths of circulation of the ascending Force (*Kundalini*) when it awakens at the lowest centre and rises from centre to centre "like a serpent" to burst open at the top into the Superconscient (this seems to be also the significance of the Uraeus or Egyptian hooded snake (Naja) which stands on the crown of the pharaohs with the solar disc, of the Mexican quetzalcoatl or plumed serpent, perhaps also of the naga serpents overhanging the head of Buddha, etc.). The characteristics of these centres scarcely interest anyone but the seer; we shall mention later certain details which are of general interest. A detailed study of this subject is found in the remarkable book of Sir John Woodroffe (Arthur Avalon) *The Serpent Power* (Ganesh & Co., Madras, 1913).

*in inner thought oblivious of our physical selves and our surround-
ings. For any one who has advanced even a little way in Yoga,
this is a most elementary proposition.* And Sri Aurobindo
adds: *As we progress and awaken to the soul in us and things,
we shall realise that there is a consciousness also in the plant, in
the metal, in the atom, in electricity, in every thing that belongs to
physical nature; we shall find even that it is not really in all respects a lower or more limited mode than the mental; on the contrary,
it is in many "inanimate" forms more intense, rapid, poignant,
though less evolved towards the surface.*[2] The task of the apprentice yogi will be then to become conscious in every way, at
all the levels of his being and all the stages of universal
existence, not only mentally; to be conscious in himself
and in others and in things, in waking and in sleep; and
finally, to learn to become conscious in what men call
"death", for to the degree that we have been conscious
in our life, we shall be conscious in our death.

But we need not take Sri Aurobindo's word for it; he
encourages us even pressingly to see for ourselves. We
must then disentangle that within us which links all our
diverse modes of being — asleep, awake or "dead" —
and allows us to contact other forms of consciousness.

The Centres of Consciousness

If we follow our experimental method based on the
silent mind, it will lead us to several discoveries which,
step by step, will put us on the track. First, we shall see
the general confusion in which we live slowly settling
down; the stages of our being will be distinguished more
and more clearly, as though we were made of a certain
number of fragments each with its individual personality

and a very distinct centre and, what is most remarkable, its own life independent of the others. This polyphony, if we may call it so, for it is rather a cacophony, is generally masked from us by the voice of the mind which covers everything, annexes everything. There is not a single movement of our being, no matter at what level, not an emotion, not a desire, not the twinkling of an eye, which is not immediately snapped up by the mind and covered with a coating of thought — that is, we *mentalize* everything. And this is the real utility of the mind in the course of our evolution: it helps us to bring to our surface consciousness all the movements of our being which would otherwise remain in a state of unformed magma, subconscious or supraconscious. It also helps us to establish a semblance of order in this anarchy and somehow coordinates all these tiny feudal states under its sovereignty. But by that very fact it veils from us their true voice and function — from suzerainty to tyranny is but one step. The overmental mechanisms are completely choked, or if something of the superconscient voices manages to come through, it is immediately falsified, diluted, obscured; the submental mechanisms become atrophied and we lose the spontaneous senses which were very useful at a former stage of our evolution and could yet be so; other minorities line up in the rebellion and others still gather secretly their little power awaiting the first opportunity to fly in our face. But the seeker who has silenced his mind will begin to distinguish all these states in their naked reality, without their mental veneer, and he will feel at the various levels of his being certain points of concentration, like knots of force, each with its particular vibratory quality or special frequency; but we have all experienced at least once in our lives different vibrations which seem to radiate from diverse levels of our being; the experience of a great revelatory vibration, for example, when a veil seems suddenly rent and we are shown an entire slice of the truth, without words, without even our knowing exactly wherein is the revelation — simply, it is something which vibrates making the world inexplicably more wide, more light, more pure; or we have had the experience of more heavy vibrations of anger or fear, vibrations of desire, vibrations of sympathy, and we know well that all these pulsate at different levels, with different intensities. Thus there is in us a whole gamut of vibratory nodules or *centres of consciousness*, each specialised in one type of vibration which can be distinguished and seized directly according to the degree of our silence and the keenness of our perceptions. And the mind is only *one* of these centres, *one* type of vibration, only *one* of the forms of consciousness, though it wants to arrogate to itself the first place.

The description of these centres as given traditionally need not detain us — better to see things for oneself — nor their localisation; the seeker will feel them himself without difficulty as soon as he becomes a little limpid. It is enough to say that these centres (called in India *Chakras*) are not situated in our physical body but in another dimension, though their concentration at certain moments may become so intense that there is the acute sensation of a physical localisation. Some of them, in fact, correspond quite closely to the different nervous plexuses we know — not all.

Roughly, there are seven centres distributed in four zones: 1) *The Superconscient*, with a centre a little above the top of the head*, which governs our thinking mind

* This centre, called "the thousand-petalled lotus" to express the rich luminosity seen when it opens, is situated, according to the Indian tradi-

and puts us in communication with higher mental planes:
illumined, intuitive, overmind, etc. 2) *The Mind*, with
two centres: one, between the eyebrows, governing the will
and the dynamism of all our mental activities when we act
through thought; this is also the centre of subtle vision
or the "third eye" certain traditions speak of; the other,
at the level of the throat, governing all forms of mental
expression. 3) *The Vital*, with three centres: one, at the
level of the heart,· governing our emotive being (love,
hatred, etc.); the second, at the level of the navel, governing our movements of domination, possession, conquest,
our ambitions, etc., and a third, the lower vital, between
the navel and the sex-centre, at the level of the mesenteric
plexus, governing the lowest vibrations: jealousy, envy,
desire, covetousness, anger. 4) *The Physical and the Subconscient*, with a centre at the base of the vertebral column,
governing our physical being and sex; this centre also
opens us, lower down, to the subconscient regions.

Generally in the "normal" man these centres are asleep
or closed or only allow the smallest little current necessary
for his bare existence to filter through; he is really walled
up in himself and communicates only indirectly with the
outer world, within a very limited circle; in fact, he does
not see other men or things, he sees himself in others,
himself in things and everywhere; he cannot get out.
With yoga the centres open. They can open in two ways,
from bottom to top or from top to bottom, according to
the methods practised: the traditional yogic and spiritual
methods or the yoga of Sri Aurobindo. By the power of
concentrations, exercises, one day we may feel an ascend-

---

tion, at the top of the head. According to Sri Aurobindo and the experience of many others, what is seen at the top of the head is not the centre itself, but the luminous reflection of a solar source which is *above* the head.

ing Force which awakes at the base of the vertebral column and climbs from level to level right up to the top of the head with an undulating movement just like a serpent; at each level this Force *pierces* (violently enough) through the corresponding centre which opens and at the same time opens us to all universal vibrations or energies which correspond to the frequency of this particular centre. With the yoga of Sri Aurobindo the descending Force opens very slowly, gently, these very centres, from top to bottom. Often enough the lower centres do not open at all till much later. This process has an advantage if we understand that each centre corresponds to a *universal* mode of consciousness or energy; if, from the very beginning, we open the lower vital and subconscient centres, we risk being now swamped not by our own small personal affairs but by universal torrents of mud; we become automatically connected with the Confusion and the Mud of the world. This is why the traditional yogas definitely required the presence of a Master who protects. With the descending Force this danger is avoided and we face the lower centres only after establishing our being solidly in the higher superconscient light. Once in possession of these centres, the seeker begins to know beings, things, the world and himself in their reality, as they are, for he no longer catches external signs, no longer doubtful words, gestures, all that immured dumb show, nor the veiled face of things, but the pure vibration in each thing, each being, at every stage, which nothing can camouflage.

But our first discovery is ourselves. If we follow a process analogous to that described for the silent mind and if we remain perfectly transparent, we shall find that not only do mental vibrations come from outside before entering our centres but that *everything* comes from outside:

vibrations of desire, vibrations of joy, vibrations of will, etc. and that our being is like a receiving station, from top to bottom: *Truly, we do not think, will or act but thought occurs in us, will occurs in us, impulse and act occur in us.*[3] If we say "I think therefore I am" or "I feel therefore I am" or "I will therefore I am", we are somewhat like the child who imagines that the speaker or the orchestra is hidden in the music-box and that the radio is a thinking organ. For all these "I's" are not ourself nor belong to us and their music is universal.

The Frontal Being

We are tempted to protest, for after all it is *our* feelings, *our* pain, *our* desires, it is *our* sensibility and it is we, not some telegraphic machine or other! And in a sense this is true, it is we; in this sense that we have acquired the habit of answering certain vibrations rather than others, of being moved, pained by certain things rather than others, and that this mass of habits seems ultimately to have crystallized into a personality which we call ourself. But looking closer, it could not even be said that it is "we" who have acquired all these habits; it is our milieu, our education, our atavism, our traditions which have chosen for us and which at every moment choose what we shall will, what we shall desire, what we shall love or not love. And everything happens as if life moved on without us. At what moment does a true "I" burst forth amid all this?

....*Universal Nature,* says Sri Aurobindo, *deposits certain habits of movement, personality, character, faculties, dispositions, tendencies in us, and that is what we usually call ourselves.*[4] Nor can we say that this "ourself" has a real fixity: *The appearance of stability is given by constant repetition and recurrence of the same vibrations and formations*[4] because it is always the same wave-lengths we hook in or rather which hook themselves on to us, according to the laws of our milieu and our education, always the same mental, vital or other vibrations recurring through our centres, which we appropriate automatically, unconsciously, indefinitely; but in reality all is in a state of *constant flux* and all comes to us from a mind vaster than ours, universal; a vital vaster than ours, universal; or from regions lower still, subconscient; or higher, superconscient. Thus this small *frontal being*[5] is surrounded, overshadowed, sustained, traversed and moved by a whole hierarchy of "worlds" as the ancient wisdom has seen — "Without effort one world moves in the other," says the Rig Veda (II.24-5) — or, as Sri Aurobindo says, by a gradation of *planes of consciousness* which range successively without break from pure Spirit to Matter and have a direct relationship with each of our centres. But we are *conscious only of some bubbling on the surface.*[6]

What is left of ourselves in the midst of all this? Not much, to tell the truth, or everything, according to the level switched on by our consciousness.

Individualisation of Consciousness

We begin to catch a glimpse of what consciousness is and to feel that it is everywhere in the universe, at all stages to which our own centres correspond but we have not yet found "our" consciousness. Perhaps because it is not something to be "found" ready-made but something to be kindled like a fire. We have all felt at certain privi-

leged moments in our lives, like a warmth in our being, a
sort of inner surge or living power which words cannot
describe, which has no reason for being there because it
springs up from nothing, without cause, naked like a need
or a flame. All our childhood bears witness to this pure
enthusiasm, this inexplicable nostalgia. But very soon we
grow out of this adolescence and the mind lays hold of this
force as it does of everything and covers it up with big
idealising words, inserts it into a work, a profession, a
Church; or the vital being seizes upon it and daubs it with
more or less noble sentiments, when it does not use it for
some adventure or for domination, conquest, possession.
Sometimes this force is sucked in lower down. And sometimes all is sunk; only a tiny shadow is left under a burden.
But the seeker who has silenced his mind and can no
longer be trapped by ideas, who has calmed his vital being
and is not swept away at every moment in the great wastage of feelings and desires, rediscovers in this clarification
of his nature, like a new state of youth, a new free *surge*.
As his concentration grows stronger by "active meditation", by his aspiration, his need, he will feel that this
surge inside him begins *to live*: "She widens bringing out
that which lives," says the Rig Veda, (I.113-8), "awakening someone who was dead" — that it gathers a more
and more precise consistency, an ever denser strength
and, above all, an *independence*, as if it were at once a force
and a being within his being. He will notice, first of all
in his passive meditations (that is, when at home, calm,
with eyes closed), that this force in him has movements,
a mass, varying intensities and that it rises and descends
within him as if it were not steady — much like the shifting
of a living substance; these inner movements can even
gather a strength sufficiently great to end the body when

the force descends or to straighten it up and draw it back when it rises. In our active meditations, that is, in the ordinary external life, this inner force becomes more diluted and gives the sensation of a small muffled vibration in the background, as we have already seen; besides, we feel it is not only an impersonal force but a presence, a *being* in our depths, as though we had a support there, something that gives us a solidity, almost a backbone, and a quiet outlook on the world. With this little vibrating thing within, one is invulnerable and no longer alone. It is there everywhere, it is there always. It is warm, close, strong. And strangely enough, when one has discovered it, it is *the same thing* everywhere, in all beings, all things; there can be a direct communication as though it were exactly alike, without a wall. We have touched then something in us which is not a toy of universal forces, not the thin and dry "I think therefore I am" but the fundamental reality of our being, ourself, truly ourself, the true centre, warmth and being, consciousness and force.*

As this surge or this inner force takes on a distinct individuality, as it grows indeed as a child grows, the seeker will become aware that it does not move at random as he had thought at first, but that it gathers itself at various points of his being according to the activities of the moment and that really it is this force which is behind each centre of consciousness: behind the mental centres when one thinks, wills, expresses himself; behind the vital centres when one feels, suffers, desires; or lower, or higher; and that it is truly this which knows — all the centres including the mind are only its openings on the different stages of the universal reality or its instruments

* We shall speak later of this centre which Sri Aurobindo calls the *psychic centre* or the *psychic being*, and which others call soul.

of transcription and expression. It is this force which is *the traveller of the worlds*,[7] the explorer of the planes of consciousness; this which links our various ways of being, from waking to sleep and to death, when the small outer mind is no longer there to inform or guide us; this which climbs and descends all the gamut of universal existence and communicates everywhere. In other words, we have discovered *the consciousness*; we have disengaged what is in the ordinary man dispersed, mixed, caught in his thousand and one activities of thought and sense. Instead of locating ourselves eternally somewhere between the abdomen and the forehead, we shall be able to shift our consciousness to profounder or higher regions, inaccessible to the mind and to our sense organs; for consciousness is not a way of thinking or feeling (in any case not exclusively that) but a power of entering into contact with the myriad rungs of existence, visible or invisible. The more our consciousness develops, the more its radius of action and the number of degrees it can encompass grow. And this consciousness, we shall see, is independent of what is thought, felt, willed by our small frontal being; it is independent of the mind, the vital nature, and even of the body, for in certain particular states (which will be mentioned later) it comes out of the body and goes for a stroll elsewhere to get experiences. Our body, our thought, our desires are only a thin film of our total existence.

Consciousness-Force, Consciousness-Joy

In discovering the consciousness we have discovered that it is a force. What is more remarkable, a current or an internal force begins to be felt even before we see that it is a consciousness. Consciousness is a force; Sri Aurobindo speaks of *consciousness-force*, for in reality the two terms are inseparable and convertible. The ancient wisdom of India knew this well and never spoke of consciousness, *Chit*, without adjoining to it the term *Agni*, heat, flame, energy, *Chit-Agni* (sometimes called also *Tapas*, which is a synonym of *Agni : Chit-Tapas*). The Sanskrit word for the various spiritual or yogic disciplines is *tapasya*, that is, what produces heat or energy or more correctly, consciousness-heat or consciousness-energy. And this *Agni* or *Chit-Agni* is the same everywhere. We speak of the descending Force or the ascending Force or the internal force or of mental force, vital force, material force, but there are not so many different forces — there is but one Force in the world, a single unique current which passes through us and through all things and which puts on one substance or another according to the level of its action. Our electric current may light up a tabernacle or a tavern, a schoolroom, a refectory, and it continues to be the same current though it illumine different objects. So too, this Force or this Heat, *agni*, continues to be the same, whether it animates or illumines our inner retreat, our mental factory, our vital theatre or our material den; from level to level it wraps itself in a more or less intense light and more or less heavy vibrations — supramental, mental, vital, material — but it is this force which links up everything, animates everything; this, the fundamental substance of the universe: *Consciousness-Force, Chit-Agni*.

If it be true that consciousness is a force, inversely, force is consciousness and all *the forces are conscious*.[8] The universal Force is a universal Consciousness. This is what the seeker discovers. When he has contacted this current of consciousness-force in himself, he can switch on to any plane whatsoever of the universal reality, to any point, and perceive, understand the consciousness there or even act upon it, because everywhere it is the same current of consciousness with different vibratory modalities, in the plant and in the reflections of the human mind, in the luminous superconscient and in the instinct of the beast, in the metal and in our profoundest meditations. If the log of wood were inconscient, the yogi would not be able to displace it by his concentration, for there would be no point of contact between them. If a single point of the universe were totally inconscient, the whole universe would be totally inconscient, because there *cannot* be two things. Einstein has taught us, and indeed it is a great discovery, that Matter and Energy are convertible: $E=mc^2$, Matter is condensed Energy. We must now discover in practice that this Energy or this Force is a Consciousness and that Matter, it too, is a form of consciousness, as the mind is a form of consciousness, as the vital and the Superconscient are other forms of consciousness. When we have found this secret, consciousness in force, we shall obtain the true mastery of material energies — a direct mastery. But we are only rediscovering very ancient truths; four thousand years ago the Upanishads knew that Matter is condensed Energy or, rather, condensed Consciousness-Energy: "By energism of Consciousness* Brahman is massed; from that Matter is born and from Matter Life and Mind and the worlds" (Mundaka Upanishad I.1.8).

And all is Consciousness down here, for all is Being or Spirit. All is *Chit*, for all is *Sat* — *Sat-Chit* — at various levels of Its own manifestation. The history of our terrestrial evolution is finally the history of a slow conversion

* *Tapas.*

of Force into Consciousness or, more exactly, a slow recollection of itself by this Consciousness engulfed in its own Force. At the first stages of evolution, the consciousness of the atom, for example, is absorbed in its whirling, as the consciousness of a craftsman is absorbed in the work he fashions, forgetful of all the rest, as the plant is absorbed in its chlorophyllian function, as our own consciousness is absorbed in a book, a desire, oblivious of all the other levels of its own reality. All evolutionary progress is finally reckoned by the capacity to disengage or unhook the element of consciousness from its element of force — this is what we mean by the individualisation of consciousness. At the spiritual or yogic stage of our evolution, the consciousness is completely freed, unglued from its mental, vital, physical turmoils and master of itself, capable of ranging through the whole scale of vibrations of consciousness, from the atom to the Spirit; the Force has completely become Consciousness, it has completely recollected itself. And to remember oneself is to remember all, because it is the Spirit in us which remembers the Spirit everywhere.

Simultaneously, as the Force recovers its Consciousness, it recovers the mastery of its force and of all forces; for, to be conscious is to be capable. The atom which spins or the man who follows the biological round and labours in his mental factory is not the master of the mental, vital or atomic force; they turn round and round; whilst at the conscious stage we are free and masters; then we verify tangibly that consciousness is a force, a *substance*, which can be manipulated as oxides or electric fields are manipulated: *If one becomes aware of the inner consciousness*, says Sri Aurobindo, *one can do all sorts of things with it, send it out as a stream of force, erect a circle or wall of consciousness around oneself, direct an idea so that it shall enter somebody's head in America, etc. etc.*[9] He explains further: *The Invisible Force producing tangible results both inward and outward is the whole meaning of the Yogic consciousness.... If we had not had thousands of experiences showing that the Power within could alter the mind, develop its powers, add new ones, bring in new ranges of knowledge, master the vital movements, change the character, influence men and things, control the conditions and functionings of the body, work as a concrete dynamic Force on other forces, modify events...we would not speak of it as we do. Moreover, it is not only in its results but in its movements that the Force is tangible and concrete. When I speak of feeling Force or Power, I do not mean simply having a vague sense of it, but feeling it concretely and consequently being able to direct it, manipulate it, watch its movements, be conscious of its mass and intensity and in the same way as of other opposing forces.*[10] At a subsequent stage Consciousness can act on Matter and transform it. This ultimate conversion of Matter into Consciousness and perhaps one day even of Consciousness into Matter is the aim of the *supramental yoga* of which we shall speak later. But there are many degrees of development of the consciousness-force, from the seeker or aspirant just awakening to the inner urge to the yogi, and even among yogis there are many grades — it is here that the true hierarchy begins.

There is an ultimate equivalence. Not only is consciousness force, not only is consciousness being, but consciousness is joy, *Ananda* — Consciousness-Joy, *Chit-Ananda*. To be conscious is joy. When consciousness is released from the thousands of mental, vital, physical vibrations in which it lies buried, there is joy. The whole being is as if filled with a mass of living force ("like a well-shaped pillar," says the Rig Veda, V.45), crystalline, immobile, aimless — pure consciousness, pure force, pure joy, for it is the same thing — a *solid* joy, a substance of joy, vast, full of peace which seems to have neither beginning nor end nor cause, which seems also to be everywhere, in things, in beings, their secret foundation and their secret need to grow — nobody likes to give up life because this joy is there everywhere. It needs nothing to be, it *is*, irrefutably, like a rock across all time, all space, like a smile behind all things and everywhere. The whole Riddle of the universe is this. There is no other. An imperceptible smile, a mere nothing that is everything. And all is joy because all is the Spirit which is joy, *Sat-Chit-Ananda*, Existence-Consciousness-Joy, eternal triad which is the universe and which we are, the secret we must discover and live across the long evolutionary journey: "From Delight all these beings are born, by Delight they exist and grow, to Delight they return" (Taittiriya Upanishad III.6).

CHAPTER SIX

QUIETING THE VITAL

Limits of Ethics

There is a zone of our being at once the source of a serious difficulty and of a great power: a source of difficulty because it jams all the communications from outside or above, opposing frantically our efforts to silence the mind, gluing the consciousness to the level of its own petty occupations and preoccupations and hindering it from travelling freely towards other regions; a source of power because it is the outcropping of the great force of life within us. This is the region located between the heart and the sex-centre, called by Sri Aurobindo *the vital*.

This is the place of all the muddles; pleasure is inextricably mingled there with suffering, pain with joy, evil with good and make-believe with truth. The various spiritual teachings of the world have found it so troublesome that they have preferred to trace a cross over this dangerous domain and to allow only the so-called religious emotions, inviting the neophyte to reject all the rest. It seems that everybody agrees about it: human nature is unchangeable. But this *moral surgery*,[1] as Sri Aurobindo calls it, brings a double inconvenience; on the one hand, it does not truly purify because the higher emotions, however refined they may be, are as mixed as the lower ones for the good reason that they are sentimental and hence partial; on the other hand, it does not truly reject — it represses. The vital is a power in itself, quite independent of our reasonings or moral arguments, and if an attempt is made to tyrannise over it or ill-treat it by a radical aske-sis or discipline there arises the danger of seeing it revolt one day at the least fissure — and it knows how to avenge itself with interest — or, if we have enough strength of will to impose our mental and moral laws, we conquer perhaps, but at the expense of drying up the force of life in us, for the vital, discontented, goes on strike and we wake up puri-fied of the evil, yes, but of the good in life as well — colour-less and odourless. Moreover, morality functions only within the limitations of mental functioning; it has no ac-cess to the subconscious or superconscious regions or to death or to sleep (which after all takes up one day out of every three of our existence, so that out of a life of sixty years we are entitled to forty years of waking moral life and twenty years of immorality; a curious arithmetic). In other words, morality does not exceed the limits of the small frontal being. It is not then a moral and radical discipline which must be imposed upon our person but a spiritual and integral one which respects every part of our nature but by liberating it from its mixture; for, in truth, there is no absolute evil anywhere, there are only mixtures.

Besides, the seeker does not think in terms of good and evil (allowing that he yet "thinks") but in terms of exacti-tude and inexactitude. When a sailor wants to take the bearings he does not make use of his love for the sea but of a sextant and he sees to it that the mirror is clear. And if our mirror is not clear, we see nothing of the reality of things and beings because everywhere we find the image of our own desires or fears, everywhere the echo of our own tumult, and not only in this world but in all the worlds, in waking and sleep and death. To *see*, evidently we must stop being in the middle of the picture. The seeker distinguishes then the things which blur his vision from those which clear it; this will be the essence of his "morality".

The Habit of Response

The first thing he discerns in his exploration of the vital is a fraction of the mind whose only function is to give a form (and a justification) to our impulsions, our sentiments, our desires; this is what Sri Aurobindo calls *the vital mind*. But we have seen already how necessary mental silence is and we extend our discipline to this lower layer of the mind. Henceforth we see things clearly; without all their mental embellishments, the various vibrations of our being show themselves in their true light and at their true level. And above all we see them coming. In this zone of silence we have now become, the least displacements of substance (mental, vital or other) act on us like signals; immediately we know that something has come and touched our atmosphere. We then become aware, spontaneously, of a number of vibrations men emanate constantly without even knowing it and we know what is going on or before whom we stand (the external gloss having mostly nothing to do with this tiny vibrating reality). Our relations with the outer world become clear, we know the why of our sympathies and antipathies or of our fears, our uneasiness, and we put things in order, correct our reactions, accept those vibrations which are helpful, reject those which obscure, neutralize those which harm. For we notice a very interesting phenomenon: our inner silence has a power. If, instead of responding to a vibration which comes to us, we remain in an absolute internal immobility, we shall see that this immobility *dissolves* the vibration; it is like a field of snow around us wherein all shocks are caught, nullified. Take the simple example of anger; instead of beginning to vibrate inside in unison with the person who is speaking, if we can remain immobile within, we shall see that the anger of the other gradually dissolves like smoke. The Mother has remarked that this inner immobility or this power not to respond can even stop the uplifted arm of an assassin or the leap of a snake. Only, one must not just wear an impassive mask and be boiling inside; one cannot disguise vibrations (the animal knows them well); what is wanted is not the so-called "self-control" which is only the mastery of appearances, but the true internal mastery. And this silence can cancel any vibration whatsoever, for the simple reason that all vibrations of whatever order are *contagious* (the highest even as the lowest; it is thus that a Master can transmit spiritual experiences or a certain power to a disciple) and it depends on us to accept the contagion or not; if we are afraid it means that we have already accepted it and thus accepted the blow of the angry man or of the serpent (a blow may be accepted through love also; there is the significant story of Sri Ramkrishna who at the sight of a carter ill-treating a bullock uttered a sudden cry of pain and found himself whipped, bleeding, with marks of the lash on his back). The same holds for physical suffering; we may allow the contagion of a painful vibration to gain on us or circumscribe the point and eventually, according to the degree of our mastery, annul the suffering, that is, disconnect the consciousness from the pain. The key of the mastery is always silence, at all the levels, because in the silence we discern the vibrations and to discern them is to be able to capture them. There are any number of practical applications and above all any number of oppor-

tunities to make progress. The ordinary external life
(which is ordinary only to those who live ordinarily) becomes a vast field of experience and of the manipulation
of vibrations; this is why Sri Aurobindo always wanted to
extend his yoga there. It is very easy when alone to live
in the perfect illusion of self-mastery.

But this power of silence or inner immobility has much
more important applications, — particularly in our own
psychological life. The vital as we know is the place of
many miseries and perturbations but also the source of
a great force; the point is then to extract — somewhat
like the swan of the Indian legend which separates milk
from water — the force of life without its complications
and without extracting oneself from life. Need it be said
that the real complications are not in life but in ourselves
and that all external circumstances are the exact image
of what we are? Now, the main difficulty of the vital is
that it identifies itself falsely with all that seems to come out
of itself; it says : "my" trouble, "my" depression, "my"
temperament, "my" desire, and takes itself for all sorts
of tiny "I"s which are not it. If we really think that all
these stories are our story, there is nothing more to do
evidently except put up with the little family until it has
finished its hysterics. But if we can be silent within, we
see quite clearly that nothing of all this belongs to us;
everything comes from outside. We always hook in the
same wave-lengths, we let ourselves be infected by all the
contagions. For example, we are in the company of such
and such a person, we are silent and still within (which does
not prevent us from talking and acting as usual outside);
suddenly in this transparency we feel something which
pulls us or tries to enter into us like a pressure or a vibration (which may translate itself into an indefinable uneasi-

ness); if we take in the vibration, we find ourselves five minutes later struggling against a depression or having a particular desire, a certain restlessness — we have caught the contagion. And sometimes it is not merely vibrations but veritable waves which fall upon us. Nor is anyone's company needed for all this; one can be alone in the Himalayas and receive just as well the vibrations of the world. Where is "our" restlessness, "our" desire in this, if not in a habit of hooking in indefinitely the same impulsions? But the seeker who has cultivated silence will not get caught in this *false identification*,[2] he has at last found what Sri Aurobindo calls *the circumconscient, the environmental consciousness*,[3] this field of snow all around which may be very luminous and strong, solid, or which may become darkened, corrupted and may even disintegrate, depending on our inner condition. It is a sort of individual atmosphere or *protecting envelope* (sufficiently sensitive to disclose to us a person's approach or to make us avoid a mishap just at the moment it is going to overtake us) and it is here that we can feel and catch the psychological vibrations *before* they enter. Generally, they have become so accustomed to entering into us as into their home, through an affinity, that we do not even feel them coming; the mechanism of appropriation and identification is instantaneous; but our practice of silence creates a transparency sufficient for us to see them come, then to stop them on the way and reject them. Sometimes, when we have rejected them, they remain circling in the circumconscient,* waiting for an opportunity to enter — we can very distinctly feel anger, desire, depression prowling about around us — but through sheer non-intervention

* Unless they sink into the subconscient. This will be mentioned again later in the study of that region.

these vibrations lose their strength and then they leave us in peace. We have unhooked ourselves. And we are quite surprised to find, one day, that certain vibrations which seemed irresistible touch us no longer; they are as though emptied of their power and pass as on a cinema-screen; we can even see beforehand with curiosity these little rogues trying once again their tricks. Or again, we find that certain psychological states break upon us at a fixed hour or recur according to certain cyclic movements (this is what Sri Aurobindo and the Mother call *formations*, that is an amalgam of vibrations which through habitual repetition finally acquires a sort of independent personality) and we see that these formations when switched on do not stop until they are reeled off from one end to the other like *a gramophone record*.[4] It is for us to determine whether we want to be taken in or not. There are thousands of experiences possible, it is a world of observations. But the essential discovery we shall have made is that there is very little of "us" in all this, except *a habit of response*.[5] As long as we identify ourselves falsely with vital vibrations, through ignorance, it is impossible to change anything in our nature except by amputation, but the day we have seen the mechanism, all can change, because we can stop all response, we can dissolve in the silence the perturbing vibrations and switch on elsewhere, if it so pleases us. Human nature can be changed despite all the dicta. There is nothing in our consciousness or nature which is ineluctably fixed, all is only a play of forces or vibrations which by their regular recurrence gives us the illusion of a "natural" necessity. And this is why the yoga of Sri Aurobindo envisages *the possibility of an entire reversal of the ordinary rule of the reacting consciousness*.[6]

Having discovered the mechanism, we shall have found

at the same time the true method of mastering the vital, a method not surgical but quieting; the difficulty of the vital is not reduced by struggling vitally against it, which would only exhaust our energies without exhausting its universal existence, but by taking another position, neutralising it through a silent peace: *If you get peace,* wrote Sri Aurobindo to a disciple, *then to clean the vital becomes easy. If you simply clean and clean and do nothing else, you go very slowly for the vital gets dirty again and has to be cleaned a hundred times. The peace is something that is clean in itself, so to get it is a positive way of securing your object. To look for dirt only and clean is the negative way.*[7]

The Adverse Forces

There is another difficulty, for the vibrations which come from people or from the universal vital are not the only ones to disturb the seeker (besides, it is scarcely possible to distinguish between them, individuals being only *ground stations*[8] of the universal vital — or the universal mind and the vibrations passing from the one to the other indefinitely, in a closed circuit); but there is one type of vibrations of a particular nature which can be distinguished by its suddenness and its violence; the seeker feels these vibrations literally swooping down upon him like a tempest; within a few moments he becomes "another man", having quite forgotten the purpose of his being, his efforts, his aim, as though everything had been swept away, bereft of meaning, decomposed. These are what Sri Aurobindo and the Mother call *the adverse forces.* They are very conscious forces whose sole aim, apparently, is to discourage the seeker or turn him from the path he has chosen. The first sign of their presence is easily perceptible: joy is veiled, consciousness is veiled and all is enveloped in an atmosphere of tragedy. As soon as suffering comes one may be sure the enemy is there. Drama is their favourite haunt, it is there that they can create the greatest havoc because they play with a very old partner in us who cannot help loving drama even when he weeps much. Their first care, generally, is to push us into sudden, extreme, irrevocable decisions which take us away as far as possible from the chosen path — it is a vibration which grows ever sharper and more pressing and wants *immediate* compliance — or they dismantle the whole mechanism of our search with a remarkable skill to prove to us that we are deluding ourselves and that our effort will come to nothing; or more often they bring about a state of depression, playing with another well-known partner whom Sri Aurobindo calls *the man of sorrows*: *a fellow…covering himself with a sevenfold overcoat of tragedy and gloom and he would not feel his existence justified if he couldn't be colossally miserable.*[9] All these vibrations of disorder which we call "our" sorrows or "our" troubles have as their immediate result the weakening or decomposing of our protecting field of snow and — the door is open to the adverse forces. They have a thousand ways of attacking us, for indeed it is an *attack*, and the more determined we are, the more relentlessly they pursue. This may perhaps seem to be an exaggeration, but only those who have never tried to progress can doubt; so long as one goes with the common herd life is relatively easy, with its spells of good and bad, without too much that is low but also without too much of the high; as soon as we want to get out of it, a thousand forces arise, very interested in seeing that we do "what everybody does"; then we discover how well organised is the imprisonment. Yet another discovery we make is that it is possible for us to descend as low down as it is possible to climb up and that in truth our lowest reaches are exactly in proportion to our capacity for the heights — many scales fall from our eyes. With a little honesty we see clearly that we are capable of anything and that finally, as Sri Aurobindo says, our *virtue is a pretentious impurity*.[10] Only those who have never gone beyond the frontal being can still cherish any illusions on the subject.

All sorts of demoniacal and "black" names have been reserved for these adverse forces in the spiritual history of the world, as though they were there solely to damn the seeker and give gratuitous trouble to good people. The reality is somewhat different, for where then is the devil if not in God? and if he is not in God, nothing much remains in God, for this world is sufficiently wicked and a good many others also, so that not much remains of the pure, save perhaps a mathematical point without any dimension, which makes no stain. But experience shows us that these perturbing forces have their place in the universal economy and that they are troublesome only on the level of our small momentary consciousness, and even here they have a fixed aim. Now, first they catch us always through the gaps in our armour; if we are solid and single-minded, they cannot shake us for a second. Then if, instead of whining and blaming the devil or the wickedness of the world, we look into ourselves, we find that each of these attacks has exposed one of our innumerable gentlemanly trickeries or, as the Mother says, has slightly drawn aside *the little cloaks we throw over things to avoid seeing*. And the small cloaks or the big ones cover not only our wounds, they are everywhere in the world, covering its little insufficiencies and its enormous sufficiencies; and if the perturbing forces pull them off a bit violently sometimes, it is not just by chance nor through wanton malice but to make us see things clearly and compel us towards a perfection at which we boggle because we have the unfortunate tendency, as soon as we have got hold of a sprig of truth or a straw of an ideal, to treble-lock it in hermetic and infallible construction and not want to budge from there. In other words, for the individual as for the world, these hardly gracious forces are instruments of progress. "By what men fall, by that they rise," says the Kulârnava Tantra in its wisdom. We protest against the apparently useless and arbitrary "catastrophes" which strike our heart and our flesh and we blame the "Enemy" but *is it not possible that the soul itself — not the outward mind, but the spirit within has accepted and* chosen *these things as part of its development in order to get through the necessary experience at a rapid rate, to hew through,* durchhauen, *even at the risk or the cost of much damage to the outward life and the body? To the growing soul, to the spirit within us, may not difficulties, obstacles, attacks be a means of growth, added strength, enlarged experience, training for spiritual victory?*[11] We cry out against the evil, but had it not been there to besiege and defy us, long ago we would have trapped the eternal Truth and made of her a tidy little well-established insipidity. Truth moves, she can run, and the princes of darkness are there to see to it, a little brutally, that she does not sleep. *God's negations are as useful to us as His affirmations,*[12] says Sri Aurobindo. *The adversary will disappear,* observes the Mother, *only when he is no longer necessary in the world. And we know very well that he is necessary, as the touchstone for gold, to find out if one is true.*

For after all, God is not perhaps a pure mathematical point outside this world; perhaps He is all this world and all this impurity which labours and suffers to become perfect and remember Itself down here.

The method in face of these adverse forces is the same as for the other vibrations: silence, inner stillness which lets the wave pass. We may not succeed perhaps at the first trial in dissolving their attacks but they will seem to take place more and more on the surface of our being; we may be shaken, upset, and yet somewhere deep down we shall feel the "Witness" in us who is not touched — who is never touched — who does not suffer. There are falls and there are risings and each time one rises up stronger. The only sin is to be discouraged. Practically, the seeker of the integral yoga will be much more exposed than others (Sri Aurobindo often used to say that his yoga was a *battle*[13]) because he wants *to embrace everything in his consciousness*, without cutting off anything, and because there is not only one passage to break through towards the beatitude of the heights, not only one guardian of the treasure to conquer, but many passages, to the right and left and below and at all the levels of our being, and more than one treasure to discover.

The True Vital

There is then a passage to cross if we want to find the true force of life behind the disturbed life of the frontal man. According to the traditional spiritual doctrines, this passage is accompanied by all sorts of mortifications and renunciations (which, by the way, magnify above all the ascetic's good opinion of himself), but we are after something else; we do not seek to leave life but to widen it; we do not seek to give up oxygen for hydrogen, or vice versa, but to study the constitution of consciousness and see under what conditions it will give us clear water and a better working. Yoga is *a greater art of life*,[14] said Sri Aurobindo. *The attitude of the ascetic who says "I want nothing" and the attitude of the man of the world who says "I want this thing" are the same,* remarks the Mother. *The one may be as attached to his renunciation as the other to his possession.* In fact, so long as one needs to renounce anything at all, one is not ready, one is still up to the neck in the dualities. Now, we can make without any special discipline a certain number of observations. To begin with, it is enough to say to the vital, "Renounce this, abandon that", for it to be seized by an immediate hunger; or if it agrees to renounce, we may be sure it expects to be paid back in another coin and, as long as it is at it, it prefers a great renunciation to a small one, because it is always itself working, negatively or positively — for it the two sides are equally nourishing, the one as much as the other. If we have unmasked this simple truth, we shall have understood the whole working of the vital, from top to bottom, that is, its total indifference to our human sentimentalisms — suffering interests it as much as joy, privation as much as abundance, hatred as much as love, torture as much as ecstasy; in every instance it feeds itself fat. For it is a Force and it is the same Force in suffering as in pleasure. Thus is bluntly shown up the absolute ambivalence of all sentiments without exception which make the niceties of our frontal being. Each sentiment is the inverse of another; at any moment it may change into its "opposite" — the disillusioned philanthropist (or rather the disillusioned vital of the philanthropist) becomes a pessimist, the zealous apostle retires to the desert, the indomitable unbeliever becomes a votary and the pure man is scandalised by all he dare not do. And we have seized another failing of the surface vital: it is *an incorrigible charlatan,*[15] it wins all along the line (we do not know if even the death of one's mother would escape its pleasure). Each time we utter a cry of reprobation or pain (any cry), a monkey within us laughs. But we know all this and yet we are as sentimental as ever. And to crown its accomplishments the vital excels in befogging everything — it is fog incarnate — it takes the force of its sentiments for the force of the truth and *substitutes for the heights a smoky volcano summit in the abyss.*[16]

Another observation which follows from the first strikes us immediately: it is the complete powerlessness of the vital to help another or simply to communicate with others except when there is a conjunction of egoisms. There is not a vital vibration emitted by us or rather relayed by us which cannot immediately change into its opposite in someone else; it suffices to wish someone well for the corresponding ill-will to awake automatically, as though it were nabbed at the same time as the other, or the corresponding resistance or the opposite will — the mechanism seems as spontaneous and unescapable as a chemical process. But in fact the vital does not care to help, it cares to take, always, in all sorts of ways. All our sentiments are tinged with grabbing. The single fact for example, of pain at betrayal by a friend (or of any pain) is a sure sign of our ego, for if truly we loved men for themselves and not for ourselves, we would love them in all possible ways, even as enemies; in every event we would have the joy of their existence. In truth our sorrows and our sufferings are always the sign of a mixture, and so always deceitful. Joy alone is true. Because the one real thing in us is the 'I' which embraces all existences and all the

possible contraries of existence. We suffer because we put
things outside us. When all is within, all is joy, because
there is no hole any more, anywhere.

Still we protest; in the name of our sentiments we say,
"But the Heart?" with a capital H. Precisely the heart,
is it not the most mixed place? Besides it gets breathless
quickly, and this is our third observation. Our capacity
for joy is small, our capacity for suffering is small, we are
soon blunted by the worst calamities, what waters have not
flowed past over our mighty troubles? We can contain
little of this great Force of Life — *we cannot hold the charge*,
says the Mother — just a breath too much and we cry out
with joy or pain, we weep, we dance, we swoon away.
Because it is always the same ambiguous Force which
flows and before long overflows. The Force of Life does not
suffer, it is not troubled, not exalted, not wicked, not good
— it just is, it flows vast and peaceful. All the contrary
signs that it puts on in us are only the vestiges of our past
evolution, for we were small, quite small and separated,
and we had to preserve ourselves from this living enormity
too intense for our smallness, and distinguish "useful"
vibrations from "harmful" vibrations, the former having
a positive coefficient of pleasure or sympathy or good, the
latter a negative coefficient of suffering or repulsion or evil;
but suffering is only a too great intensity of the same
Force and too intense a pleasure changes into its painful
"opposite": These *are conventions of our senses*,[17] says Sri
Aurobindo; *it is enough just to shift the needle of the consciousness a little*, says the Mother. *To cosmic consciousness in its
state of complete knowledge and complete experience all touches
come as joy*, Ananda.[18] Only the narrowness, the insufficiency of consciousness is the cause of all our evils, moral
and even physical, and of our impotence and of that

sempiternal tragi-comedy of existence. But the remedy is not to cripple the vital as the moralists would like to, but to enlarge it; not to renounce but to accept more, always more, and to widen one's consciousness. For that is the very meaning of the evolution. The only thing in fact which must be renounced is our ignorance and our pettiness. When we cling frantically to our small frontal being, to its comedies and its sentimental viscosity and its sanctified sorrows, we are not truly "human", we are the outdated laggards of the Pleistocene, we *defend our right to sorrow and suffering*.[19]

The seeker will no longer be the dupe of the equivocal play enacted in his surface vital but he will yet keep for quite a long time the habit of responding to the thousands of small biologico-sentimental vibrations which circle around him. It is a fairly long passage, like passing from the twaddling mind into mental silence, and this transition may be accompanied by periods of intense fatigue because the organism loses the habit of renewing its energies at the common superficial source (which very soon appears to be gross and heavy when one has tasted of the other energy) without having yet the capacity to remain constantly connected to the true source, whence certain "holes"; but here too he will be helped by the descending Force which will contribute powerfully in establishing a new rhythm in him — he will find with an ever-renewed surprise that if he but takes one small step forward, the Help from above takes ten towards him, as though he were expected. It would be quite wrong to think that it is a negative task; the vital of course is pleased to say that it makes huge efforts to struggle against itself, which is a clever way of protecting itself on every side, but in reality the seeker does not obey an austere and negative command, he follows a positive urge of his being; for he is really growing and the norms of yesterday or the pleasures of the day before seem to him as meagre as the diet of a suckling — he is no longer at ease in all this, he has to do better, to live better. This is why it is so difficult to explain the path to one who has not tried; he will see only his point of view of today or rather the loss of his point of view. And yet, if we only knew how each loss of one's viewpoint is a progress and how life changes when one passes from the stage of the closed truth to the stage of the open truth — a truth like life itself, too great to be trapped by points of view, because it embraces every point of view and sees the utility of each thing at every stage of an infinite development; a truth great enough to deny itself and pass endlessly into a higher truth.

Behind this infantile, restless, quickly spent vital, we discover a vital which is calm and powerful — what Sri Aurobindo calls *the true vital* — a vital which contains the very essence of the Force of Life without all its sentimental and sorrowful excrescences. We enter a state of tranquil, spontaneous concentration, even as the sea may be under the play of the waves. And this fundamental immobility is not a nervous numbness, even as mental silence is not a cerebral torpor, it is the basis of action. It is a concentrated strength which can set going all acts, bear all shocks, even the most violent and the most prolonged, without losing its peace. All sorts of new capacities can emerge in this vital immobility, according to the degree of our development, but first of all an inexhaustible source of energy — as soon as there is fatigue it is a sure sign of our having relapsed into the superficial agitation. The capacities of work or even of physical effort become tenfold, food and sleep are no longer the unique and all-absorbing source of the renewal of energy (sleep changes its nature, we shall see, and food may be reduced to a hygienic minimum avoiding all the dullness and disease it usually brings). Other powers also, considered often "miraculous", may manifest, but they are *miracles with a method*; it is not possible to speak of them here, it would be better to make the experiment for oneself. We may just say that if anyone is capable of controlling a single vital vibration in himself, he is automatically capable of controlling the same vibration everywhere it is met with in the world. Then, in this immobility another sign will be permanently established: the absence of suffering and a sort of unalterable joy. As soon as the ordinary man receives a shock, whether physical or moral, his immediate reaction is to withdraw into himself; he shrinks back, begins to boil inside and increases tenfold the evil. On the contrary, the seeker who has established some immobility in himself will find that this immobility dissolves all the shocks, because it is *wide*, because he is no longer a small individual doubled up on himself as on a stomach-ache but a consciousness overflowing the limits of his body — the calm vital like the silent mind universalises itself spontaneously: *In yoga experience the consciousness widens in every direction, around, below, above, in each direction stretching to infinity. When the consciousness of the yogi becomes liberated, it is not in the body, but in this infinite height, depth and wideness that he lives always. Its basis is an infinite void or silence, but in that all can manifest — Peace, Freedom, Power, Light, Knowledge, Ananda.*[20] As soon as there is suffering of any kind, it is the immediate sign of a narrowing of the being and a loss of consciousness.

A very important corollary follows upon this widening of the being which will make us understand the absolute necessity of this vital immobility, not only for the clarity of communication or for the power of our action or the joy of living, but simply for our security. So long as we live as the small frontal fellow, the vibrations are small, the shocks are small, the joys are small and we are protected by our very smallness; but when we emerge into the universal Vital, we find the same vibrations or rather the forces on a gigantic, universal scale, for it is these which make the world dance, even as they make us dance, and if we have not acquired a perfect *equality* or inner immobility, we are swept away. And this is true not only of the universal Vital but of all the planes of consciousness, for one can and one must (at least the integral seeker must) realise the cosmic consciousness at all the levels, in the Superconscient, the mental, the vital and even in the body; now, when he will rise into the Superconscient, the seeker will understand that the intensities of the Spirit also can be overpowering (in reality, it is always the same Force, the divine Force, the same Consciousness-Force above and below, in Matter or Life or Mind or higher up, but the more It descends the more it is obscured, deformed, broken up by the media through which It passes) and if the seeker, getting out of his heavy denseness, wishes to rise up too rapidly, to force the stages without having taken care to establish an unshakable and clear basis, he may explode like a boiler. Vital transparency is not then a problem of morality but a technical problem, if we may say so, or even organic. In truth, the great Solicitude is always there to stop us from premature experiences; perhaps we are narrow and small only as long as we have need to be narrow and small?

Finally, when we have mastered vital immobility, we find that we can begin to help others with some efficacy.

For, to help others is not a question of sentiments or charity but a question of power; a matter of vision, a matter of joy. In this tranquillity, not only is there a radiating joy but a vision which dispels all shadows; spontaneously we shall perceive all the vibrations, and to be able to distinguish them is to be able to manipulate, quiet, avert them or even to change them. *Tranquillity*, says the Mother, *is a very positive state; there is a positive peace which is not the contrary of strife — a peace active, contagious, powerful, which dominates and calms, puts everything in order, organises.* An example of this "contagious peace" anticipates a little an event in Sri Aurobindo's life: It was in Pondicherry, many years ago, in that season when the tropical rains, sometimes cyclones, sweep down suddenly and work havoc. Doors and windows have to be barricaded with stout bamboo laths. That night a cyclone had burst with torrents of rain and the Mother had hastily come to Sri Aurobindo's room to help him shut the windows. He was seated at his desk as usual (Sri Aurobindo spent twelve hours writing, from six in the evening to six next morning, for years together; then for eight hours he used to walk up and down "for yoga") the windows were wide open, not a drop of rain had entered. The peace which reigned in that room, relates the Mother, was so solid, so compact, that the cyclone *could not* enter.

CHAPTER SEVEN

THE PSYCHIC CENTRE

We are not the mind, for all our thoughts come from a
Mind vaster than ours, universal; we are not the vital
nor our sentiments nor our acts because all impulsions
come from a Vital wider than ours, universal; and we
are not this body either, for its components come from
a Matter and obey laws greater than ours, universal.
What then is this thing in us which is not our milieu,
our family, our traditions, our marriage, our profession,
which is not the plaything of universal Nature or of circumstances and which is the reason why each of us would
be "I", even if everything else crumbled down? and above
all, which is "I" when everything else crumbles, because
it is the hour of *our* truth.

In the course of our reconnoitring, we have observed various centres and levels of consciousness and seen that
behind these centres there is a consciousness-force which
moves and links our diverse states of being (one of the
first results of mental silence and of the calming of the vital
has even been to separate this consciousness-force from
mental and vital activities wherein it is usually embedded)
and we have felt that this current of force or of consciousness is the fundamental reality of our being behind all
our states. But this consciousness-force is the consciousness of *someone*. Who then is conscious in us? What is the
centre, who the master? or are we simply the marionettes
of some universal Being who would be our true centre
because all these mental, vital, physical activities are in
fact universal activities? The truth is twofold and under

no condition are we marionettes except when we persist in taking the frontal being for ourselves, for that is the real marionette. We have an individual centre which Sri Aurobindo calls *the psychic being* and a cosmic centre or *central being*. Stage by stage we must find the one and the other and become Masters of all our states. For the moment, we are only in search of our individual centre, the psychic, which others call soul.

This is at once the simplest thing in the world and the most difficult. The simplest, because a child understands it, or rather *lives* it, spontaneously — he is lord, he laughs! he lives in his psychic being.* The most difficult, because this spontaneity is very soon covered over by all sorts of ideas and sentiments. Then we begin to speak of "soul" which means that we no longer understand anything about it. All the suffering of adolescence is just the story of a slow imprisonment of the psychic (we speak of a "crisis of growth" but it is perhaps a crisis of suffocation, maturity being attained when the suffocation has become a natural state) and all the difficulties of the seeker are the inverse story of a slow extirpation of all mental and vital mixtures. However, it is not only a backward journey, first because one never goes back, then because the psychic child found at the end of the journey (an end which is always the beginning) is not a momentary caprice but a *conscious* royalty. For the psychic is a being, it grows — it is the miracle of an eternal childhood in an ever-vaster kingdom. It is "within as a child to be born", says the Rig Veda (IX.83.3).

---

* There are exceptions and degrees, but they are almost visible to the naked eye.

The Psychic Birth

The first manifestations of the psychic are love and joy — a joy which may be extremely intense and powerful but without exaltation, calm, deep like the sea, and without an object. Psychic joy has no need of anything to be, it *is*, even in the depths of a prison it cannot help being, it is a state not a sentiment, like the river which flows and sparkles wherever it passes, over mud or rocks, through the plains or the mountains. A love which is not the contrary of hatred and which also needs nothing to be, it *is*; it burns calm in all it meets with, all it sees, all it touches, because it cannot help loving, that is its state; nothing is low for it nor high, nor pure nor impure; its flame cannot be tarnished nor its joy. Other signs also reveal it: it is light, nothing is a burden to it, as though the world were its play; it is invulnerable, nothing touches it, as though it were for ever beyond all tragedies, already safe from all accidents; it is the magus, it sees; it is tranquil, tranquil as a tiny breeze in the depths of the being; vast as though it were the sea through millions of years. For it is eternal. And it is free, nothing can catch it; neither life, nor man, nor ideas, nor doctrines, nor countries — it is beyond, always beyond, and yet innumerably at the heart of each being, as if it were one with all. For it is God in us.

To the eye which sees, this is how the psychic appears: *When one looks at somebody who is conscious of his soul and lives in his soul,* says the Mother, *there is the impression of descending, of entering deep, deep into the person, far, far, very far within; whilst generally, when one looks into the eyes of people (there are eyes one cannot enter, closed like a door; but still there are eyes which are open), one enters; then, quite close behind, one meets something which vibrates, which sometimes shines, which sparkles. And if deceived, one says, "Oh, he has a living soul"— it is not that: it is his vital. To find the soul one must step back from the surface, withdraw deep within, and enter, enter, go down, far down into a very deep hole, silent, still; and then down there, is something warm, tranquil, rich in contents and very still, and very full, like a sweetness — this is the soul. And if one persists and is conscious in oneself, a sort of plenitude comes which gives the impression of something complete holding unfathomable profundities. And one feels that if one entered there many secrets would be revealed, like the reflection in calm, peaceful waters of something which is eternal. And the limits of time are no more. One has the impression of having always been and of being for eternity.*

But these are only signs, an outward translation of something which is self-existent and which we want to experience directly. How to open the doors of the psychic? for it is well hidden. And before all, it is hidden by our ideas, our sentiments, which plunder it and mimic it mercilessly; we have so many ideas about what is high and low, pure and impure, divine and undivine, so many small sentimental bolts and bars against what is lovable and unlovable, that this poor psychic has not much of a chance to show itself, the place is already taken up by all this clutter; as soon as it shows its face, it is immediately pounced upon by the vital which uses it for its own brilliant exaltations, its "divine" and palpitating emotions, its selfish loves, its grasping generosities, its gaudy aesthetics; it is shut up in a cage by the mind which uses it for its exclusive ideals, its infallible philanthropies, its padlocked moralities; and Churches, innumerable Churches put it into article and dogma. Where is the psychic within all that? It is there, yet, divine, patient, striving to pierce through all the crusts and making use of everything, in truth, everything that is given to it or imposed upon it — "it does with what it gets," as we say. And this precisely is the big danger-rock; when it comes out of its hiding place, for a second, it throws such a glory upon all it touches, that we naturally confuse its luminous truth with the circumstances of the revelation. One who has had the revelation of his psychic, listening sometime to Beethoven, will say: music, nothing but music is true and divine down here; another who has felt his soul in the immensity of the ocean will make a religion of the great open sea; and another still will say: my prophet, my chapel, my gospel. And each builds his construction around a core of experience. But the psychic is free, marvellously free of all things; it needs nothing for its existence, it is the very essence of Liberty and uses all our small or great music, our Scriptures sublime or less sublime, to make just a hole in this human cuirass through which it may escape; it lends its strength and its love, its joy, its light, its irresistible open Truth to all our ideas, our sentiments, our doctrines, because this is the only chance it is given to see the light, the only means it has to express itself; but in this very act, these emotions, these ideas, these doctrines draw from it all their assurance; they appropriate it and wrap it up, they imbibe from this element of pure Truth their indisputable certitudes, their exclusive profundity, their one-way universality, and *the very strength of the element of truth increases the strength of the element of error*.[1] The burial of the psychic is so complete, finally, the mixture so perfect, that one is quite at sea and cannot extirpate the counterfeit without destroying the very fact of the truth — and the world goes thus, weighed down with half-truths which are more heavy than lies. The true difficulty, perhaps, is not in liberating oneself from the evil, for we know well what kind of a thing it is — it cannot resist the least little sincerity — but in liberating oneself from that good which is only the reverse of evil and which has for ever shut its doors on even a particle of truth.

If we want to have the direct experience of the psychic in its crystalline purity, so marvellously fresh, as it exists irresistibly outside all the traps we set for it, outside all we think of it, feel about it, say about it, we must create a transparency within — Beethoven, the sea, the chapel were only instruments of that transparency — for it is ever the same: as soon as one is clear the Truth emerges sponta-neously and the vision, the joy, — all is there without one's needing to do anything, because Truth is the most natural thing in the world; it is all the rest which jam everything — the mind and the vital with their disordered vibrations and their wise complications. All spiritual disciplines worth the name, all *tapasya* must finally tend only towards this completely natural point where there is no need of effort — effort is yet another jamming, another thickening of the being. The seeker will not try then to enter the jam-ming of the moral mind or the impossible task of sorting out the good from the evil in order to release the psychic, for, after all, the utility of the good *and* the evil is intimately linked with their mutual harmfulness (*my lover took away my robe of sin and I let it fall, rejoicing; then he plucked at my robe of virtue, but I was ashamed and alarmed and prevented him. It was not till he wrested it from me by force that I saw how my soul had been hidden from me*[2]); he will simply try his best to pour everything out into the silence, for silence is in it-self clean, it is lustral water. "Do not try to wash off one by one the stains on the robe," says a very ancient Chal-dean tradition, "change it altogether". This is what Sri Aurobindo calls a *change of consciousness*. In this trans-parency, in fact, the old creases of the being are quietly

smoothed out and we feel another station of the consciousness — not intellectual but a centre of gravity. At the level
of the heart but deeper than the vital centre of the heart
(which only covers up and copies the psychic), we feel a
zone of concentration intenser than the others which seems
to be their point of convergence — this is the *psychic centre*.
Already we had felt a current of conciousness-force taking
shape within us, individualising itself, circulating in the
body and becoming more and more intense as it slowly
disengaged itself from its mental and vital activities, but
at the same time something was kindled at the centre like
a fire — *Agni*. This is the true 'I' in us. We say that we
have "a need to know", "a need to love", but who is it
within us that has the need? not the little ego, surely, so
satisfied with itself, not the mental chap who turns round
and round, nor the vital fellow who tries to take and ever
take more, but behind there is this fire which does not
slacken, it is this which has the need, for it remembers
something else. One speaks of "the presence" but it is
rather a poignant absence, like a living hole one carries
within, which warms, burns, pushes up more and more
and finally becomes real and the only reality in a world
where one wonders if men truly live or only pretend to.
This is the self of fire, the only true self in the world, the
only thing which does not crumble: "A conscious being
is the centre of the self, who rules past and future; he is
like a fire without smoke.... That, one must disengage with
patience from one's own body", says the Upanishad.*
This is "the boy suppressed in the secret cavern" of which
the Rig Veda speaks (V.2.1), "the son of heaven by the
body of the earth" (III.25.1), "he that is awake in those
who sleep" (Katha Upanishad V.8). "He is there in the

* *Katha Upanishad* IV. 12, 13; VI. 17.

middle of his house" (Rig Veda 1.70.2), "He is as if life and the breath of our existence, he is as if our eternal child" (1.66.1), he is "the shining King who was hidden from us" (1.23.14). This is the Centre, the Master, the place where all things communicate:

> *The sunlit space where all is for ever known.*[3]

If we have felt this Sun within, this flame, this living life — there are so many dead lives — even for a second in one existence, everything is changed; it is a remembrance before which all the others look pale. It is *the* Remembrance. And if we are faithful to this *Agni* which burns, it will grow ever stronger like a living being in our flesh, like an inexhaustible need. And it will be concentrated more and more within, enclosed, poignant like something that cannot burst out: *A terrible sensation of something which prevents sight and entry; one tries to pass through and finds oneself before a wall. And then one knocks and knocks and knocks and yet cannot pass*, says the Mother. Then by force of need, by force of will and all choked up in this imprisonment, the psychic tension one day reaches its reversal-point and we have the experience: *The pressure becomes so great, the intensity of the problem so strong that something tips over in the consciousness. Instead of being outside and trying to see within, one is within; and the moment one is within, absolutely everything changes, completely. All that appeared true, natural, normal, real, tangible, all this immediately appears very grotesque, very droll, quite unreal, quite absurd. But one has touched something supremely true and eternally beautiful; and this, one never loses this again.* "O Fire, when thou art well borne by us thou becomest the supreme growth and expansion of our being, all glory and beauty are in thy desirable hue and thy perfect vision. O Vastness, thou art the plenitude that carries us to the end of our way; thou art a multitude of riches spread out on every side" (Rig Veda II.1.12). The true life opens as though one had never before seen daylight: *Place the prism in one position*, says the Mother, *the light is white; turn it over, and the light is broken up. Well, this is exactly what happens; you restore the white. In the ordinary consciousness there is the decomposition and you restore the white.* And the Mother once again explained the experience thus: *One is seated as it were before a closed door, a heavy door of bronze, and one remains there with the will that it open, to pass through to the other side. Then all the concentration, all the aspiration gathers into a single beam and starts pushing, pushing against this door, pushing harder and harder, with an ever-increasing energy, until suddenly the door gives way. And one enters, as if precipitated into the light.*

Then one is truly born.

Psychic Growth

Of all the experiences when the door of the psychic opens, the most immediate and most irresistible is that of having always been and of being for ever. One emerges into another dimension where one sees oneself old as the world and eternally young and that this life is *one* experience, *one* link, in an uninterrupted succession of experiences which stretch out behind us and are lost in the future. All widens to the dimensions of the earth; what man have we not been? what fault have we not borne? All the values are reversed; what is not ours in all these pettinesses and these grandeurs, where is the stranger, where the traitor, where the enemy? O divine comprehension, compassion absolute. And everything breathes anew, as though one had passed from a life of the caverns to a life of the high plateaus; all is linked and gathers together as though the old riddle were ripped up in the winds of light — death is no more, the ignorant alone can die, how should that which is conscious suffer death? *Whether I live or die, I am always.*[4] "Old and outworn he grows young again and again," says the Rig Veda (II.4.5.), "It is not born nor dies," says the Gita; "nor is it that having been it will not be again. It is unborn, ancient, everlasting; it is not slain with the slaying of the body. As a man casts from him his wornout garments and takes others that are new, so the embodied being casts off its bodies and joins itself to others that are new. Certain is the death of that which is born and certain is the birth of that which dies."*

What is commonly called reincarnation is not particular to the teaching of Sri Aurobindo; all the ancient wisdoms have spoken of it, from the Far East to Egypt and the Neo-Platonists† but Sri Aurobindo gives it a new meaning. For the minute one gets out of the little momentary vision of a single life cut short by death, two attitudes are possible: either one may think, with the exclusive spiritualists, that all these lives are a painful and futile chain from which it is essential to liberate oneself at the earliest to rest in God, in Brahman or some Nirvana; or one may believe with Sri Aurobindo — a belief founded on experience — that the aggregate of these lives represents a growth of consciousness which culminates in a *terrestrial* fulfilment or, to put it otherwise, that there is an evolution,

* Gita II. 18, 20, 22, 27.
† It is interesting to note that the Fathers of the Church at the Alexandrian Council also discussed whether reincarnation should be admitted in their doctrines.

an evolution of the consciousness behind the evolution of the species and that this spiritual evolution must end in a realisation, individual and collective, on the earth. One may ask how the traditional spiritualists, being enlightened sages, did not see this terrestrial realisation. To begin with, the question refers to the relatively modern spiritualists, for the Veda (whose secret Sri Aurobindo has found) and perhaps other traditions so far badly deciphered attest the contrary; it would seem that here the spirituality of our historic epoch is marked by an obscuration of the consciousness parallel to its mental development. Then, it would be quite surprising if the spiritualists could arrive at conclusions different from their premises; having started with the idea that the terrestrial world is an illusion or an intermediate realm more or less given up to the flesh and the devil, they could not but come to where their premises led them: it was outside the world they naturally sought liberation or salvation. Instead of exploring patiently all human resources, mental, vital, physical and psychic, to free them from their gangue and enlarge them, in a word, to divinise them, as the Vedic sages had done and perhaps those of all the ancient Mysteries, not to speak of Sri Aurobindo, they have rejected everything and wanted *to shoot at once from pure mind to pure spirit*,[5] and so naturally they could not see what they refused to see. The materialists have skipped over things from the other end; they have explored a tiny bit of physical reality and rejected all the rest; starting from the idea that matter alone is real and all the rest a hallucination, they could not but end up where their premises led them. But if we start quite simply, without preconceptions, as Sri Aurobindo did, armed with an open truth and a total confidence in the integral possibilities of man, we shall perhaps have a chance to arrive at an integral knowledge and so at an integral life.

Seen from the point of view of an evolution of the consciousness, reincarnation ceases to be the futile round some have seen in it or the imaginative extravagance others have made of it. With a clarity typical of the West, Sri Aurobindo rids us of this *spiritual romancing*, as the Mother calls it, into which so many serious learnings have degenerated since the end of the Age of the Mysteries, and he invites us to an experimentation, not extra lucid but just lucid. It is not a question of "believing" in reincarnation but of experiencing it and, first of all, of knowing under what conditions the experience is possible. Here is a practical question concerning our integral development through all time. Now, it is not the small frontal being which reincarnates, though this may disappoint those who picture themselves immortally as Mr. Smith, in Elizabethan gaskins, then in satin breeches, then in synthetic trousers — it would be tedious besides. The meaning of reincarnation is at once deeper and more vast. The whole façade disintegrates at the time of death; the aggregate of mental vibrations which were amalgamated around us due to their habitual repetition and formed our mental ego or mental body, disintegrates and returns to the universal Mind; in the same way the vital vibrations which form our vital ego or vital body disintegrate into the universal Vital, even as the physical body disintegrates into its natural constituents in universal Matter. Only the psychic stays; it is eternal, as we have seen. Our experience of reincarnation depends then on the discovery of the Centre and psychic Master who carries his memories from one life to another and on the degree of our psychic development. And if our psychic has remained buried all our life under our mental, vital and physical activities, it has no memories to take with it — it returns again and again precisely to emerge on the surface of our being and become openly conscious. To remember, first it is necessary to stop being amnestic, that is evident. It is hardly possible, then, to speak of reincarnation below a certain stage of development, for what is the good of saying that the psychic reincarnates, if it is not conscious? This becoming conscious is the very sense of the evolution.

From life to life the psychic grows silently behind the frontal being, it grows through the thousand sensations of our body, the thousand shocks of our sentiments, the innumerable thoughts which stir in us; it surges up through our soarings and our falls, our sufferings and our joys, our good and our evil — these are its antennae for feeling the world; and when this exterior amalgam dissolves, it carries away only the *essence* of all its experiences, certain general tendencies which have stood out more strongly and become the first embryo of the *psychic personality* behind the frontal being;* it brings certain results from the past life, for all our acts have a dynamism which tends to perpetuate itself (what is called *karma* in India); certain imprints which are translated in another life into special predispositions, particular difficulties, innate tastes, inexplicable hauntings, irresistible attractions, and sometimes certain circumstances which repeat themselves

* The psychic or true personality expresses the unique destiny of each being (perhaps we should say the unique angle) behind its cultural, social or religious clothings. Thus a particular individual could successively be a navigator, a musician or a revolutionary, Christian, Musulman or atheist, but each time he will express the same angle of love, for example, or of conquering power or of joy, of purity, which will give a special colouring to all he undertakes, and each time this angle will become more precise, purified, wider.

almost mechanically as if to put us before the same problem to be resolved. Each life represents then one type of experience (we believe we have many experiences but it is always the same) and it is by an accumulation of innumerable types of experience that slowly the psychic acquires an individuality, stronger and stronger, more and more conscious and more vast, as if it had not really begun to exist before it had run through the whole gamut of human experiences. And the more it grows, the more the consciousness-force individualises itself in us, the more the psychic tension increases, pushes through, till one day it needs no longer its frontal chrysalis and springs up into full daylight. Then it can become directly aware of the world around; it becomes the master of the nature instead of being its sleeping prisoner; consciousness becomes the master of its force instead of being glued down in the force. Yoga is precisely that point of our development at which we pass from the interminable meanderings of natural evolution to an evolution that is conscious and self-directed : it is *a process of concentrated evolution.*

There are then all the degrees from the ordinary man in whom the psychic is just a latent possibility to the awakened being. Without reincarnation it is difficult to explain the immense difference of degree between souls, between that of the pander, for example, and that of a Dante or a Francis of Assissi or even simply that of a man who seeks and of an *economic philistine,* as Sri Aurobindo calls him, unless spiritual development is considered as a question of education, milieu and heredity, which manifestly is not true; or must we believe that only the sons of respectable families have a soul and that three-fourths of inconscient humanity is doomed to an eternal damnation? *The very nature of our humanity,* says Sri Aurobindo, *supposes a varying constituent past for the soul as well as a resultant [terrestrial] future.*[6] And if one wants to think, despite everything, that man has but one life at his disposal, one runs into an absurdity: *Plato and the Hottentot, the fortunate child of saints or Rishis* and the born and trained criminal plunged from beginning to end in the lowest fetid corruption of a great modern city have equally to create by the action or belief of this one unequal life all their eternal future. This is a paradox which offends both the soul and the reason, the ethical sense and the spiritual intuition.*[7] But even among the awakened ones, there are enormous differences of degree; there are souls, consciousness-forces, just born, and others who have an individuality already well-formed; souls who are in the first radiant blaze of their discovery but who do not know much outside their own radiating joy, who have not even precise memories of their past, not even any consciousness of the worlds they carry within, and others, rare ones, who seem charged with a consciousness as vast as the earth. For one may be a luminous yogi or a saint who lives in his soul, and yet have a crude mind, a suppressed vital, a body which is despised and treated like an ass, and a completely blank superconscient. "Salvation" has perhaps been realised but not the plenitude of an integral life.

Upon the discovery of the psychic must then follow what we could call metaphorically "the psychic colonisation" or more soberly *the psychic integration*. Contemporary psychology also speaks of integration, but it may be asked around what it wants to integrate; for integration a centre is necessary. Integrate around the convulsions of the mental and vital ego? as well moor a boat to the tail of an eel. Patiently, slowly, after having

* Sages of the Vedic Age, at once seers and poets, who composed the Vedas.

discovered the inner psychic kingdom, it is necessary to colonise and adjoin to it the outer realm; all our mental and vital activities and even, we shall see, all our physical nature if we want a terrestrial realisation, must be integrated around this new centre. It is on this condition alone that they will survive: only those activities which are "psychicised" participate in the immortality of the psychic. All that goes on outside the psychic goes on really outside us and has not a longer duration than the body. There are lives where no one is found. The psychic must be present in our exterior activities to be able to remember exterior things, otherwise it is like a blind king. Then and then alone can we begin to speak of reincarnation and the remembrances of things past — remembrances not necessarily of the doughty deeds more or less showy and glorious (how many Napoleons, how many Caesars, if one may believe the romancers of reincarnation!) but memories of *soul-moments*,[8] because for the psychic nothing is glorious or non-glorious, nothing high or low, and the conquest of Everest is not greater than the daily walking down to the tube when this is consciously done. It is in itself all glory.

These "soul-moments" may retain the impress of the physical circumstances which accompanied them; we may remember a setting, a place, a costume which we wore then, a banal detail which is as it were stamped with eternity at the same time as the inner revelation; but we have all known, in this very life, these moments of pure transparency or of a sudden flowering and, twenty, forty years later we find intact this snapshot with the faintest colour of the sky which clung to it, even the pebble which lay there on the road or the absurd daily round, as if all this was there for eternity — and it is not "as if", *it is* for eternity, truly ; these are the only moments we have lived, in which a true "I" has emerged in us from all those hundreds of hours of inexistence. In tragic circumstances also the psychic can emerge, when the whole being gathers together at one go in a great poignant intensity and something is torn apart; then may be felt a kind of presence behind which makes us do things we would normally be quite incapable of doing. And this is the other face of the psychic, not only of joy and sweetness but of calm strength, as though it were for ever above all possible tragedies, an invulnerable master. Here too the details of the scene can be indelibly imprinted. But what passes on into the next life is not so much the details as the essence of the scene; we meet certain junctures or circumstances, certain deadlocks which strike us suddenly with their look of "a play already acted" and appear enveloped in a halo of fatality: what we have not conquered in the past returns again and again, each time with slightly different faces but fundamentally always the same, until we have confronted the ancient knot and untied it. This is the law of inner progress.

But generally the precise memory of physical circumstances does not tend to perpetuate itself, for these are of little importance after all, although our little surface consciousness makes much of them. There is even a spontaneous mechanism which effaces the crowd of useless memories of the past, just as in this present life their crowd dissolves. If we look behind us in a single snatching glance, without thinking, what actually is left over of our present life? A greyish mass with two or three images afloat; all the rest is blotted out. It is the same with the soul and its past lives. There is an immense sorting. And this mechanism of forgetfulness works very wisely for a long time, for if we were to recall prematurely our former lives we would risk being constantly hampered; already in our present lives there are so many useless memories which stand like a wall in the way of our progress because they freeze us in the same inner attitude, the same contraction, the same denial, the same revolt, the same bias. To grow we need to forget. And in our outer consciousness, irremediably childish as it is, if we happened to remember for instance having been once a certain virtuous banker and if we found ourselves suddenly in the skin of a needy scamp, we would make nothing of it! for we are yet too young, perhaps, to understand that our soul had need to know the contrary of virtue or rather that it has allowed the abscess hidden by its virtue to be pierced. Evolution does not lie in becoming more and more saintly or more and more intelligent but more and more conscious. Many ages must pass before the capacity to bear the truth of past lives comes.

All depends then on the degree of our development and the extent to which our psychic being has participated in our outer life; the more we have "colonised" the exterior, the more memories we carry away. Unhappily, most frequently we are content with an "inner life", they say, and outside we live no matter how, by habit. This is the contrary of an integral yoga. But if from the beginning, instead of rejecting all worldly activities in order to plunge into the exclusive quest of the soul, we have embraced everything in our search, all the levels of our being, all life, we would have an integral and integrated life where we would be the same outside as within; whilst if one has excluded everything to arrive at so-called "spiritual" goals, it is very difficult afterwards to retrace one's steps and descend from these fragile heights to set free the mind and universalise it, release the vital and universalise it, clean the subconscient and work finally in the physical dirt to divinise it; one is too well-established up there to stir all this bog and, to tell the truth, one *can no longer do it*. In fact, one does not think about it, for how could one have the idea of undertaking this enormous task if, to begin with, one considers the mind perishable, the vital perishable, the body perishable, and the sole aim of life to get out of it and find one's salvation?

The psychic realisation or discovery of the soul is not then the end for the seeker, it is only the very small beginning of another voyage which is made in consciousness instead of in ignorance — in an ever vaster consciousness, for the more the psychic being grows and enters into our wordly activities, the more its mental, vital, physical memories become clear, precise, continuous from one life to another — then we begin to understand what immortality means — the more its births also become concerted, willed, efficacious. We are free, we are awake for ever. Death is no longer that grinning mask which reminds us that we have not found ourselves but a calm passage from one mode of experience to another; we have caught once for all the thread of consciousness and we pass hither and thither as from one country to another and back again to the old earth until the day when, perhaps, as Sri Aurobindo declares, we are sufficiently grown up not only to assure the continuity of our mental and vital existence but to infuse enough consciousness into the body so that it also participates in the psychic immortality. For everything, always, is a question of consciousness, for our mental, vital and physical life as for our sleep and our death and our immortality. Consciousness is the means, consciousness is the key, consciousness is the end.

CHAPTER EIGHT

INDEPENDENCE FROM THE PHYSICAL

After the mind and the vital, the physical, the third instrument of the Spirit in us, plays a particular role in the
yoga of Sri Aurobindo, for without it a *divine life* is not
possible on earth. We shall take up now only some prepa-
ratory points of experience, the very ones discovered by
Sri Aurobindo at the commencement of his yoga; the yoga
of the body, in fact, necessitates a much greater development of consciousness than that envisaged so far — the
more one descends towards Matter, the more one needs
high powers of consciousness, for the resistance also increases. Matter is the place of the greatest spiritual difficulty
— but also *the place of the Victory*. The yoga of the body
lies outside the scope of our vital or mental power and
comes under a *supramental yoga* of which we shall speak
later.

Independence from the Senses

Matter is the starting point of our evolution; enclosed
in it consciousness has gradually evolved; so the more the
consciousness emerges, the more it must recover its sovereignty and affirm its independence. This is the first step
(not the end, let us note). Now, we are in an almost total
subjection to the needs of the body in order to live and to
the organs of the body to perceive the world; we are
very proud, and rightly, of our machines, but it is enough
that our own is a little out of order in the head for

everything to get jammed, and if we do not have at our disposal the complicated arsenal of our wireless, telephones, television, etc., we are incapable of knowing what goes on around or even of seeing further than the end of our street. We are the hyper-civilised who have not physically gone beyond the state of the savage. Possibly our machinery is not the symbol so much of a mastery as of a terrible powerlessness. The blame lies equally with the materialists who have not believed in the power of the inner Spirit and the spiritualists who have not believed in the reality of Matter. This impotence, however, is not beyond remedy, it is due above all to the fact that we believe ourselves impotent; we are somewhat in the position of one who having inherited from his ancestors a pair of crutches has no longer any faith in his legs. In short, it is a question of believing in our own consciousness — it has not only legs but millions of eyes and arms, and even wings.

In the very history of our evolution, the consciousness, submerged in Matter, has grown accustomed to depend on a certain number of outer organs to perceive the world and because we have seen the antennae appear before the master of the antennae, we have concluded, puerilely, that it is the antennae which have created the master and that without the antennae there is no master, no perception of the world. But this is an illusion. Our dependence on the senses is only a habit, millennial it is true, but not more ineluctable than the chipped flint implements of the Chellean man: *It is possible for the mind — and it would be natural for it, if it could be persuaded to liberate itself from its consent to the domination of matter, — to take direct cognisance of the objects of sense without the aid of the sense-organs.*[1] We can see, we can feel across the continents as though distances did not exist, because distance hampers only the body and its organs not the consciousness which can be everywhere it wishes in a second if it has learnt to widen itself — there is another space, more airy, where all is gathered in a lightning-point. Perhaps we expect here some sort of a "recipe" of clairvoyance and ubiquity, but recipes are yet another machinery of a second order. That is why, besides, we like them. Certainly hatha yoga has its efficacy like all the methods, more or less yogic, which consist in staring at a lighted candle (*tratak*), working out infallible dietetics, doing respiratory exercises and stifling oneself scientifically (*pranayama*).... Everything is useful, everything can be useful. But these methods have the disadvantage of being long and limited in compass; besides, they are always uncertain and sometimes dangerous when handled by those insufficiently prepared or purified — it is not enough to want power, the machine must not crack when it receives the power; it is not enough to "see", we must also be ready to understand what is seen. Practically our task would be much simplified if only we could understand that it is *the consciousness* which makes use of all these methods and acts through all the methods and that if we go directly to the consciousness we get hold of the central lever. With this advantage that the consciousness does not deceive. Even if it were given as a method a piece of wood, the consciousness would end up by making it into a magic wand — but this would not be the merit of the piece of wood or the method. Even if it were shut up in the depths of a cavern, it would finish by finding a means to look outside — this is, besides, the whole history of the evolution of consciousness in Matter.

For the integral seeker, the work on the body naturally comes to accompany his work on the mind and the vital;

for convenience we have described one after another the various stages of being but all march abreast and each victory, each discovery on any plane whatever, has its repercussions on all the other planes. When working on the silence of the mind, we have observed successively several mental layers which we have reduced to silence: a *thinking mind* which constitutes our normal ratiocination, a *vital mind* which justifies our desires, our sentiments, our impulsions; there is also a *physical mind* which will give us a lot of trouble, but its conquest is as important for physical mastery as is the conquest of the thinking mind or of the vital mind for vital or mental mastery. It seems, decidedly, that this mind is the scapegoat of the integral yoga, we hunt it down everywhere; actually it was a very precious help in the course of our evolution and continues still to be the indispensable agent for many, but all our helps, no matter which, no matter how high, how divine, change one day into obstacles because their value is only for one step and we have many steps to take and more than a truth to conquer. If we accept this simple proposition throughout our ladder of values, without forgetting to include in it the ideal to which we are attached at present, we go very fast on the path of evolution. This physical mind is the most stupid thing, it is the vestige in us of the first appearance of the Mind in Matter; a microscopic mind, stubborn, fearful, limited, conservative (this was its evolutive utility) which makes us verify ten times if necessary that we have locked a door properly which we certainly know we have closed, which becomes panicky at the least scratch and sees itself consigned to the most frightful diseases as soon as something goes wrong, which is imperturbably sceptical about all that is new and raises mountains of difficulties when it must change ever so little its routine — it repeats and repeats in us like a muttering old spinster. We have all at one time or another made its acquaintance and it is such a matter of shame for us that we send it packing, but it is still there, down below, muttering all alone; the full sonority of our habitual household is necessary to shut out its voice. When the thinking mind and the vital mind have been silenced, we find it is there all right and that it is frightfully sticky. It is not even possible to reason with it, it is too stupid. It must, however, yield, for if the thinking mind is a screen against the widening of our mental consciousness, the vital mind an obstacle to the universalisation of our vital consciousness, the physical mind puts up a solid wall against the expansion of our physical consciousness which is the basis of all physical mastery. Not only that, but it jams all the communications and calls in all the misfortunes; it is enough — and this point is of enormous importance — to think of something or someone for us to be *instantaneously* in communication (most often unconsciously) with all the vibrations which represent this thing or this person and all the consequences of these vibrations. Now, the physical mind, precisely by its gnomish fears, puts us in constant contact with the most annoying possibilities. It always imagines the worst. This craze has only a relative importance in man's ordinary life where the activities of the physical mind are lost in the general hubbub and where we are protected by our very lack of receptivity, but when we have worked systematically to create a transparency within us and to increase our receptivity, the jammings of the physical mind become a serious obstacle and even dangerous.

This mental, vital and physical transparency is the key of a twofold independence. Independence from the sensations, for the consciousness-force, disengaged from its innumerable dispersions at the various levels of our being and gathered up in a dirigible beam, can at will be disconnected from any point whatever, from cold, from hunger, from pain, etc. Independence from the senses, for liberated from its immediate absorption in our mental, vital and physical activities, this same consciousness-force can extend beyond the bodily frame and by a sort of inner projection contact things, beings and events at a distance. Generally a state of sleep or hypnosis is necessary to see a little farther in space or in time and to disengage oneself from immediate sensations, but these primitive and cumbrous means are not at all needed if the mental tumult is hushed and we are masters of our consciousness. Consciousness is in truth the *only organ*.[2] It is this which feels, sees, hears. Sleep and hypnosis are simply very rudimentary means of lifting the curtain of the surface mind. And it is but normal! If we are full of the noise of our desires and our fears, what else indeed can we see but the innumerably repeated image of our desires and fears? As the calm mind and the quieted vital universalise themselves, so the clarified physical universalises itself spontaneously. We are our own prisoners; the world is waiting all wide at our doors, if only we would consent to pull aside the screen of our small constructions. To this capacity of widening of the consciousness must naturally be joined a capacity of concentration, so that the widened consciousness may settle, immobile and silent, on the object contemplated and in some way *become* this object. But concentration or widening are spontaneous corollaries of the inner silence. In the inner silence, the consciousness sees.

Independence from Illness

When we are freed from the tension of the thinking mind and its buzzing, from the tyranny of the vital mind and its restlessness, its insatiable exigencies, from the denseness and the fears of the physical mind, we begin to understand what the body is without all these tiring overloads and we discover that it is a marvellous instrument — docile, enduring, full of an inexhaustible good will. It is of all the most misunderstood instrument and the most illtreated. In this general clarification of our being, we observe first that the body is never ill, simply it gets worn out, but even this wearing out is not perhaps irremediable as we shall see with the supramental yoga. It is not the body which is ill, it is the consciousness which is wanting; as one advances in yoga, one sees in fact that each time illness comes or even each time there is an outer "accident", it is *always* the result of inconscience or of a wrong attitude, of a psychological disorder. This study is all the more interesting because the moment we set foot on the path of yoga something in us is immediately *alerted* which, every minute, makes us see, even touch palpably, our errors and the cause of all that happens to us, as if "someone" was in truth taking seriously our seeking — nothing is left in the darkness; and we discover more and more, sometimes with stupefaction, a rigorous correlation between our inner state and the outer circumstances (illnesses, for example, or "accidents"), as though the course of life did not unwind from outside inwards but from inside outwards, the within fashioning the outer, even the most banal outer circumstances — in fact, nothing is banal any more and the daily life seems a network crowded with signs awaiting our exploration. Everything holds together, the world is a miracle. We commit a childish mistake, perhaps, in imagining that the spiritual life means seeing visions, apparitions, and contemplating "supernatural" phenomena — the Divine is nearer us than we think, the "miracle" less flagrant and more profound than all this coloured pasteboard imagery. When we have deciphered a single one among these small signs which cross us, guessed but once the imperceptible link which binds all things, we are nearer the great Miracle than if we had touched the heavenly manna. For the miracle perhaps is that the Divine is also natural. But we do not pay heed.

The seeker then becomes aware of this reversal of the current of life, from inside outwards and for a good reason: the psychic Master has come out of his imprisonment, he deciphers these daily signs and sees that the inner attitude has the power of shaping outer circumstances in two ways, good and bad; when we are in a state of harmony and our action corresponds to the deep truth of our being, it seems that nothing can offer resistance; even the "impossibilities" dissolve, as though another law had been superimposed upon the "natural" law (in reality it is the true naturalness which emerges from its mental and vital complications) and we begin to taste a royal freedom; but when there is an inner disorder, mental or vital, we find that this disorder irresistibly *calls* in annoying outer circumstances, the intrusion of an illness or an accident. The reason for this is simple: when we are in a bad inner state, we emit a certain type of vibration which, automatically, calls up and contacts all the other vibrations of the same type, at all levels of our being; it is a general jamming which disturbs all the outer circumstances and makes everything go wrong. And not only does the bad inner state cause a jamming but it weakens the circumconscient protecting envelope we have mentioned; that is, instead of being guarded by a certain vibratory intensity, we are left open, vulnerable — there is nothing better than a vibration of disorder to make *holes* in our protecting envelope or rather to decompose it — and anything may enter. Besides, this bad inner state is contagious: there are people who always draw accidents or troubles. When we have undergone ten times, a hundred times, the same experience, which may range from the common cold or a commonplace fall to a serious accident, according to the inner state, we come to know well that neither our body nor the so-called "luck" have anything to do with all this, and that the remedy too is not in any outer drug but in the recovering of the right attitude, in the inner order, in the consciousness. If the seeker is conscious, he can pass through the midst of any epidemic, drink all the dirt of the Ganges if it so please him, nothing will touch him, for what could touch the awakened Master? Bacteria and viruses have been isolated but we have not understood that they are only the agents and that the illness is not the germ but the force which makes use of it and, if we are clear, all the viruses of the world can do nothing to us because our inner force is greater than this force or, better, because our being vibrates at an intensity too high for that low intensity. Only the similar can enter the similar. And this is also why cancer may be eliminated, for instance, after other medieval maladies have been eliminated, but the *forces* of illness will not be eliminated and they will make use of something else, of another agent, another virus, once their present medium has been tracked down. Our medicine touches only the surface of things, not the source. There is but one illness, inconscience. At a more advanced stage, when we have established sufficiently well the inner silence and are capable of perceiving mental and vital vibrations as they enter into our circumconscient, we shall be able to perceive similarly the vibrations of illness and to throw them out before they enter: *If you can become conscious of this environmental self of yours*, wrote Sri Aurobindo to a disciple, *then you can catch the thought, passion, suggestion or force of illness and prevent it from entering into you.*[3]

Two other categories of illness need yet to be noted, illnesses which are not related directly to our errors: those which come from a subconscious resistance (we shall speak of this later with the purification of the subconscient) and those which may be called "yogic illnesses", which come from a rift between the development of the higher stages of our consciousness and the development of our physical consciousness. It may happen that our mental or vital consciousness widens considerably and receives new intensities whilst our physical consciousness still lags behind in the old vibratory movement and cannot bear this increased intensity. This leads to an upsetting of equilibrium which may bring an illness, not through the intrusion of an outer agent, a microbe or some virus, but through a rupture in the normal relations between the inner elements: allergies, colloidal disorders of the blood, etc. or nervous and mental troubles. Here we border on the problem of the receptivity of matter to the higher forces of consiousness, one of the big problems of the supramental yoga. In any case, this is one of the reasons why Sri Aurobindo and the Mother insist so much on the development of our physical basis; without this, we may go into an ecstasy and shoot up straight into the Absolute, perhaps, but not bring down the intensities and the amplitude of the Spirit into our "lower" kingdom, mental, vital and material, to create there a divine life.

Independence from the Body

The consciousness can then be independent of the sense-organs, independent of illness, independent to a large extent of food and sleep, when it has discovered the inexhaustible reservoir of the great Force of Life. And it can be independent even of the body. When the current of consciousness-force in us is sufficiently individualised, we find that not only can we detach it from the senses and the objects of the senses but also from the body. In our meditations first of all, for this is the first field of training before the natural mastery comes, we observe that this consciousness-force becomes particularly homogeneous, compact and that after disengaging itself from the mind and vital, it withdraws itself slowly from all the rustlings of the body which becomes perfectly still like a transparent block or like something that occupies no place, has no weight, something almost inexistent; the respiration becomes more and more imperceptible, the beatings of the heart more and more delicate; then, suddenly, there is an abrupt breaking free and we find ourselves "elsewhere", outside the body. This is what is called in technical language "exteriorisation".

There are all kinds of "elsewheres", as many as the planes of consciousness, and we may go out here or there according to the level at which our consciousness is fixed (already we know the universal Mind and the universal Vital), but the most proximate elsewhere which borders our physical world and resembles it with a greater intensity is what Sri Aurobindo calls *the subtle physical*. This knowledge is as old as the world and is not peculiar in any way to the yoga of Sri Aurobindo; it simply is a part of our integral development and prepares us for the day when we shall leave our body for a longer period in what men ignorantly call "death". This may be made more clear by the following experience of the subtle physical as it was recounted by a young boy of the Ashram at Pondicherry when he had gone out for the first time from his body: "I was stretched out on my easy-chair, in concentration, when all at once I found myself at my friend's house; he was playing music with several others. I could see very clearly, even more clearly than in the physical, and I moved about very quickly, without hindrance. I remained there a good while, watching; I even tried to draw their attention but they were not conscious. Then, suddenly, there was something that pulled me, like an instinct: I must go back. I had the sensation of a pain in the throat. I remember that to come out of their room which was all closed except for a small opening in the ceiling, my form seemed to vaporise (because I still had a form but it was not as of matter, it was more luminous, less opaque) and I went out like a smoke by the open window. Then I found myself back again in my room near my body and I saw that my head was lying askew, rigid against the cushion, and that I was breathing with difficulty; I wanted to re-enter my body, — impossible. This time I was seized with fear. I entered by the legs and then, having come as far as the knees, it was as if I was slipping out; twice, thrice, thus; the consciousness climbed up, then slipped out like a spring. I told myself: If only I could turn over this stool (there was a small stool under my feet), it would make a noise and I would wake up! Nothing doing. And I breathed more

and more heavily. I was terribly afraid. Suddenly I remembered Mother and I called: Mother! Mother! and I
found myself back in my body, awake, with a stiff neck."*
Thus, after many cycles of burial and awakening and innumerable shocks which compel it to remember itself and
get hold of itself and close itself in to grow up sheltered,
the consciousness, having become a formed individuality,
breaks its shell and affirms its independence. This independence, writes Sri Aurobindo, *will come to be so much the
normal attitude of the whole being to the physical frame that the
latter will feel to us as if something external and* detachable *like
the dress we wear or an instrument we happen to be carrying in our
hand. We may even come to feel that the body is in a certain sense
non-existent except as a sort of partial expression of our vital force
and of our mentality. These experiences are signs that the mind is*

---

* Three observations may be made. First, that it was by quite an
amusing inexperience that this boy tried to re-enter his body "by the legs"!
— it is not surprising that he had so much trouble. It is generally through
the heart-centre that one goes out and returns. One may also go out
through the top of the head, but this is scarcely recommended. When the
yogis wish to leave their bodies definitively (what is called in India *iccha-
mrityu*, or death at will), they go out through the top of the head. Then
we observe that when one is exteriorised, the body grows cold, the circulation is reduced to a minimum; this chilling may go as far as a complete
catalepsy with all the outer signs of death, according to the "distance" of
the consciousness in relation to the physical level. This is an opportunity
to verify very concretely that if the consciousness withdraws, the force withdraws, because it is the same thing. When we swoon the consciousness
withdraws also, because we cannot bear certain intensities, but as we have
not learnt to build a conscious bridge between our various states of being,
our involuntary retreat is translated by a blank. The last observation is
that the single fact of remembering his Master, that is, here, the Mother,
was sufficient to restore order in the disorder of fear and to help the
disciple to make the correct movement for re-entering the body: by
thinking of the Mother, he instantaneously switched on the true vibration,
which put everything straight. Here is, roughly, one of the mechanisms of
the protection or help of the Master to the disciple.

coming to a right poise regarding the body, that it is exchanging the false viewpoint of the mentality obsessed and captured by physical sensation for the viewpoint of the true truth of things.[4] For the true viewpoint, always, is that of the Master, the psychic, the Spirit in us — each time we feel an impossibility or a limitation, a barrier, we may be sure it is our victory of tomorrow, for if we did not feel the obstacle we would not be on our way to conquer it, and we are made to conquer all and live all our dreams, for it is the Spirit that dreams in us. And the first of these dreams, perhaps, in a world where bans close down more and more upon us like an iron cage, is to sail at large, unlimited by the body and the frontiers. Then we no longer need passports, we are the stateless, heirs of all the nations of the world, without a rubber-stamp; we know a delightful freedom and wideness of life: "O Vastness"...says the Rig Veda.

CHAPTER NINE

SLEEP AND DEATH

The Planes of Consciousness

Everyone is not capable of consciously leaving his body or of consciously widening his mind or vital but many do it unconsciously in their sleep, that is, precisely when the little "I"s of the frontal being are less of a hindrance and less narrowly absorbed in their superficial preoccupations. These various "I"s express a fraction of the reality, that seen by the naked eye, but immense domains stretch far behind; already we have heard of a universal Mind, a universal Vital, a subtle Physical behind this physical film; it is a question then of recovering the integrality of our universal reality. There are three methods or three stages of doing it; the first, which is at everybody's disposal, is sleep; the second, rarer, is conscious exteriorisation or profound meditation; the third represents an already advanced degree of development in which everything is simple: it is possible to do without sleep and meditation and to see in any way, even with eyes wide open in the very midst of other activities, as though all the stages of universal existence were present before our eyes and accessible by mere shiftings of the consciousness, somewhat as when one adjusts his sight from an object that is nearby to a far-off object. Sleep, then, is a first instrument of work; it can become conscious, more and more conscious, until the moment we are sufficiently developed to be continuously conscious, here or there, and when sleep as also death is no longer a return to the vegetative state or a dispersion into our natural components, but simply a passage from one mode of consciousness to another. Because, in truth, the line of separation we have traced between sleep and waking, life and death, answers perhaps to an observation of external appearances but has no essential reality any more than the reality of our national frontiers for physical geography or the reality of the coloured, fixed, external object for nuclear physics. In fact, there is no separation *except for our inconscience,* and the two worlds (or rather this one and innumerable others) coexist constantly, are constantly intermingled, and it is only a certain way of perceiving *the same thing* which makes us say in one case "I live" and in the other "I sleep" or "I am dead" (if we are conscious enough to notice this) as it is possible in a way to have different experiences of the same object according to the particular level from which it is seen, sub-atomic, atomic, molecular or external — the "elsewhere" is everywhere here. We have attached a unique and exclusive value to the various symbols which form our outer physical life because they are found just here under our nose, but they are not more nor less valid than the other symbols which constitute our extra-physical life — the atomic reality of an object does not nullify and is not separated from its external reality, and vice versa. And not only are the other symbols as valid as our physical symbols but we understand nothing, truly, of our own symbols if we do not understand *all* other symbols. Without the knowledge of the other degrees of reality, our knowledge of the ordinary human world remains as incomplete and as false as would be a study of the physical world without a knowledge of molecules, atoms and particles. Nothing is understood until all is understood.

There is thus an infinite gradation of coexistent, simultaneous realities, upon which sleep opens for us a natural skylight. For after all, if we get out of the superficial life-death-sleep classification to follow an essential classification of the universe, we see that from top to bottom (if there is such a thing as top and bottom) this universe is nothing else but a continuum of consciousness-force or, as Sri Aurobindo says, a gradation of *planes of consciousness* which range uninterruptedly from pure Matter to pure Spirit — subtle Physical, Vital, Mental, Supramental (we may use other words if we like, another terminology, but the fact remains the same) — and that everything takes place in the midst of these planes, our life and our sleep and our death; there is nowhere to go outside this; and not only is everything located there but everything coexists there, without separation. Life, death, sleep are simply different *stations* of the consciousness amidst this same gradation. When we are awake, we receive mental or vital vibrations which are translated into certain symbols, certain ways of seeing, of understanding or of living; when we are asleep or "dead", we receive *the same* mental, vital and other vibrations which will be translated by other symbols, other ways of seeing, understanding or living *the same reality*. In all these instances, the key of our existence, here or elsewhere, is always our capacity of consciousness; if we are unconscious in our life, we shall be unconscious in every way; death will be truly a death and sleep truly a torpor. To become aware of these various degrees of reality is then our fundamental task; and when we have done this work integrally, the lines of artificial demarcation which separate our diverse modes of living will crumble and we shall pass without break or without a gap in the consciousness from life to sleep and to death; or, more precisely, there will no longer be death or sleep as we understand it but various ways of perceiving continuously the total Reality, and perhaps finally an integral consciousness which will perceive everything simultaneously. Our evolution is not over. *Death is not a denial of Life but a process of Life.*[1]

This physical life in a physical body assumes consequently a special importance among all our modes of living because it is in this that we become conscious — this is *the place of the work*, says the Mother, the point where all the planes meet in a body. The place of the work because this is the zero point, or almost, of the evolution and because it is starting from the body, slowly, across innumerable lives, that a "we", undifferentiated at first, individualises itself by contacting planes of consciousness more and more elevated and, on each plane, ever vaster reaches of consciousness. There are then as many different deaths or sleeps as there are different lives because it is the same thing; all depends on the degree of our evolutionary development; and all the degrees are possible, as in life, from total nullity to the perfectly awakened and individualised consciousness. No general laws, then, can be made for sleep and death because all things are possible. At the most some lines of development may be indicated.

We are constituted, we have said, of a certain number of centres of consciousness which range from the top of the head right down, and that each of these centres, somewhat like a receiving station corresponding to various wave-lengths, is linked to different planes of consciousness from which we receive constantly, unknown to us most often, all sorts of vibrations, subtle physical, vital, mental, or higher or lower, which determine our manner of thinking, feeling, living, the individual consciousness being like a filter and selecting certain vibrations rather than others in conformity with its milieu, its traditions, its education, etc. The general principle is that we go at the moment of sleep or death, by affinity, to the places or planes with which we have already established a link. But at this elementary stage the consciousness is not truly individualised, though it may be very refined and cultured mentally; it thinks more or less what everybody thinks, feels what everybody feels and lives as everybody lives; it is simply a temporary aggregate which has no other continuity than that of the body around which it is centred. When this corporal centre dies, everything gets scattered into small vital, mental and other fragments which go and rejoin their respective environments because they have no longer a centre. And when this centre is asleep, all is more or less asleep because the non-corporal and mental elements do not exist truly except in relation to the corporal life and for it. In this embryonic state, then, the consciousness falls back into the subconscient when it is asleep (using the word as Sri Aurobindo uses it, in the etymological sense, that is, that which is historically sub-conscient, not below the level of our waking consciousness, but below the conscious stage of the evolution, as in animal or plant[2]), in other words the consciousness returns to its evolutive past which may send it all sorts of chaotic images fabricated by the fanciful combination of innumerable fragments of memories and impressions unless it continues in a more or less unregulated way its habitual waking activities; from there the consciousness sinks into a more distant past, vegetative or larval, which is, truly speaking, its sleep, as that of plants and animals. Many stages will be necessary before the true centre, the psychic, and its consciousness-force are formed and give some coherence and continuity to this volatile amalgam. But from the moment the body stops being the principal centre and one begins to have an inner life independent of physical circumstances and of the physical life and, above all, when one does Yoga which is a process of accelerated evolution, life truly changes, death also and sleep also — one begins to exist. This is even the first thing noticed, as if external visible changes were preceded by inner mutations of a more subtle order which are translated notably into dreams of a particular kind. We pass from animal sleep to a conscious sleep or *sleep of experience* and from a rotting death to a death which lives. The partitions which broke up our integral life crumble. Instead of being thrown into a complete dispersion for want of a centre, we have found the Master and caught the thread of the consciousness-force which links all the stages of the universal reality.

Sleep of Experience

There are many degrees in this new sleep, according to the development of our consciousness, from the rare spasmodic flashes on one plane or another to a continuous vision, master of itself, which can move at will from bottom to top or from top to bottom,* wherever it deems best. All depends here too on our waking consciousness. Normally, through an affinity we go to the planes with which we have established a link; the vital, mental or other vibrations we have accepted and which are translated in us into ideas, aspirations, desires, baseness or nobility, constitute this

---

* We use here a tri-dimensional language which has no true sense, for there is neither within nor without, nor top nor bottom; our mental language is flat, photographic, and does not express much of the reality of the world, but what is to be done?

link and, when out of the body, we go to the source —
an extraordinarily living and striking source; our mental
and vital translations in the physical world seem poor and
almost abstract beside this original there. Then we begin
to become aware of immense, innumerable worlds which
penetrate and envelop and overshadow our little terrestrial planet and which determine its destiny and ours.
It is evidently not possible to describe these worlds in a few
pages nor even in several volumes; one may as well wish
to describe the earth by a glimpse of Normandy. Besides,
we do not intend to describe them but to give only some
indications to help the seeker to check up with his own
experience. The essential quality for this exploration, as Sri
Aurobindo often insisted, is a *clear austerity* and the absence
of desire, the silence of the mind, otherwise we become
the toy of all sorts of illusions. Patiently, through repeated
experiences, we learn first to recognise on what plane
our experience takes place, then, on what level of each
plane. This localisation is as important for our inquiry
as to distinguish on the earth the nature of the milieu
where we find ourselves and the country through which
we travel. Then we learn to understand the meaning
of our experiences; this is a foreign language and even
several languages together which we must assimilate
without mixing up with them our own mental tongue;
one of the big difficulties, actually, comes from the fact that
the mental is the only terrestrial language we know and
its transcriptions when we awake tend unconsciously to
jam or deform the purity of the experience. If no enlightened guide is there who can unravel this complicated
skein, it is necessary to learn to remain as silent as possible
mentally when waking and to feel intuitively the meaning
of these other languages; this is acquired quite quickly

as the consciousness develops and the experiences multiply. It is at the beginning like a virgin forest or a Chinese market-place, everything seems the same; then, after some months, some years, one ends up by recognising roads and faces, places, signs, and a more crowded diversity than on earth.

But how to remember one's sleep? For most people it is an absolute blank — a joint is missing. In fact, there are a number of joints or *bridges*, as the Mother says — as though we were made of a series of countries linked each to each by a bridge. It is possible then that we may easily keep the memory of certain parts of our being and their travels whilst others are left in oblivion for want of a bridge with the rest of our consciousness. When one passes across this void or this ill-trained part of the consciousness one forgets (this is what generally happens to those who fall into an "ecstasy"; we shall come back to it). In principle, a sufficiently developed being travels through the whole gamut of the planes of consciousness in his sleep and goes right up to the supreme Light of the Spirit, *Sat-Chit-Ananda*, most often unconsciously, and those few minutes there are his real sleep, the true repose in the absolute relaxation of Joy and Light. Sri Aurobindo used to say that the real justification of sleep is the spontaneous rejoining with the Source and being reinvigorated there. From there we come down slowly through all the planes, Mental, Vital, subtle Physical and Subconscient (the last we remember most easily) and each part of our being has there its corresponding experiences. In the midst of each plane there are also many zones, each with a bridge. The chief difficulty is in establishing the very first bridge, that with the external waking consciousness — and there is but one way: a total immobility and a complete silence at the moment of awakening. If one turns over or stirs ever so little, all vanishes or rather everything is covered up by little ripples on the great lake of sleep and nothing is seen any more; and if one begins to think, not little ripples but muddy swirls veil everything; thought has nothing to do in this affair, it is not with the mind one ought to try to remember. One must remain leaning over this vast tranquil lake as in an objectless but very sustained contemplation, as though this dark blue thickness had to be pierced through sheer gazing at it. And suddenly, if we persevere sufficiently long, we see an image float up under our eyes or perhaps just a trace, a breath as of a far land loaded with fragrance, very familiar, but uncapturable. Then we have not to precipitate ourselves upon this trace, for it will immediately vanish, but let it little by little, of its own accord, grow clear, take shape, and finally we shall get back a scene. When we have caught the thread well, it is sufficient in principle to pull slowly, without trying to think about it, without seeking to understand (understanding will come afterwards; if we start interpreting on the way, we cut all the communications) and the thread leads us from country to country, from memory to memory. Sometimes we remain stuck for years on the same point of the route, as if there were a hole in the memory, a few yards away. To construct the missing bridge, there is scarcely anything to do except be patient and want it again and again; if one persists, the road will at last be traced, as in a virgin forest. But the recall on waking is not the only method; it is possible also to concentrate in the evening before going to sleep, with the will to remember and to wake up at fixed intervals, once or twice in the night, to catch the thread at different levels. This method is particularly efficacious.

We all know it is enough to want to wake up at a certain hour for the machinery to function perfectly, almost to the minute; this is what is called "making a formation". These formations are like little vibratory nodules emanated by the will which acquire an independent existence of their own and do their work very accurately*. We may make formations more or less powerful, more or less durable (which may be recharged from time to time) for all sorts of purposes and specially for remembering and for waking up at regular intervals. And if we persist for months, for years if necessary, we end up by being automatically alerted each time an important event takes place on some plane of our sleep. Then, in the sleep itself, we stop, repeat twice or thrice the memory to register it well, then set out again.

In this enormous field of experience it is possible to stress only some practical points of a general order which may strike the seeker at the beginning of his quest. First of all, ordinary dreams from the subconscient must be clearly distinguished from *experiences*. Experiences are not dreams, though we have the habit of mixing up everything; they are real events in which we have shared on a particular plane; they are distinguished from ordinary dreams by their special intensity. All the events of the outer physical world, no matter how exceptional, seem *pale* by the side of these events; these leave a profound im-

---

* We all make formations, involuntarily, with our desires, our thoughts (good or bad) and we forget them, but these formations do not forget, and they come back two or ten years later, with their work done, the realisation of the desire, of the thought, the organisation of circumstances, when we no longer think of this; we do not even recognise the result of our thought and our desires. We are thus besieged by all sorts of small living entities which continue to want to realise themselves whilst we no longer want them.

pression and a *more vivid* memory than any of our terrestrial memories, as though we had suddenly touched a
richer mode of living — not necessarily richer in external
representation or in colour, which however may be of an
unbelievable brilliance (specially in the Vital), but in contents. When the seeker on waking has this overbrimming
impression, as of having bathed in a world charged with
signs which want to say more than one thing at a time
(our events of the physical world want to say only one thing
at a time, rarely more) and before which it is possible to
remain a long while without exhausting their meaning, so
much do they seem to be charged with invisible ramifica-
tions and terraced depths; or when he has been present
at or shared in certain scenes which seem infinitely more
real than our physical scenes, always so flat, as though they
came up immediately against a hard and slightly photographic background, he will know he has had a veritable
experience and not a dream.

> *Unreal-seeming yet more real than life,*
> *...truer than things true*
> *If dreams these were or captured images,*
> *Dream's truth made false earth's vain realities.*[3]

There is another remarkable thing: the more one rises
in the scale of consciousness, the more the quality of the
light changes — the differences of luminosity are a *very
sure* indication of the place where one finds oneself and
even of the meaning of things — and there is the whole
gamut, from the dirty tones of the subconscient, grey,
maroon and black, the vibrating tints of the subtle Physical, the brilliant colours of the Vital which have always
a slight tinge of hard artifice and tinsel (this is the most

deceptive region possible), to the lights of the Mind which become more and more powerful and pure as one rises towards the Origin; from the Overmind upwards there is a radical difference of vision: the objects, beings or things seen seem no longer lit up from outside, flatly, as we are by the sun; they are luminous *in themselves*; and finally it is not so much an "exteriorisation" as an ecstasy in a Light immobile, resplendent, cleared of all the din and sensational incidents of the lower planes. When one can enter into contact with this Light, one reposes as well within a few minutes as in eight hours of sleep; it is thus that yogis can do without sleep; it is also thus that a few minutes of concentration in the day can give as much rest as a walk in the open air. The body has an unbelievable endurance; it is psychological agitation which tires.

Besides the events of a universal order with which we may be intermingled, we find that sleep is a mine of information about our own individual state; all the stages of our being are lit up with an exact light, as if outside during the waking hours we had lived like the deaf and dumb or like men of plaster and as if suddenly everything awakes to a life more true than life. These various inner levels can be seen as rooms or as houses of which the least details are revelatory: *When one sets out to explore the inner being,* says the Mother, *and the different parts which consti-tute it, one has very often the impression of entering a hall or a room and, according to the colour, the atmosphere, the things there, one has a very clear perception of the part of being that is visited. Then one may go into deeper and deeper rooms each of which has its special character.* Or sometimes, instead of rooms we may find beings of all kinds — an entire little family, in-deed a menagerie — which are the expression of the various forces or vibrations we have made it a habit to

welcome into us and which constitute "our" nature. And
these are not "dream-beings", these are real beings whom
we shelter: the forces are conscious, the vibrations are
conscious — beings or forces, consciousness or force, are
two simultaneous faces of the same reality. We see thus
in a singularly vivid way what we want or no longer want
to allow in us.

Another observation will strike the seeker by its almost
daily recurrence. He will find, too late, that he had
during the night the exact premonition of all the important psychological events which took place in the day.
First he will think it pure coincidence or he will not see
much of a link, then, after this has been repeated hundreds of times, he will begin to be on his guard and at last
when he is quite awake, he will be able to see what is
coming and take protective measures beforehand. For
example, we have undergone a crisis of depression in the
day or have been seized by a violent fit of anger, have had
a movement of revolt, a sexual obsession, etc. or, to take
an example of an apparently different order, we have just
missed falling down twice or thrice and breaking a limb
or have caught a fine fever — and we find that each of
these little incidents, quite banal, corresponds exactly to
other incidents, most often symbolic (symbolic because
it is not the exact fact but a mental transcription on
waking) of which we have had the experience the preceding night, whether we were attacked in "dream" by
an enemy, mixed up in untoward events, or saw at times
exactly all the details which surrounded the psychological
scene the next day. It would seem decidedly that "someone" was altogether awake in us and very careful to make
us finger tangibly all the whys and all the hidden wheels
of our psychological life, all the reasons of our falls or our

progress. For inversely, we can have a premonition of all the happy psychological movements which are translated the next day into some progress, an opening of the consciousness, a lightness, an inner widening, and we see that the night before there was a certain light, a certain ascension, the crumbling of a wall or house (symbolic of our resistances and the mental constructions which enclosed us). And we shall the more be struck that these premonitions usually are not related to events considered important on our physical plane, like the death of a parent or a worldly success (though these premonitions may also come), but to details without any external importance, quite trivial, but always very useful for our inner progress. This is the sign that our consciousness is developing; instead of receiving unconsciously the mental, vital or other vibrations which go to shape our life without our knowing anything about them, and which we ingenuously take for ours (we say this is *our* anger, *our* depression, *our* sexual obsession or *our* fever), we shall begin to see them coming; this will be the visible proof, supported by hundreds of experiences night after night, that all the play of our frontal nature comes from outside, from a universal Mind, a universal Vital or from higher regions if we are capable of switching on to these. And this will be the beginning of the mastery, for once we have seen, and even foreseen, we can change the course of circumstances. The terrestrial life is the place, simultaneously, of the most rigorous, the most blind determinism and of conquered liberty — all depends on our consciousness. A disciple had written to Sri Aurobindo relating his "dreams" and this sort of bizarre coincidence between the nocturnal and diurnal incidents. Here is the answer: *Understand that these experiences are not mere imaginations or dreams but actual happenings.... It is a mistake to think that we live physically only, with the outer mind and life. We are all the time living and acting on other planes of consciousness, meeting others there and acting upon them, and what we do and feel and think there, the forces we gather, the results we prepare have an incalculable importance and effect, unknown to us upon our outer life. Not all of it comes through, and what comes through takes another form in the physical — though sometimes there is an exact correspondence; but this little is at the basis of our outward existence. All that we become and do and bear in the physical life is prepared behind the veil within us. It is therefore of immense importance for a yoga which aims at the transformation of life to grow conscious of what goes on within these domains, to be master there and be able to feel, know and deal with the secret forces that determine our destiny and our internal and external growth or decline.*[4]

Sleep of Action

From animal sleep we have passed to conscious sleep or the sleep of experience, thence we pass on to the sleep of action; this is the third stage. For a long time, in fact, however conscious it may be, our sleep remains a passive state; we are only the witnesses of events, the impotent spectators of what happens in such and such a part of our being — for always it is just *one part* of our being, though we could have the impression, at the moment of experience, that it is our entire being which suffers, fights, travels, etc.; even as we may have the impression, when discussing politics or philosophy with a friend, that it is the whole of ourselves which discusses, whilst really it is only a mental or vital fraction. As our sleep becomes more conscious, we pass from impressions to striking realities (where is the "concrete", on which side the "objective"? one wonders) and we see that we are constituted of an incongruous mass of mental, vital and other fragments which have an independent existence, with their independent experiences, each on its particular plane. In the night, when the link of the body is no longer there or the tyranny of the mental mentor, this independence bursts out in a very remarkable fashion; the little vibrations agglutinated by us, constituting "our" nature, disperse into small beings of our being which run hither and thither, and we discover all kinds of unknown folk in us whose existence we never suspected. In other words, these fragments are not integrated around the true centre, the psychic, and not being integrated, we are powerless to intervene and modify the course of circumstances. We are passive, for the real "we" is the psychic and the majority of these fragments have no link with the psychic.

The necessity of integration is seen very quickly if we want to become the masters, not only here, but there and in every way. For instance, when we come out of our body and go into certain regions of the lower Vital (which corresponds to the low zones of the navel and sex centres), the part of our being which is exteriorised in this domain encounters there most often very disagreeable experiences; it is attacked by all sorts of voracious forces and we have what is conventionally called a "nightmare" from which we escape by re-precipitating ourselves as quickly as possible into our body where we are sheltered. If this very part of our being consented to integrate itself around the psychic centre, it could without peril go out into these very regions, infernal enough, for it would be armed with a psychic light — the psychic is a light, it is a fragment of the great original Light; it is enough that it remembers this light (or the Master, which comes to the same thing) at the moment it is attacked, for all the adverse forces to disperse. In remembering, it calls the true vibration which has the power to dissolve or scatter all vibrations of a lesser intensity. There is even a stage of transition, very instructive, when helpless we take part in terrible pursuits, for instance; then, all of a sudden, in its distress this fragment of ourselves remembers the light (or the Master) and the situation is reversed. In the same way we can meet on these planes all sorts of people, known or unknown, near to us or far, living or dead, — *the ever-living whom we name as dead*[5] — who are as if on the same wavelength, and be the witness or the helpless partner of their misadventures (which as we know, can be translated into terrestrial events troublesome for the living — all the blows down there are blows to be received here; all that happens there prepares what happens here), but if at the moment of the experience, this fragment of ourselves which is with the corresponding fragment of these friends, these unknown or "dead" ones, remembers the Light, that is, if it is integrated around the psychic, it can reverse the course of the circumstances, help a friend or a stranger in distress, a disembodied being to cross a difficult passage or to come out of a bad place and liberate himself from certain unhealthy associations (there are so many places where we are really prisoners). Here is a single example, chosen deliberately as a negative one, as banal as possible: X "dreams" that she is walking with a friend along the banks of a pond with (apparently) marvellously clear waters, when suddenly a snake springs up from the bottom of the pond and bites her friend in the throat. She makes several attempts to protect her friend but then feels afraid and, pursued in her turn by the serpent, flies "back home" (into the body). The next day she learns that her friend is ill, completely speechless, and she herself is pursued the whole day by a series of small abortive accidents, inner and outer. If she had been actively conscious, centred, nothing would have happened, the adverse force would have fled; indeed there are many instances in which accidents have been "miraculously" avoided because they have been conquered the night before by a conscientious friend if not by oneself. We can thus participate usefully in all kinds of activities which prepare our personal tomorrows or vaster tomorrows according to our capacities: "A conscious being, no larger than a man's thumb, stands in the centre of our self; he is Master of the past and the present...he is today and he is tomorrow", says the Katha Upanishad (IV. 12, 13). Numerous experiments must be made, with verifications whenever possible, to understand to what extent these dreams are not dreams. There are imprisonments here which cannot be broken through until we have broken the imprisonments down there. The problem of action is then linked with a problem of integration.

This integration is all the more indispensable because when we have no longer a body, that is, when we are supposedly dead, these fragments have no more the recourse of re-precipitating themselves into our body for protection. If they are not integrated, they suffer much unpleasantness. Here lies, no doubt, the origin of our stories of hell, which concern — it cannot be repeated enough — only some lower *fragments* of our nature. For the lower planes (notably the lower Vital, which corresponds to the navel and sex regions, the most difficult to integrate naturally) are peopled with famished forces; as it was put by a young disciple of Pondicherry who, prematurely dead, had come to relate to his friend in sleep what had happened on the journey: "Just behind your world there is no law and order" — a proper British laconism for hell. And he added: "I had with me Mother's light (the Master's) and I crossed over." As the experience is typical of many deaths, perhaps it should be made clear that the meeting of the two friends took place in the higher Vital regions (which correspond to the heart-centre), in the midst of those beautiful coloured gardens which are often met with there and which constitute one of the innumerable so-called "paradises" of the other world — they are paradises which hang low. Generally, the disembodied one remains there as long as he wishes, then he gets tired and goes to the place of true rest, into the original Light, with his soul awaiting the hour of return. To say that an individual goes to "eternal hell" is a cruel absurdity; how could the soul, that Light, ever be a prisoner of those low vibrations? As well say that the infra-red is master of the ultra-violet. The similar goes with the similar, always and everywhere, down here or elsewhere. And what could be "eternal", truly, except the soul, except joy? *If there were an unending Hell, it could only be a seat of unending rapture,* says Sri Aurobindo, *for God is joy,* Ananda *and than the eternity of His bliss there is no other eternity.*[6]

Thus, as our being gets integrated around the psychic, it passes from a passive to an active sleep, if one may yet speak of "sleep", and from a difficult death to an interesting journey or to another form of work. But here too there are all the degrees according to the amplitude of our consciousness, from the small action limited to a close circle of people, living or dead, whom we know, or the worlds which are familiar to us, to the universal action of some great beings whose psychic has in a sense colonised vast stretches of consciousness, and who by their silent light protect the world.

To end these brief generalities which are, however, mere trials for the seeker, a last observation may be made. This is about premonitions. Perhaps it has not been sufficiently pointed out that the single fact of having a premonition is a fair sign that the events exist *already somewhere* before taking place here — they do not exist in the air. We who are so scrupulous about material realities, we grant to the phenomena of less material worlds the quite gratuitous benefit of an incoherence or a vagueness which is the result entirely of our own mind. Now, it is found in experience that everything is perfectly rational, if not reasonable: not only is the luminosity more intense as one climbs the steps of consciousness, but time becomes more and more fast, it covers a wider and wider space, if we may put it thus, for farther and farther events (in the future or in the past) and finally one emerges into this still Light in which all *is* there already. Simultaneously, or as a corollary, one observes that according to the plane of consciousness where our premonitory vision is located, the terrestrial fulfilment is more or less near or far. When one sees, for instance, an event in the subtle Physical which borders our world, the terrestrial transcription is almost immediate — a few hours or a day later; one sees an accident and the next day one is caught in an accident; and the vision is very precise to the least detail. The more one rises in the scale of consciousness, the farther is the date of the vision and the more universal its scope, but the details of working are less visible, as though the fact seen was certainly ineluctable (on condition that our vision be sufficiently free from all egoism), but with a margin of incertitude for the modalities of realisation — this margin of incertitude represents in a way the peripeteia or deformations of the truth from above when it descends from plane to plane to find a terrestrial realisation. All kinds of interesting conclusions can be drawn from this observation but specially the fact that the more one is conscious on the earth, that is, capable of climbing high in the scale of consciousness and drawing close to the Origin, the nearer to the earth one brings also the land of the Origin, annulling the deforming determinisms of the intermediary planes. This may have not only considerable individual consequences for the mastery and transformation of our own life but general results for the transformation of the world. The problem of freedom and determinism has been much discussed, but it is a problem wrongly viewed. There is not freedom or determinism, there is freedom *and* a number of determinisms. We are subject to a series of *superimposed determinisms*, physical, vital, mental and higher, says Sri Aurobindo, and the determinism of each plane can modify or annul the determinism of the immediately lower degree. For instance, in the microcosm good health and a given longevity can be modified by the vital determinism of "our" passions and "our" disorders, which again can in its turn be modified by the mental determinism of our will and our ideal, which can be modified by the greater law of the psychic, and so on. The freedom is to move on to a higher plane. And similarly for the destiny of the earth: it is the same forces which move the microcosm and the macrocosm. And if we, who are decidedly the point of insertion of all these determinisms into Matter, are capable of lifting ourselves to a higher plane, we contribute automatically to the modification of all the lower determinisms and to the accession of the earth to a greater freedom — till the day when through the instrumentality of the pioneers of evolution we can lift ourselves to a *supramental* plane, which will modify the present destiny of the world as the Mind modified its destiny somewhere about the tertiary age. And perhaps, finally — if there is anything final — the earth will touch the supreme Determinism which is the supreme Freedom and the perfect accomplishment. We are each one of us, by our work of consciousness, agents of resistance to the fatalities which weigh upon the world and a ferment of the earth's freedom or divinisation. For the evolution of consciousness has a meaning for the earth.

CHAPTER TEN

THE REVOLUTIONARY YOGI

Such were the mental, vital, physical and psychic discoveries Sri Aurobindo made alone, step by step, between the age of twenty and thirty, simply by following the thread of consciousness. The remarkable thing is that his yoga was practised in all circumstances where usually it is not, in the midst of his lectures in French and English at the State College of Baroda, during his work at the Court of the Maharaja, and more and more in the very heart of his secret and revolutionary activities. The hours of the night which were not devoted to the study of his mother-tongue and Sanskrit or to political work were spent in writing poetry: "Aurobindo had the habit of writing poetry till one o'clock in the night," notes his Bengali teacher, "and consequently he did not get up very early in the morning.... He would concentrate for a minute before starting, then poetry would flow from his pen like a stream." From poetry Sri Aurobindo went on to his experimental sleep. He had married Mrinalini Devi in 1901 at the age of twenty-nine and wanted her to share his spiritual life: *I am experiencing all the signs and symptoms*, he writes in a letter found in the archives of the British police. *I should like to take you with me along this path.* Mrinalini did not understand; Sri Aurobindo remained alone. We would search in vain in the life of Sri Aurobindo for those touching and miraculous stories which adorn the lives of the great sages or mystics, in vain also for sensational yogic methods; every thing there is apparently so ordinary that one sees nothing there, as in life itself. Perhaps he had found more miracles in ordinary than in extraordinary things: *With me all is different, all is uncommon,* he wrote in a letter to Mrinalini — *all is deep and strange to the eyes that see,*[1] he was to say in *Savitri* later. And perhaps it is this that he wants us to discover, through his life, his work, his yoga, all these unknown riches under the ordinary crust: *Our lives [are] a deeper mystery than we have dreamed.*[2] If we only knew how hollow our "miracles" are, how meaningless, a sort of jugglery for adults! — as soon as one has a twopence and a half worth of knowledge one sees easily how they are devised — and how the Truth is so much more simple than this supernatural technicolour. As he progressed in his yoga, Sri Aurobindo left all this imagery for what he called a *spiritual realism,*[3] not through any distrust of beautiful images — he, the poet! — but because he saw that these images would be more beautiful still if they incarnated on the earth and the supraphysical became our normal physical, with the eyes wide open. This naturalisation of the beyond and the tranquil mastery of life which Sri Aurobindo attained were possible only because he never separated the two worlds: *My own life and my yoga have always been since my coming to India both this-worldly and other-worldly without any exclusiveness on either side,* he says in a letter to a disciple. *All human interests are, I suppose, this-worldly and most of them have entered into my mental field and some, like politics, into my life, but at the same time, since I set foot on the Apollo Bunder in Bombay, I began to have spiritual experiences, but these were not divorced from this world but had an inner and infinite bearing on it, such as a feeling of the Infinite pervading material space and the Immanent inhabiting material objects and bodies. At the same time I found myself entering supraphysical worlds and planes with influences and an effect from them upon the material plane, so I could make no sharp divorce or irreconcilable opposition between what I have called the two ends of existence and all that lies between them. For me all is Brahman and I find the Divine everywhere.*[4]

Problem of Action

It is in his revolutionary activities that we find at first the spiritual realism of Sri Aurobindo. A programme was quickly drawn up in four stages: to awaken India to the concept of independence, for which journalism and political speeches were sufficient; to keep men's minds in a state of constant revolt — and he, with another great hero of India, Tilak, was undoubtedly one of the first at the opening of the century to speak of complete liberation, passive resistance and non-cooperation (Gandhi did not come on the Indian political scene till fifteen years later); to transform the Indian Congress and its timid demands into an *extremist movement* parading unambiguously the ideal of complete independence; and finally to prepare secretly an armed insurrection. With his younger brother Barin, he began then to organise guerrilla bands in Bengal under the cover of sport and cultural groups; he even sent a representative to Europe at his own expense to study the manufacture of bombs. When Sri Aurobindo said, *I am neither an impotent moralist nor a weak pacifist,*[5] these words made sense. He had studied sufficiently well the history of France and of the Italian and American revolutions to know that armed revolt can be right; neither Joan of Arc nor Mazzini nor Washington were apostles of "non-violence". When Gandhi's son came to Pondicherry in 1920 to pay him a visit and discussed non-violence, Sri Aurobindo answered with this simple, very matter-of-fact question: "What would you do if tomorrow the northern frontiers of India were invaded?" Twenty years later, in 1940, Sri Aurobindo and the Mother publicly took the side of the Allies whilst Gandhi, in an undoubtedly praiseworthy outburst of feeling sent an open letter to the English people, adjuring them not to take up arms against Hitler and to use only "spiritual force". It would therefore be well to clarify the spiritual position of Sri Aurobindo with regard to violent action.

War and destruction, he writes, are not only a universal principle of our life here in its purely material aspects, but also of our mental and moral existence. It is self-evident that in the actual life of man intellectual, social, political, moral, we can make no real step forward without a struggle, a battle between what exists and lives and what seeks to exist and live and between all that stands behind either. It is impossible, at least as men and things are, to advance, to grow, to fulfil and still to observe really and utterly that principle of harmlessness which is yet placed before us as the highest and best law of conduct. We will use only soul-force and never destroy by war or any even defensive employment of physical violence? Good, though until soul-force is effective, the Asuric force in men and nations tramples down, breaks, slaughters, burns, pollutes, as we see it doing today, but then at its ease and unhindered, and you have perhaps caused as much destruction of life by your abstinence as others by resort to violence .... It is not enough that our own hands should remain clean and our souls unstained for the law of strife and destruction to die out of the world; that which is its root must first disappear out of humanity.* *Much less will mere immobility and inertia unwilling to use or incapable of using any kind of resistance to evil, abrogate the law; inertia, tamas, indeed, injures much more than can the [dynamic] rajasic principle of strife which at least creates*

* Emphasis ours.

more than it destroys. Therefore, so far as the problem of the individual's action goes, his abstention from strife and its inevitable concomitant destruction in their more gross and physical form may help his own moral being, but it leaves the Slayer of creatures unabolished.[6]

The whole evolution of Sri Aurobindo's thought and of his practical attitude towards war, from his secret activities in Bengal to his retreat to Pondicherry in 1910, turns around the problem of *means*: How to assail most surely this "Slayer of creatures", "the Eater", as the Vedic rishis called him? And from the independence of India, Sri Aurobindo passed on to the independence of the world. Indeed, as he advanced in his yoga, he found more and more by experience that the hidden forces are not only at the base of our own psychological disorders but of the disorders of the world — all comes from elsewhere, as we have seen — and that if our abstention leaves unabolished the Slayer of creatures, our wars do not conquer him either, though it be necessary in practice to soil one's hands in these. In the very midst of the war of 1914, Sri Aurobindo noted down with a prophetic force: *The defeat of Germany... could not of itself kill the spirit then incarnate in Germany; it may well lead to a new incarnation of it, perhaps in some other race or empire, and the whole battle would then have to be fought over again. So long as the old gods are alive, the breaking or depression of the body which they animate is a small matter, for they know well how to transmigrate. Germany overthrew the Napoleonic spirit in France in 1813 and broke the remnants of her European leadership in 1870; the same Germany became the incarnation of that which it had overthrown. The phenomenon is easily capable of renewal on a more formidable scale.*[7] We have found today that the old gods know how to transmigrate. Gandhi himself, seeing all those years of non-violence ending in the terrible violence which marked the partition of India in 1947, observed with grief a little before his death: "The attitude of violence which we have secretly harboured now recoils on us and makes us fly at each other's throats when the question of distribution of power arises .... Now that the burden of subjection is lifted, all the forces of evil have come to the surface." For neither violence nor non-violence goes to the root of the Evil. And in the midst of the war of 1940, even while Sri Aurobindo publicly stood on the side of the Allies,* because, *in practice*, it was there that action was necessary, he wrote to a disciple: *You write as if what is going on in Europe were a war between the powers of the Light and the powers of Darkness — but that is no more so than during the Great War. It is a fight between two kinds of Ignorance.... The eye of the yogin sees not only the outward events and persons and causes, but the enormous forces which precipitate them into action. If the men who fought were instruments in the hands of rulers and financiers, etc., these in turn were mere puppets in the clutch of these forces. When one is habituated to see the things behind, one is no longer prone to be touched by the outward aspects — or to expect any remedy from political, institutional or social changes.*[8] Sri Aurobindo had become aware of these "enormous forces" behind and of the constant infiltration of the supraphysical into the physical; his energies no longer turned around a moral problem, finally so superficial — violence or non-violence — but around a problem of efficacy; and he saw clearly, always through experience, that to cure the world's evil it is necessary to cure first "what is at its roots in man" and one can cure nothing

* At the risk of incurring the censure of his compatriots (it must be remembered that India had suffered enough under the domination of the British not to be disinterested in their fate in Europe under the German attack).

outside if one does not first cure within, for it is the same thing; one cannot master the without if one does not master the within, for it is the same thing; one cannot transform outer matter without transforming our inner matter, for it is again and always the same thing — there is but one Nature, but one world, one matter and so long as we go at it the wrong away, we shall arrive at nothing. And if we find the remedy difficult, then there is no hope for man nor for the world, for all our outer panaceas and our rose-water moralities are ultimately doomed to nothingness and to destruction by these hidden powers: *The only way out,* says Sri Aurobindo, *is through the descent of a consciousness which is not the puppet of these forces but is greater than they are and can force them either to change or disappear.*[8] It was towards this new consciousness, the supramental, that Sri Aurobindo was on his way in the very midst of his revolutionary work.

> ....*We may find when all the rest has failed*
> *Hid in ourselves the key of perfect change.*[9]

Nirvana

In 1906 Sri Aurobindo left Baroda State to plunge into the heart of the political agitation in Calcutta. The mistakes of Lord Curzon, governor of Bengal, had precipitated the wrath of the students; it was the moment of action. With another great nationalist, Bepin Pal, Sri Aurobindo launched an English daily, *Bande Mataram* ("I bow to Mother India"), which was the first newspaper to proclaim publicly the goal of complete independence and to contribute powerfully to the awakening of the whole of

India; he founded an *extremist party*, established a programme of national action: boycott of British goods, boycott of British law-courts, boycott of British schools and
universities. He became the principal of the first National
College in Calcutta and agitated so much that less than a
year later he was under arrest. Unhappily for the British,
the articles and speeches of Sri Aurobindo were legally
unassailable; he did not preach racial hatred, did not
even attack the government of His Majesty, simply he
proclaimed the right of nations to independence. The
prosecution fell through for lack of evidence: only the prin-
ter, who did not know a single word of English, was sentenced to six months' jail. This narrow escape made Sri
Aurobindo famous; he was henceforth the recognised leader of the nationalist party and came forward from behind
the scene where, however, he would have preferred to
remain: *I do not care a button about having my name in any
blessed place*, he was to say later; *I was never ardent about
fame even in my political days; I preferred to remain behind the
curtain, push people without their knowing it and get things
done*.[10] But it would be wrong to imagine a fanatical Sri
Aurobindo; all his contemporaries were struck by this
"calm young man who with a single word silenced a tumultuous meeting." It was in the midst of this external
bubbling, in between political meetings and the newspaper to bring out every morning, and under the constant
threat of the secret police, that on the 30th December,
1907, Sri Aurobindo met a yogi by the name of Vishnu
Bhaskar Lele, who was to bring him a paradoxical experience in his already paradoxical life.

This was the first time Sri Aurobindo was meeting a
yogi, at least voluntarily, after thirteen years in India!
It would be enough to say that he distrusted asceticism and

spiritualists. His first requisition is, besides, typical: *I want to do Yoga but for work, for action, not for sannyasa (renouncing the world) and Nirvana.*[11] Lele's reply is strange and deserves to be remembered: "It would be easy for you as you are a poet." The two men retired to a solitary room for three days. Thenceforth the yoga of Sri Aurobindo was to follow an unforeseen curve which seemed to take him further away from action, but only to lead him to the secret of action and of changing the world. *The first result,* writes Sri Aurobindo, *was a series of tremendously powerful experiences and radical changes of consciousness which he had never intended ... and which were quite contrary to my own ideas, for they made me see with a stupendous intensity the world as a cinematographic play of vacant forms in the impersonal universality of the Absolute Brahman.*[12]

> *In the enormous spaces of the self*
> *The body now seemed only a wandering shell....* [13]

In a moment, the whole integral yoga of Sri Aurobindo crumbled down, all his efforts at mental, vital and physical transformation and his faith in a perfect terrestrial life were annulled in an enormous Illusion — nothing remained now except empty forms. *It threw me suddenly into a condition above and without thought, unstained by any mental or vital movement; there was no ego, no real world — only when one looked through the immobile senses, something perceived or bore upon its sheer silence a world of empty forms, materialised shadows without true substance. There was no One or many even, only just absolutely That featureless, relationless, sheer, indescribable, unthinkable, absolute, yet supremely real and solely real. This was no mental realisation nor something glimpsed somewhere above, — no abstraction, — it was positive, the only positive reality — al-*

though not a spatial physical world, pervading, occupying or rather flooding and drowning this semblance of a physical world, leaving no room or space for any reality but itself, allowing nothing else to seem at all actual, positive or substantial ....What it (this experience) brought was an inexpressible Peace, a stupendous silence, an infinity of release and freedom.[14] At the first shot, Sri Aurobindo had entered into what the Buddhists call Nirvana or the Hindus the Silent Brahman, That; the *Tao* of the Chinese, the Transcendent, Absolute, Impersonal of the Westerners. He had reached that famous "liberation" (mukti) which is considered the "summit" of the spiritual life — what could be there then beyond the Transcendent? And Sri Aurobindo verified the words of the great Indian mystic, Sri Ramakrishna: "If we live in God, the world disappears; if we live in the world, God exists no longer"; the gulf between Matter and Spirit he had tried to bridge had opened again under his unsealed sight; the spiritualists were right, in the West as in Asia, for assigning as the sole destination of man's effort a life beyond — paradise, Nirvana or liberation — elsewhere, not in this vale of illusion or of tears. The experience of Sri Aurobindo was there, irrefutable under his eyes.

But this experience which is considered final was to be for Sri Aurobindo the starting-point of new experiences, *much higher*, which reintegrated in a total Reality, continuous and divine, the truth of the world and the truth of the beyond. We are here before a central experience the understanding of which is of importance to the very meaning of our existence, for there are two alternatives: either the supreme Truth is not down here, as all the religions of the world seem to say, and we are wasting our time with futilities, or there is something other than all we have been told. And the question is all the more important because it is not a matter of theory but of experience. Here is what Sri Aurobindo records: *I lived in that Nirvana day and night before it began to admit other things into itelf or modify itself at all ... in the end it began to disappear into a greater Superconsciousness from above .... The aspect of an illusionary world gave place to one in which illusion is only a small surface phenomenon with an immense Divine Reality behind it and a supreme Divine Reality above it and an intense Divine Reality in the heart of everything that had seemed at first only a cinematic shape or shadow. And this was no reimprisonment in the senses, no diminution or fall from supreme experience, it came rather as a constant heightening and widening of the Truth .... Nirvana in my liberated consciousness turned out to be the beginning of my realisation, a first step towards the complete thing, not the sole true attainment possible or even a culminating finale.*[15]

What then is this Transcendent which seems to be situated not at the summit but at a very average height? We may say, to use a rather plain but true analogy, that sleep represents a transcendent state when compared with waking but that it is not either higher or more true than waking, or less true. Simply, it is another state of consciousness. If we withdraw from mental and vital movements, naturally everything vanishes; when one takes an anaesthetic, one can feel nothing, as a simpleton would say. We are inclined naturally to conclude that this immobile and impersonal Peace is superior to our tumult but, after all, this tumult also is entirely of our own making. The superior or inferior does not depend on the change of state but on the quality or altitude of our consciousness in the given state. Now the passage into Nirvana is not at the summit of the ladder any more than are sleep and death at the top of the scale; it can occur at *any level whatsoever of our consciousness*; it can come about through a concentration in the mind, a concentration in the vital and even through a concentration in the physical consciousness; the hatha-yogi bent over his navel or the Basuto dancing around his totem can all of a sudden pass elsewhere, if that is their destiny, into another transcendental dimension where all this world is reduced to nothingness; so too the mystic absorbed in his heart; so too the yogi concentrated in his mind. Because in reality one *does not rise up* when one passes into Nirvana — one pierces a hole and goes out. Sri Aurobindo had not gone beyond the mental plane when he had the experience of Nirvana: *I myself had my experience of Nirvana and silence in the Brahman long before there was any knowledge of the overhead spiritual planes.*[16] And it was precisely after having risen to other superconscious planes that he had higher experiences than of Nirvana, wherein this illusionist, immobile and impersonal aspect melted into a new Reality embracing simultaneously the world and the beyond. Such was the first discovery of Sri Aurobindo. *Nirvana cannot be at once the ending of the Path with nothing beyond to explore... it is the end of the lower Path through the lower Nature and the beginning of the Higher Evolution.*[17]

From another point of view we may also ask ourselves if the goal of evolution is really to get out of it, as the adepts of Nirvana would believe and all those religions which have fixed a beyond as the end of our efforts; for if we go above the sentimental reasons on which our belief or un-belief is founded and look only at the evolutionary process, we are obliged to note that Nature would have easily been able to operate this "exit" when we were at an elementary mental stage and lived yet like instinctively intuitive, open, malleable beings. The humanity of Vedic times or of the Mysteries of ancient Greece or even that of the Mid-dle Ages was closer to the "exit" than we are and, if this was truly the goal of evolutionary Nature, granting that evolution does not uncoil itself haphazardly but according to a Plan, it is this type of man it ought to have cherished; one could easily *outleap the intellect*,[18] as Sri Aurobindo observes in his *Human Cycle*, and pass from this instinctively intuitional stage to an ultra-mundane spiritualism. The intellect is a perfectly useless excrescence if the goal of evolution is to get out of it. Now, on the contrary, it seems that Nature has discountenanced this primitive intuition, has covered it over as on purpose with a mental layer, thicker and thicker, more and more complex and universal and more and more useless from the point of view of the exit; we all know how the marvellous intuitive efflorescence of Upanishadic India at the beginning of history or of Neo-Platonic Greece at the beginning of our era was levelled down in favour of a human mentalisation less high, certainly, and quite thick, but more general. We can just put the question without trying to solve it. We ask ourselves if the meaning of evolution is simply to indulge in the luxury of the mind only to demolish it later and go back to a sub-mental or non-mental religious stage or, on the contrary, to develop the mind to the extreme,* as evolution pushes us to do, until it exhausts its smallness and its superficial tumult to emerge into its higher, superconscient regions, at a spiritual and supramental stage where the Matter-Spirit contradiction will vanish like a mirage and we shall no longer need to "go out" of it because we shall be everywhere Within.

---

* We must note that the yoga of Sri Aurobindo, which seeks to go beyond the Mind, is supposed to begin *at the end* of the curve of the intellect and would be impossible, as we shall see, if all the intermediate degrees have not been traversed. To speak of "mental silence" to an aboriginal of the Fiji Islands or to a Breton peasant would evidently not have much sense.

It would however be wrong to think that the experience of Nirvana is a false experience, a sort of illusion of an illusion; first, because there are no false experiences, there are only incomplete experiences, then because Nirvana divests us rather of an illusion. Our habitual way of seeing the world is warped, it is a sort of very efficacious optical illusion, as efficacious as the broken stick in water but as erroneous. We must "cleanse the doors of perception", said William Blake, and Nirvana helps us in the cleansing, a little radically, it is true. We see a flat world in three dimensions with a multitude of objects and beings *separated* one from another as are the parts of the stick in water, but the reality is quite different when we climb to a higher rung, into the Superconscient, as it is also different when we descend to a lower rung, to the nuclear stage. The only difference between the broken stick and our habitual vision of the world is that in one instance it is an optical illusion and in the other a serious illusion. We persist in seeing as broken a stick which is whole. That this serious illusion is adapted to our present practical living and to the superficial level on which our existence unrolls itself is perhaps a justification of the illusion but it is also the reason why we are powerless to master life, because to see falsely is to live falsely. The scientist who is not troubled by the vision of appearances sees better and masters better but his vision also is incomplete and his mastery uncertain; he has not mastered life, not even the physical forces, he has only made use of certain effects of these forces, the most immediately visible effects. This problem of vision is then not only a problem of agreement; it is not a question of seeing better so as to have beautiful visions in pink and blue which, besides, are not so very high, but of having a true mastery of the world and of circumstances and of ourselves, which is of course the same thing, for nothing is separate. So far, those who have had some access to this higher mode of vision (there are many rungs) have scarcely used it except for themselves or have not known how to *incarnate* what they saw because all their effort aimed precisely at going out of this incarnation; but this nebulous attitude is not inevitable. Sri Aurobindo will show us this; he had not prepared in vain all this basis, material, vital, mental and psychic.

Nirvana represents thus an intermediate stage, useful but not indispensable, in this passage from the ordinary vision to the other vision; it divests us of the complete illusion in which we live: "As if by an enchantment they see the false as the true," says the Maitri Upanishad (VII. 10). Sri Aurobindo does not use the word illusion, he simply says that we live in *Ignorance*. Nirvana rids us of our Ignorance but to fall into another Ignorance, because the eternal difficulty with men is that they run from one pole to the other; they believe themselves always obliged to deny one thing in order to affirm another; hence an intermediary stage is taken for the end, as so many other great spiritual experiences have been also taken for an end. Whilst really there is no end but *a constant heightening and widening of the Truth*.[19] We could say that the nirvanic or in general the religious stage, to the extent to which it is fixed on the beyond, represents a first stage of evolution, which turns us away from a certain false way of seeing the world, and that its utility is essentially pedagogic. The awakened man, truly *born*, must prepare himself for the next evolutionary stage and pass from the religious centred on the other world to the spiritual centred on the Totality. Then nothing is excluded, all is widened. So the integral seeker must be on his guard, for inner experiences, touching the intimate substance of our being, are always irrefutable and final when they occur; they are dazzling at any level — remember Vivekananda speaking of Nirvana: "An ocean of infinite peace, without a ripple, without a breath" — and the temptation to anchor there is great, as in an ultimate haven. We only put down here this advice of the Mother to all seekers: *Whatever be the nature, the power and the marvel of the experience, you must not be dominated by it to the point of its governing your entire being . . . . When you enter in some way into contact with a force or a consciousness which is beyond yours, instead of being entirely subjugated by this consciousness or force, you must always remember that this is but one experience among thousands and thousands of others and that, consequently, it is not in any way absolute. No matter how beautiful it be, you can and you must have better ones; no matter how exceptional it be, there are others which are yet more marvellous; and however high it be, you can always climb higher in the future.*

Sri Aurobindo lived for months in this Nirvana before emerging elsewhere. The strange thing is that he could continue in this state editing a daily, running secret meetings and even making political speeches. The first time he was to speak in public in Bombay, he expressed his difficulty to Lele: *He asked me to pray, but I was so absorbed in the Silent Brahman consciousness that I could not pray. He replied that it did not matter; he and some others would pray and I had simply to go to the meeting and make Namaskar (bow) to the audience as Narayan* and wait and speech would come to me from some other source than the mind.*[20] Sri Aurobindo did exactly as he was told and *the speech came as though it were dictated. And ever since all speech, writing, thought and outward activity have so come to me from the same source above the brain-*

* One of the names of the Supreme.

mind.[21] Sri Aurobindo had made a first contact with the Superconscient. This speech given at Bombay is, besides worth remembering. *Try to realise the strength within you*, said he to the militant nationalists, *try to bring it forward; so that everything you do may be not your own doing but the doing of that Truth within you. . . . Because it is not you, it is something within you. What can all these tribunals, what can all the powers of the world do to That which is within you, that Immortal, that Unborn and Undying One, whom the sword cannot pierce, whom the fire cannot burn? . . . Him the jail cannot confine and the gallows cannot end. What is there that you can fear when you are conscious of Him who is within you?*[22]

On the 4th May, 1908, at dawn, the British police came, revolver in hand, to pull him out of his bed. Sri Aurobindo was thirty-six. An attempt on the life of a British magistrate of Calcutta had just failed; the bomb had been manufactured in the garden where Barin, his brother, was training "disciples".

CHAPTER ELEVEN

ONENESS

Sri Aurobindo had to pass a year in the jail at Alipore awaiting the verdict. He had had no hand in that unsuccessful attempt; the organisation of the rebellion had nothing to do with individual acts of terrorism. *When I was arrested and hurried to the Lal Bazar police station I was shaken in faith for a while, for I could not look into the heart of His intention. Therefore I faltered for a moment and cried out in my heart to Him, "What is this that has happened to me? I believed that I had a mission to work for the people of my country and until that work was done, I should have Thy protection. Why then am I here and on such a charge?" A day passed and a second day and a third, when a voice came to me from within, "Wait and see". Then I grew calm and waited, I was taken from Lal Bazar to Alipore and was placed for one month in a solitary cell apart from men. There I waited day and night for the voice of God within me, to know what He had to say to me, to learn what I had to do. . . . I remembered then that a month or more before my arrest, a call had come to me to put aside all activity, to go into seclusion and to look into myself, so that I might enter into closer communion with Him. I was weak and could not accept the call. My work* was very dear to me and in the pride of my heart I thought that unless I was there it would suffer or even fail and cease; therefore I would not leave it. It seemed to me that He spoke to me again and said, "The bonds you had not the strength to break, I have broken for you, because it is not my will nor was it ever my intention that that should continue. I have had another thing for you to do and it is for that I have brought you here, to teach you what*

* For the liberation of India.

you could not learn for yourself and to train you for my work".[1]
This "work" was to be the realisation of the cosmic consciousness or Oneness and the exploration of planes of consciousness above the ordinary mind, or the superconscient,
which was to put Sri Aurobindo on the trail of the Great
Secret. *What happened to me during that period I am not impelled
to say, but only this that day after day, He showed me His wonders.
... That knowledge He gave to me day after day during my twelve
months of imprisonment.*[2]

Cosmic Consciousness

Sri Aurobindo had lived for months in a sort of phantas-
magoric and empty dream standing out against the one
static Reality of the Transcendent; however, strangely
enough, it was in the midst of this Void and as if coming
out of it that the world once again burst forth with a new
face, as though it were necessary each time to lose all in
order to rediscover all in a higher integer: *Overpowered
and subjugated, stilled, liberated from itself, the mind accepts
the Silence itself as the Supreme. But afterwards the seeker discovers that all is there for him contained or new-made. . . then the
void begins to fill, there emerges out of it or there rushes into it all
the manifold Truth of the Divine, all the aspects and manifestations and many levels of a dynamic Infinite.*[3] Having seen only
a static Infinite, we have seen but one face of God, and we
have excluded Him from the world (and perhaps it is
better to have a world empty of God as we say than a world
full of a solemn and judge-like God), but when the Silence
has washed away our solemnities, both small and great,
leaving us for a time caught in a pure whiteness, the world
and God are there once again at every step and at every

point as though they had never been separated except by an excess of materialism or spiritualism. It was in the courtyard of Alipore that this new change of consciousness set in, during the hour of walking: *I looked at the jail that secluded me from men and it was no longer by its high walls that I was imprisoned; no, it was* Vasudeva* *who surrounded me. I walked under the branches of the tree in front of my cell but it was not the tree, I knew it was* Vasudeva, *it was* Sri Krishna* *whom I saw standing there and holding over me his shade. I looked at the bars of my cell, the very grating that did duty for a door and again I saw* Vasudeva. *It was* Narayana* *who was guarding and standing sentry over me. Or I lay on the coarse blankets that were given me for a couch and felt the arms of* Sri Krishna *around me, the arms of my Friend and Lover....* *I looked at the prisoners in the jail, the thieves, the murderers, the swindlers, and as I looked at them I saw* Vasudeva, *it was* Narayana *whom I found in these darkened souls and misused bodies.*[4] This experience was never to leave Sri Aurobindo. During the six months the trial lasted, with its two hundred odd witnesses and its four thousand filed documents, Sri Aurobindo was every day shut up in an iron cage in the middle of the court, but it was no longer a hostile crowd that he saw nor the judges: *When the case opened... I was followed by the same insight. He said to me, "When you were cast into jail, did not your heart fail and did you not cry out to me, where is Thy protection? Look now at the Magistrate, look now at the Prosecuting Counsel". I looked and it was not the magistrate whom I saw, it was* Vasudeva, *it was* Narayana *who was sitting there on the bench. I looked at the Prosecuting Counsel and it was not the Counsel for the Prosecution that I saw; it was* Sri Krishna *who sat there and smiled. "Now do you fear?" he said, "I am in all men and overrule their actions and their*

* One of the names of the Divine.

words".[5] For, in truth, God is not outside His world, He has not "created" the world — He has *become* the world, says the Upanishad: "He became knowledge and ignorance, He became the truth and the falsehood.... He became all this whatsoever that is" (Taittiriya Upanishad II. 6). "This whole world is filled with beings who are His members," says the Swetaswatara Upanishad (IV. 10). *All to the eye that sees is One, to a divine experience all is one block of the Divine.*[6]

We are inclined to believe that here is an altogether mystical vision of the universe without anything in common with the hard reality of things; at every step we come up against ugliness, against evil; this world is full of suffering, it brims over with obscure cries; where then is the Divine in all this? — the Divine, this barbarity ever ready to open its camps of torture? the Divine this sordid egoism, this villainy which hides or spreads itself? God is pure of all these crimes, He is perfect, He cannot be all this — *neti neti* — God is so pure that He is not of this world, there is no place for Him in all this squalor where already we are stifling! *We must look existence in the face if our aim is to arrive at a right solution whatever that solution may be. And to look existence in the face is to look God in the face; for the two cannot be separated.... This world of our battle and labour is a fierce dangerous destructive devouring world in which life exists precariously and the soul and body of man move among enormous perils, a world in which by every step forward, whether we will it or no, something is crushed and broken, in which every breath of life is a breath too of death. To put away the responsibility for all that seems to us evil or terrible on the shoulders of a semi-omnipotent Devil, or to put it aside as a part of Nature, making an unbridgeable opposition between world-nature and God-nature, as if Nature were independent of God, or to throw the responsibility on man and his sins, as if he had a preponderant voice in the making of this world or could create anything against the will of God, are clumsily comfortable devices.... We erect a God of Love and Mercy, a God of good, a God just, righteous and virtuous according to our own moral conceptions of justice, virtue and righteousness, and all the rest, we say, is not He or is not His, but was made by some diabolical Power which He suffered for some reason to work out its wicked will or by some dark Ahriman counter-balancing our gracious Ormuzd, or was even the fault of selfish and sinful man who has spoiled what was made originally perfect by God.... We have to look courageously in the face of the reality and see that it is God and none else who has made this world in His being and that so He has made it. We have to see that Nature devouring her children, Time eating up the lives of creatures, Death universal and ineluctable and the violence of the* Rudra* *forces in man and Nature are also the supreme Godhead in one of his cosmic figures. We have to see that God the bountiful and prodigal creator, God the helpful, strong and benignant preserver is also God the devourer and destroyer. The torment of the couch of pain and evil on which we are racked is his touch as much as happiness and sweetness and pleasure. It is only when we see with the eye of the complete union and feel this truth in the depths of our being that we can entirely discover behind that mask too the calm and beautiful face of the all-blissful Godhead and in this touch that tests our imperfection the touch of the friend and builder of the spirit in man. The discords of the world are God's discords and it is only by accepting and proceeding through them that we can arrive at the greater concords of his supreme harmony, the summits and thrilled vastnesses of his transcendent and his cosmic* Ananda†. *... For truth is the foundation of real spirituality and courage is its soul.*[7]

---

* One of the forms of the Divine.

† Divine joy.

The wound is then healed which seemed to cut the world for ever into two between Satan and the heavens as though there were nothing else but Good and Evil, and yet again the Evil and the Good, and we in between like *an infant coddled and whipped into virtuous ways.*[8] All duality is a seeing in the Ignorance; everywhere, there is but *the innumerable One*[9] — and the "discords of God" to unfold the godhead within us. Even so, an abyss yet remains between this imperfection, perhaps divine, and the ultimate Perfection; this cosmic Divine, is he not a rather thinned-out Divine? is it not elsewhere that one must strain, towards an untainted Divine, transcendent and perfect? *If there is an opposition between the spiritual life and that of the world, it is that gulf which he [the integral seeker] is here to bridge, that opposition which he is here to change into a harmony. If the world is ruled by the flesh and the devil, all the more reason that the children of Immortality should be here to conquer it for God and the Spirit. If life is an insanity, then there are so many million souls to whom there must be brought the light of divine reason; if a dream, yet it is real within itself to so many dreamers who must be brought either to dream nobler dreams or to awaken; or if a lie, then the truth has to be given to the deluded.*[10]

But our spirit is not at rest; perhaps we accept to see God in all this evil and suffering, to understand that the obscure Enemy who torments us is truly the builder of our force, the secret smith of our consciousness; perhaps we accept to be the "warriors of the Light" in this darkened world, like the rishis of old, but precisely why this obscurity? why has He whom we conceive of as eternally pure and perfect, become this world apparently so faintly divine; what need had He of Death and Falsehood and Suffering? if this is a mask, why the mask, and if an illusion, why this cruel game? Perhaps it is a benediction after all that the Lord has not made the world in accordance with our idea of perfection, for we have so many ideas about what is "perfect", about what God ought to be and, above all, about what He ought not to be, that nothing would finally remain behind in our world after clipping all the extra fringes, except an enormous Zero which would not even tolerate the impurity of our existence — or a regimented barrack. *Virtue*, observes the Mother, *has always passed its time in suppressing many elements in life, and if all the virtues of the different countries of the world were put together, there would remain very few things in existence.* Because so far we know only one kind of perfection, that which eliminates, not that which comprehends all; but perfection is a *totality*. Because we see only one second of Eternity and this second does not contain all that we would wish to see and have, we complain and say that this world is ill-made, but if we come out of our second and enter into the Totality everything changes and we see Perfection in the making. This world is not finished, it is *becoming*, it is a progressive conquest of the Divine by the Divine for the Divine, in order to become *the endless more that we must be.*[11] Our world is in evolution and evolution has a spiritual meaning:

Earth's million roads struggled towards deity.[12]

What do we know truly of the great terrestrial journey? It appears to us tortuous, cruel, impure, but we have just been born! we have hardly come out of Matter, muddy, small, suffering, like a god in a tomb who knows no longer and who seeks, who knocks against everything — but what other birth, what recollected memory, what rediscovered power does not await us farther down our road?

This world is on its way, we do not yet know the whole wonder-tale.

> *Seek Him upon the earth...*
> *For thou art He, O King. Only the night*
> *Is on thy soul*
> *By thy own will. Remove it and recover*
> *The serene whole*
> *Thou art indeed...*[13]

The Central Being. The Universal Person

"Thou art He", this is the eternal truth — *Tat tvam asi*, thou art That. This is the Truth which the ancient Mysteries taught and the later religions forgot. Having lost the central secret, they fell into all the aberrant dualisms, substituting obscure mysteries for the great all-simple Mystery. "I and my Father are one," said Christ, (John 10, 30), "I am He," say the sages of India — *so'ham* — because this is the truth *all* liberated men discover, whether they be of Asia or of the West, of the past or the present. Because this is the eternal Fact which we all have to discover. And this "me", this "I" which declares its identity with God is not that of any privileged individual — as though there were yet room for a small personal and exclusive "I" in this triumphant opening, as though the sages of the Upanishads, the Vedic rishis or the Christ had annexed for themselves alone the divine parentage — it is the voice of all men fused into one cosmic consciousness and we are all sons of God.

There are two ways of making this Discovery or two stages. The first is to discover the soul, the psychic being, eternally one with the Divine, the little light from that great Light: "The Spirit who is here in man and the Spirit who is there in the Sun, lo, it is One Spirit and there is no other," says the Upanishad;* "whoever thinks 'Other is he and I am other,' he knows not."† It is this discovery of the Spirit within that the Vedas, some six or seven thousand years ago, called "the birth of the Son": "The red-glowing mass of him is seen: a great god has been delivered out of the darkness" (Rig Veda V. 1.2) and in a language of dazzling power the Vedic rishis affirmed the eternal identity of the Son and the Father, and the divine transmutation of man: "Rescue thy father, in thy knowledge keep him safe, thy father who becomes thy son and bears thee" (Rig Veda V. 3.9).

And the moment we are *born*, we see that this soul in us is the same in all human beings, and not only in beings but in things, latent, unrevealed: "He is the child of the waters, the child of the forests, the child of things stable and the child of things that move. Even in the stone he is there" (Rig Veda I. 70.2). All is one because all is the One. Did not Christ say, "This is my body, this is my blood," choosing these two most material, most earthy and matter-of-fact symbols of the bread and wine to convey that this Matter also is the body of the One, this Matter the blood of God?§ And if He had not been already there in the stone, how would He have come to be in man, by what miraculous fall from the skies? We are the result of an evolution, not of a succession of arbitrary miracles: *All the earth-past is there in (our human nature)... the very nature of the human being presupposes a material and a*

---

* Taittiriya Upanishad X.
† Brihadaranyaka Upanishad I.4.10.
§ See Sri Aurobindo, *Eight Upanishads*, X, XI.

*vital stage which prepare his emergence into mind and an animal
past which moulded a first element of his complex humanity. And
let us not say that this is because material Nature developed by
evolution his life and his body and his animal mind, and only
afterwards did a soul descend into the form so created... for that
supposes a gulf between soul and body, between soul and life,
between soul and mind, which does not exist ; there is no body without soul, no body that is not itself a form of soul ; Matter itself
is substance and power of spirit and could not exist if it were anything else, for nothing can exist which is not substance and power
of the Eternal[14].... The dumb and blind and brute is That and
not only the finely, mentally conscious human or the animal existence. All this infinite becoming is a birth of the Spirit into form.[15]*

When we have opened the doors of the psychic, a first
stage of cosmic consciousness is unveiled. But the growing
psychic, the consciousness-force individualising itself and
becoming more and more compact and dense within, is
not for long satisfied with this narrow individual form;
feeling itself one with That, it wants to be vast like That,
universal like That, and rediscover its inner Totality.
*To be and to be fully is Nature's aim in us... and to be fully is
to be all that is.[16]* We need totality because we *are* the Totality; the ideal which beckons us, the goal which guides our
steps, is not really in front; it does not draw us, it pushes us,
it is behind — and before and within. Evolution is the
eternal blossoming of a flower which was a flower from all
eternity. Without this seed in the depths, nothing would
stir, for nothing would have need of nothing — this is
the Need of the world. This is our *central being*. This is the
brother of light who emerges sometimes when all seems
lost, the sunlit memory which turns and re-turns us and
will give us no peace until we have rediscovered all our
Sun. This is our cosmic centre as the psychic was our indi-

vidual centre. But this central being is not located somewhere at a point; it is at all points; it is inconceivably
at the heart of each thing and embraces all things at the
same time; it is supremely within and supremely above,
and below and everywhere — it is a *giant point*.[17] And
when we have found it, all is found, all is there; the adult
soul regains its origin, the Son becomes once again the
Father or more truly, the Father, who had become the
Son, becomes Himself once more: *There is a pushing back
and rending or a rushing down of the walls that imprisoned our
conscious being; there is a loss of all sense of individuality and
personality, of all placement in Space or Time or action or law of
Nature; there is no longer an ego, a person definite and definable,
but only consciousness, only existence, only peace and bliss; one
becomes immortality, becomes eternity, becomes infinity. All that
is left of the personal soul is a hymn of peace and freedom and bliss
vibrating somewhere in the Eternal*.[18]

We had believed ourselves small and separated from one
another, a man and a man in the midst of separate things,
and we needed this separation to grow under our shell,
else we would have remained an undifferentiated mass in
the universal plasma, members of the flock without our
own life. Through this separation we have become conscious; through this separation we are incompletely conscious; and we suffer, for our suffering is in being separated
— separated from others, separated from ourselves, separated from things and from all, because outside that
single point where all things unite.

*The only way of putting everything right is to become
consciousness once more; and this is very simple.*

There is but one origin.
This origin is the perfection of the Truth,
for that is the only thing which truly exists.
And by exteriorising, projecting, scattering itself,
that has produced what we see
and a crowd of little heads, very gentle, very brilliant,
in search of that they have not yet found
but which they can find,
because what they seek is within them.

*The remedy is at the centre of the evil.**

When we have suffered enough, lives after lives of this long evolution, grown up enough to recognise that everything comes to us from outside, from a Life greater than ours, a Mind, a Matter vaster than ours, universal, the hour comes to find again consciously what we unconsciously were always — a universal Person: *Why shouldst thou limit thyself? Feel thyself also in the sword that strikes thee and the arms that embrace, in the blazing of the sun and the dance of the earth ... in all that is past and all that is now and all that is pressing forward to become. For thou art infinite and all this joy is possible to thee.*[19]

Knowledge by Identity

We may think perhaps that this cosmic consciousness is a sort of poetic and mystical super-imagination, a pure subjectivity without any practical bearing. But first, we could ask ourselves what "objective" and "subjective" signify, for if we take the so-called objective as the sole

* The Mother, in a conversation with the children of the Ashram.

criterion of the truth, this entire world is in danger of slipping through our fingers as our art, our painting and even
our science for the last fifty years do not cease proclaiming,
leaving us only a few crumbs of sure victuals. Certainly
roast beef is more universally verifiable and hence more
objective than the joy of Beethoven's Last Quartets; but
we have denuded the world, not enriched it. Really this
is a false opposition; the subjective is an advanced or pre-
paratory stage of the objective; when everyone will have
verified the cosmic consciousness or even simply the joy of
Beethoven, we shall have perhaps the objective phenomenon of a less barbarous universe.

But Sri Aurobindo was not the man to be satisfied with
cosmic reveries. The authenticity of the experience and
its practical efficacy can immediately be verified by a very
simple test, the appearance of a new mode of knowledge,
by identity — one knows a thing because one *is* that thing.
The consciousness can shift to any point whatsoever of *its*
universal reality, can repair to any being, any event whatsoever and know it there and then, intimately, as one
knows the beating of one's own heart, because all takes
place within, nothing is outside or separate any longer.
But the Upanishad has already said: "When That is
known, all is known".* The first symptoms of this new
consciousness are quite tangible: *One begins to feel others
too as part of oneself or varied repetitions of oneself, the same self
modified by Nature in other bodies. Or, at the least, as living in
the larger universal self which is henceforth one's own greater reality.
All things in fact begin to change their nature and appearance; one's
whole experience of the world is radically different from that of
those who are shut up in their personal selves. One begins to know
things by a different kind of experience, more direct, not depending*

* Shandilya Upanishad, II.2.

*on the external mind and the senses. It is not that the possibility
of error disappears, for that cannot be so long as mind of any kind
is one's instrument for transcribing knowledge, but there is a new,
vast and deep way of experiencing, seeing, knowing, contacting
things; and the confines of knowledge can be rolled back to an almost unmeasurable degree.*[20]

This new mode of knowledge is not truly different from
ours; indeed, secretly, all experience, all knowledge, of
whatever order it be, from the most material level to the
metaphysical heights, is a knowledge by identity — we
know because we *are* what we know. *True knowledge*, says
Sri Aurobindo again, *is not attained by thinking. It is what
you are; it is what you become.*[21] Without this secret identity, this underlying absolute oneness, we would be able to
know nothing of the world and of beings; Ramakrishna
crying out with pain and bleeding from the cut of the whip
which lashed the bullock beside him, or the seer who
knows that a particular object is hidden in a particular
place, the yogi who cures his sick disciple hundreds of
miles away or Sri Aurobindo stopping the cyclone from
entering his room, are only striking illustrations of a natural phenomenon — the natural thing is not separation, not
differentiation, it is the indivisible oneness of all things. If
beings and objects were different from us, separated from
us, if we were not in essence this cyclone or this bullock,
this hidden treasure, this sick disciple, not only would we
be unable to act upon them, to feel them, but they would
be quite simply invisible and inexistent for us. Only the
similar can know the similar, only the similar can act
upon the similar. We can know only what we are: *Nothing
can be taught to the mind which is not already concealed as potential
knowledge in the unfolding soul of the creature. So also all perfection of which the outer man is capable, is only a realising of the*

eternal perfection of the Spirit within him. We know the Divine and become the Divine, because we are That already in our secret nature. All teaching is a revealing, all becoming is an unfolding. Self-attainment is the secret; self-knowledge and an increasing consciousness are the means and the process.[22]

We have separated from the world and beings across the millenniums of our evolution, we have egotized, hardened some atoms of this great Body, and asserted "we-me-I" against all the others similarly hardened under an egoistic crust; and having separated ourselves, we could no longer see anything of what was *ourself*, formerly, in the great Mother-Unity. Then we invented eyes, hands, senses, a mind to rejoin what we had excluded from our great Being, and we believed that without those eyes, those fingers, that head, we could know nothing; but this is our separatist illusion; our indirect knowledge covers up and hides from us the immediate knowledge without which our eyes, our fingers, our head and even our microscopes would be able to perceive nothing, understand nothing and do nothing. Our eyes are not organs of vision, they are organs of division, and when the Eye of Truth opens in us there is no longer any need of these glasses or these crutches. Our evolutionary journey, finally, is a slow reconquest of what we had exiled, a revival of Memory; our progress is not measured by the sum of our inventions, which are so many means of artificially bringing back what we have estranged, but by the reintegrated sum of the world which we recognise as ourselves.

And this is joy — *Ananda* — for to be all that is, is to have the joy of all that is.

The bliss of a myriad myriads who are one.[23]

"Whence shall he have grief, how shall he be deluded, who sees everywhere the Oneness?"*

* Isha Upanishad 7.

CHAPTER TWELVE

THE SUPERCONSCIENT

The Riddle

A triple change of consciousness marks then our voyage on
the earth: the discovery of the psychic being or immanent
Spirit, the discovery of Nirvana or the transcendent Spirit
and the discovery of the central being or cosmic Spirit.
Here is probably the true meaning of the Father-Son-Holy
Ghost trinity of which Christian tradition speaks. We
have not to compare the excellence of one or other of these
experiences but to verify them for ourselves: *Philosophies
and religions dispute about the priority of different aspects of God
and different Yogins, Rishis and Saints have preferred this or that
philosophy or religion. Our business is not to dispute about any of
them, but to realise and become all of them, not to follow after any
aspect to the exclusion of the rest, but to embrace God in all His
aspects and beyond aspect*[1] — this is the very meaning of the
integral yoga. But we may ask ourselves if there is nothing
beyond this triple discovery, for however great each may
seem to experience, none gives us the integral plenitude to
which we aspire, at least if we consider that the earth also
and the individual ought to form a part of this plenitude.
Indeed, if we discover the psychic being, it is a great realisation, we become aware of our divinity, but it is limited to
the individual, it does not break the personal walls wherein
we are shut up; if we discover the central being, this is a
very vast realisation, the world becomes our being, but we
lose at the same time the individual, for it would be quite

erroneous to think that it is Mr. Smith who is seated in
the midst of his cosmic consciousness and who enjoys the
view — there is no longer a Mr. Smith; and if we discover the Transcendent, this is a very high realisation but
we lose both the individual and the world — there is nothing else but That for ever beyond this play. We may say
theoretically that Father-Son-Holy Ghost are one — theoretically one may say anything one likes — but practically,
in experience, each of these changes of consciousness seems
to be cut off from the other by a gulf. And so long as we
have not found the path of experience permitting us to
reconcile this triple hiatus between the pantheist, the individualist and the monist, there will not be any plenitude,
either for the individual or for the world. It is not enough
for us to find our individual centre without the totality of
the world, or the totality of the world without the individual, and yet less to find the supreme Peace if it dissolves the
world and the individual — "I do not wish to be sugar,"
exclaimed the great Ramakrishna, "I want to eat sugar!"
In this chaotic, tormenting world, where we must become,
act, bear, we need to be also. Without this being, our becoming is scattered in the throng. But without this becoming our being vanishes into a *blissful Zero*.[2] And without
the individual what meaning would all the marvellous
realisations have for us, for we are no longer there. It is
this contradiction that has to be resolved, not in philosophical terms but in terms of life and power of action. Till
today this reconciliatory path seems inexistent or unknown; this is why all religions and all spiritualities have
put the transcendent Father at the summit of the hierarchy, outside this unfortunate affair, and invite us to seek
elsewhere the totality to which we aspire. However, intuition tells us that if we, beings in a body, aspire to the

totality, it means that the totality *is there*, that it is possible in a body, otherwise we would not aspire to it; what we call "imagination" does not exist — there is no such thing as imagination, there are only deferred realities or truths which await their hour. Jules Verne, in his own way, witnesses this. Is there not then another discovery to be made, a fourth change of consciousness which will change everything?

In his iron cage in the middle of the court-room, Sri Aurobindo had reached the end of the road; by turns he had realised the Immanent, the Transcendent, the Universal — that cage scarcely enclosed anything more than a body: he was everywhere he wished to be in his consciousness. But perhaps he remembered an individual Aurobindo who, since Cambridge and the years in the West, had not stopped gathering consciousness into this body, and now here was the Infinite Consciousness, but this body remained a body among a million others, subject to the same laws of Nature, continuing to be hungry and thirsty, perhaps, and ill at times, like all other bodies, and to advance slowly but surely towards disintegration. The consciousness is vast, luminous, immortal, but underneath everything continues. And because he saw clearly, because he was no longer the dupe of all the masks superimposed by morality and decency, he saw perhaps also in the subconscient the animal grimace under the infinite Consciousness and the material grossness intact under the beautiful aureole — underneath everything continues, nothing is changed. Perhaps he saw still all those other himselfs, behind the cage, who continued to judge and hate and suffer. Who is saved? Nothing is saved if all is not saved! And what did this infinite Consciousness do for all this world, its world? It sees, it knows, but what

can it *do*? Had he not started on his way, one day in
Baroda, for action, for power? And he looked everywhere
in his infinite consciousness, he experienced the vast joy
above, felt *joy laugh nude on the peaks of the Absolute*,[3] but what
can this joy do if the above is not everywhere below? Below all continues, all suffers, all dies. He did not even
listen to the judges, he did not reply to the questions on
which however his life depended, he heard only the Voice
which repeated: *I am guiding, therefore fear not. Turn to
your own Work for which I have brought you to jail*, and Sri
Aurobindo kept his eyes closed in that cage. He was
seeking. Was there not a totality above which could
be the totality down below also? Had the road then come
to an end with this *golden impotence*?[4] What was the
meaning of all this journey?

The soul, which for some inexplicable reason had
descended into this Matter or rather become this Matter,
evolves slowly in the course of ages; it grows, individualises
itself through its senses, its mind, its experiences, it remembers more and more its lost or submerged divinity,
its consciousness amidst its force, then discovers itself and
finally returns to its Origin, transcendent and nirvanic,
or cosmic, according to its destiny and its taste. Is all this
story then only a long and laborious transit of the Divine
to the Divine across the obscure purgatory of Matter?
But why this purgatory, why this Matter? Why did He
ever enter into it if it was only to get out again? We may
be told that the cosmic or nirvanic beatitudes of the end
are well worth all the trouble we have taken; perhaps,
but meanwhile the earth suffers; we shine up above in
our sublime beatitude, but the tortures, the illnesses, death
proliferate and batten — our cosmic consciousness does
not make an atom of difference to the destiny of the earth,

and still less our Nirvana. We may be told that others
have only to do the same and awaken also from their error
— very well, but yet once again why this earth, if it is simply to awaken from the error of the earth? We speak of "the
fall", of Adam and Eve or some absurd sin which has
spoilt what God had created so perfect in the beginning
— but all is God! the serpent of paradise, if there was one,
was God, and Satan and his Pomps and his Works; there
is nothing but He! Would He then be so clumsy that He
falls without knowing it or so impotent that He suffers
without willing it or so sadistic that He plays at error to
have the bliss of getting out of His error? is the earth
then only an error? For if this earth has no meaning *for
the earth*, if the suffering of the world has no meaning
for the world, if it is only a field of transit to purge oneself
of some absurd fault, then nothing and no one, no ultimate bliss, no final ecstasy could ever excuse this useless
interlude — God had no need to enter into Matter if it
was to get out of it, God had no need of Death or of Suffering or of Ignorance, if this Suffering, this Death and this
Ignorance did not carry *in themselves* their meaning, if this
earth and this body finally are not the place of a Secret
which changes everything but the instrument of a purga-
tion and a flight.

> *I climb not to thy everlasting Day,*
> *Even as I have shunned thy eternal Night...*
> *Thy servitudes on earth are greater, king,*
> *Than all the glorious liberties of heaven...*
> *Too far thy heavens for me from suffering men.*
> *Imperfect is the joy not shared by all.*[5]

But if we yet look at this enigma, this soul-centre around which turns all the mystery, we are obliged to see that *it* does not need to be "saved" as it is said, it is for ever free, pure, all saved in its radiance — the moment one enters within, with the eyes wide open, one can well see that it is marvellously divine and light, untouched by all the mud thrown upon it! It is the earth that must be saved, because it hangs heavy; it is life that must be saved, because it dies. Where then is the seed of this Deliverance? where the Power which will deliver? where the true salvation of the world? The spiritualists are right in wanting to make us taste the supreme lightness of the soul; but so too the materialists who dig into Matter and would draw out marvels from that thickness. But they do not have the Secret, nobody has the Secret. The marvels of these have no soul and those of the others no body.

The body, yes, which at first seemed only an obscure instrument for the liberation of the Spirit, is perhaps precisely, paradoxically, the place of an unknown wholeness of the Spirit: *These seeming Instrumentals are the key to a secret without which the Fundamentals themselves would not unveil all their mystery.*[6] "Turn to your own work," said the Voice, and this Work was not at all to swim in the cosmic beatitudes but to find down here, in this body and for the earth, a new path which would bring together in one and the same consciousness the liberty of the Transcendent, the living immensity of the Cosmic and the joy of an individual soul on a perfected earth and in a truer life. For *the true change of consciousness*, says the Mother, *is that which will transform the physical conditions of the world and make of it a new creation.*

Conditions of the Discovery

If we want "to transform the physical conditions of the world", that is, the so-called natural "laws" which govern the world's existence and ours, and if we want to work out this transformation by the power of consciousness, two conditions must be fulfilled: on one side, to work in one's own individual body without escaping into the beyond, since this body is the point of insertion of the consciousness into Matter and, on the other, to discover that principle of consciousness which will have the power to transform Matter. Now, none of the consciousnesses or levels of consciousness known so far to humanity have had the power to operate this change, neither mental consciousness nor vital consciousness nor physical consciousness, as we well know. It is true that by sheer force of discipline certain individuals have been able to defy natural laws, to triumph over weight, over cold, hunger, illness, etc. but first it was a question of individual changes which at no moment have been transmissible; then these are not truly transformations of Matter: the laws which govern the body remain essentially what they are; only certain particular effects, apparently supernatural, are superposed more or less temporarily on the natural. We may give the example of that other revolutionary yogi, companion of Sri Aurobindo, who was once bitten by a mad dog; using the force of his consciousness, he checked immediately the effects of the virus and lived on without bothering about it (let us note in passing that if this yogi had been in a perfect state of consciousness he *could not* have been bitten). Then one day, in the course of a particularly stormy political meeting, he lost patience and became violently angry with one of the speakers. A few hours later he died in the terrible pains of rabies. His power depended only on the *control* of his consciousness and the moment this consciousness gave way everything returned as before because the laws of the body had not been changed, they had been merely muzzled. Consequently, for the transformation envisaged by Sri Aurobindo and the Mother, it is not a question of acquiring "supernatural" powers more or less momentary which plaster the natural, but of changing the very nature of man and his physical conditioning; it is not a question of control, but truly of a transformation. Besides, if we want a realisation for the entire earth, this new principle of existence which Sri Aurobindo calls supramental must *establish itself* definitively among us, in a few of us first, then through radiation in all those who are ready, even as the mind-principle and the life-principle have definitively established themselves on the earth. In other words, the need is to create a divine supermanhood on the earth which will no longer be subject to the laws of ignorance, suffering and decomposition.

The undertaking may seem to us grandiose or fantastic, but only because we see in the perspective of a few decades; it is completely in conformity with the evolutionary line. If we consider, in fact, that all this terrestrial becoming of the Spirit into forms, all these human births are a growth of the soul or the Spirit in man, we may doubt whether the Spirit would always be satisfied with human narrowness, as we may doubt, the journey being over, whether It would wish simply to return into its supraterrestrial Glory and Joy, whence after all It had no need to come out — the Light is there, eternal, it is already there, it is always there, immutable; this is not a conquest for It — but Matter, here is a heaven to build! Perhaps, It wants to know this very Glory and Joy precisely in conditions apparently opposed to its own, in a life besieged by death, ignorance, obscurity, and in the innumerable diversity of the world instead of in a blank unity? Henceforth this life and this Matter would have a meaning; it would no longer be a purgatory or a vain transit towards the beyond, but a *laboratory* in which, step by step, through Matter, plant, animal, then more and more conscious man, the Spirit works out the superman or god: *The soul has not finished what it has to do by merely developing into humanity; it has still to develop that humanity into its higher possibilities. Obviously, the soul that lodges in a Caribbee or an untaught primitive or an Apache of Paris or an American gangster, has not yet exhausted the necessity of human birth, has not developed all its possibilities or the whole meaning of humanity, has not worked out all the sense of Sachchidananda in the universal Man; neither has the soul lodged in a vitalistic European occupied with dynamic production and vital pleasure or in an Asiatic peasant engrossed in the ignorant round of the domestic and economic life. We may reasonably doubt whether even a Plato or a Shankara marks the crown and therefore the end of the outflowering of the spirit in man. We are apt to suppose that these may be the limit, because these and others like them seem to us the highest point which the mind of man can reach, but that may be the illusion of our present possibility.... The soul had a prehuman past, it has a superhuman future.*[7]

Sri Aurobindo is not a theoretician of evolution but a practitioner of evolution. All that he has been able to say or write on evolution, has come *after* his experience, we have only forestalled him to explain more clearly his tentative seekings in the Alipore jail. Now, he saw quite well that this cosmic, beatific immensity was not in truth the place of the work, and that it was necessary to go down towards the body, humbly, and search there. However, we may ask: if it is by the power of consciousness that "the transformation" has to be worked out and not by some external mechanism, what higher consciousness can there be than the cosmic consciousness? has not the summit of the ladder been reached and hence the limit of power? The question is important if we want to understand the practical process of the discovery and eventually to make the experiment ourselves. We may reply by making two observations. First, it is not enough to attain high powers of consciousness, what we yet need is *someone* who embodies them, else we are like the hunter who won marvellous treasures at the end of his binoculars. Where is the "someone" in the cosmic consciousness? There is no one.... A present-day analogy will explain things better: one may send a rocket into the sun, perhaps, and the summit of the world is reached but not the summit of man who will not have moved an inch. Our rocket will have gone out of the terrestrial field. The yogi, in the same way, concentrates on one point of his being, he gathers all his energies like the cone of a rocket, he makes a hole in his shell and emerges elsewhere, in another dimension, cosmic or nirvanic:

He mounted burning like a cone of fire. *

But *who* has realised the cosmic consciousness? Not the yogi — the yogi continues drinking, eating, sleeping, being ill at times like all human animals, and dies — it is not he but a minute point in his being which has realised the cosmic consciousness, that upon which he has concentrated himself with so much desperation to come out of it. And all the rest, all this human and terrestrial nature

* *Savitri*, p. 90.

which he has excluded, which he has suppressed or morti-
fied to concentrate on this single point of escape, does not
share in his cosmic consciousness except by an indirect
radiation. Sri Aurobindo established then this first very
important fact, that a linear realisation at a point does not
suffice and that what we need is a *global realisation*, at all
points, which includes the total existence of the individual:
If you want to transform your nature and your being, says the
Mother, *and if you want to participate in the creation of a new
world, this aspiration, this sharp and linear point does not suffice
any longer; one must englobe all and contain all in one's consciousness.* Hence the integral yoga or "complete yoga", *purna
yoga*. We wanted to get rid of the individual as of an en-
cumbering weight hindering us from flitting about at ease
in the spiritual and cosmic spaces, but without him we
can do nothing for the earth, we cannot draw down those
our treasures on high: *There is something more than the mere
self-breaking of an illusory shell of individuality in the Infinite.*[8]
And Sri Aurobindo leads us to a first conclusion: *The
stifling of the individual may well be the stifling of the god in man.*[9]

A second observation, more important still, compels
recognition. To use again the analogy of the rocket, this
can make a hole at any point whatever of the terrestrial
atmosphere; it can go off from New York or the equator
and quite as easily reach the sun; it is not necessary to
scramble to the summit of Everest and perch up there the
launching-pads! In the same way, the yogi can realise
the cosmic consciousness in any part of his being, at any
level whatsoever, in his mind, his heart and even in his
body, because the cosmic Spirit is everywhere, at all
points of the universe, and the experience can begin anywhere, at any stage whatever, in concentrating upon a
stone or a swallow, upon an idea, a prayer, a feeling or

upon what we disdainfully call an idol. The cosmic consciousness is not the supreme point of human consciousness; we do not take a step atop the individual to reach there but a step outside; it is not necessary to rise in the consciousness, not necessary to be Plotinus, to see the universal Spirit; on the contrary, the less mental one is, the easier is the experience — a shepherd underneath the stars or a fisherman of Galilee has a better chance than all the thinkers of the world together. What then is the use of all this development of human consciousness, if a rustic mysticism can do better? We are compelled to say that either we are all on the wrong path or that these mystical escapes are not the whole sense of the evolution. However, if we admit that the evolutionary line to follow is that of the high summits of earth-consciousness — that of a Leonardo da Vinci, of a Beethoven, an Alexander the Great, a Dante — we are obliged to acknowledge that none of these altitudes has been able to transform life. The summits of the mind or the heart do not bring us, any more than do the cosmic summits, the key of the riddle and the power to change the world; another principle of consciousness is necessary. But another principle *without break of continuity* with the preceding ones, for if there is a rupture of the line or the loss of the individual, we fall back yet again into the cosmic or mystical outbursts, without a link with the earth. Certainly the consciousness of unity and the transcendent consciousness are the indispensable basis of all realisation (without these we may as well build a house without a foundation) but they must be acquired in other ways which respect the evolutionary continuity — what is needed is an evolution, not a revolution. In short, it is a question of getting out of it without getting out. Instead of a rocket which goes to its annihilation in the sun, what is necessary is a rocket which harpoons the Sun of the supreme consciousness and has the power to make it descend at all points of our terrestrial consciousness: *The ultimate knowledge is that which perceives and accepts God in the universe as well as beyond the universe and the integral Yoga is that which, having found the Transcendent, can return upon the universe and possess it, retaining the power freely to descend as well as ascend the great stair of existence.*[10] This double movement of ascension and descent of the individual consciousness constitutes the basic principle of the supramental discovery. But on the way Sri Aurobindo was to touch an unknown spring which would upset everything.

Ascension of Consciousness

It is not enough to say in what lies the discovery of Sri Aurobindo, we must yet know how it is accessible *to us*. Now, it is very difficult to give a diagram and assert "Here is the road", because spiritual development is always in accordance with each one's nature — and for a good reason: it is not a question of learning something foreign but of learning oneself, and there are no two natures exactly alike. Sri Aurobindo has pointed this out often: *The ideal I put before our yoga does not bind all spiritual life and endeavour. The spiritual life is not a thing that can be formulated in a rigid definition or bound by a fixed mental rule; it is a vast field of evolution, an immense kingdom potentially larger than the other kingdoms below it, with a hundred provinces, a thousand types, stages, forms, paths, variations of the spiritual ideal, degrees of spiritual advancement.*[11] We can hence give only a few indications, hoping that each man may find the

sign that lights up *his own road*. One should always remember that the true system of yoga is to catch the thread
of one's *own* consciousness, that "shining thread" the rishis
spoke of* and to hold on to it and go to the very end.

Cosmic consciousness and Nirvana do not bring us the
evolutionary key we are seeking, so we take up once again
our quest, with Sri Aurobindo, at the point where he had
left it at Baroda, before his two great experiences. The
ascension into the Superconscient is the first stage. As the
seeker establishes silence in his mind, as he calms his
vital, liberates himself from his absorption in the physical,
the consciousness disengages itself from the thousand
activities wherein it was indiscernably fused, scattered, and
it acquires an independent existence. It is like a being
within, a compact Force vibrating more and more intensely. And the more it grows, the less is it satisfied with being
shut up in a body; we find that it radiates, in sleep at first,
then in our meditation, then with eyes wide open. But this
lateral movement, if it may be called thus, in the universal
Mind, the universal Vital, the universal Physical, is not
its only movement. It wants to climb. This ascending
surge is not even necessarily the result of a conscious
discipline, it may be a natural spontaneous need (it must
never be forgotten that our effort in this life is only the continuation of many other efforts in many other lives, whence
the unequal development of individuals and the impossibility of fixing rules). Instinctively we can feel something
above the head which draws us like a vastness or a light,
or like a pole which is the source of all our acts and
thoughts or like a zone of concentration at the top of
the skull. The seeker has not silenced his mind simply for
the pleasure of being like a log, his silence is not dead,

* Rig Veda X. 53.

it is living; he has switched on up above because he feels it is alive up there. Silence is not an end, it is a means, like the sol-fa to capture music, and there are many musics. Day after day, as his consciousness concretises itself, he has hundreds of tiny experiences, almost imperceptible, which spring forth from this Silence above: he is thinking of nothing and suddenly a thought crosses him — not even a thought, just a click — and he knows exactly what must be done, how it must be done, in the least details, like the pieces of a puzzle which fall into their place in the twinkling of an eye, and with a massive certitude (down below all is complete incertitude; things can always be otherwise); or sometimes a tiny knock strikes him: "Go to see so-and-so" — he goes and "by chance" this person needs him; or "Don't do this", he persists and has a bad fall; or, without any reason he is thrust towards a certain place and meets exactly the circumstances which can help him; or a certain problem presents itself, he remains immobile, silent, calls above and the answer comes, clear, irrefutable. Or if he speaks, if he writes, he can feel very concretely an expanse above whence he draws his thought like the thread from a luminous cocoon — he does not stir; simply he keeps under the current and transcribes; nothing passes in his head. But if he mingles in the least his mind there, everything vanishes or rather gets falsified because the mind tries to copy the intimations (it is an inveterate monkey) and it takes its own will-o'-the-wisps for illuminations. And the more the seeker learns to listen above, to follow these intimations (which are not imperious, not noisy, which are almost imperceptible like a breath, hardly thought out, only felt, but terribly rapid), the more numerous, exact, irresistible they become; and gradually he sees that all his acts, the very least, can be sovereignly guided by this silent source above, that all his thoughts come from there, luminous, beyond dispute, that a sort of *spontaneous knowledge* is born in him. He begins to live constant little miracles. *If mankind only caught a glimpse of what infinite enjoyments, what perfect forces, what luminous reaches of spontaneous knowledge, what wide calms of our being lie waiting for us in the tracts which our animal evolution has not yet conquered, they would leave all and never rest till they had gained these treasures. But the way is narrow, the doors hard to force, and fear, distrust and scepticism are there, sentinels of Nature to forbid the turning away of our feet from less ordinary pastures.*[12]

Once this expanse above becomes concrete, living, like a shore of light up there, the seeker feels the need to enter into direct communication and to spring up in the open, for he feels also with a growing sharpness that the life down below, the mind down below are narrow, untrue, a sort of caricature; he has the impression of knocking against everything, of not being at home anywhere, and that all is false, grating — words, ideas, feelings; that it is not *that*, never *that* — it is always beside the point, always approximate, always beneath. Sometimes in sleep, as a heralding sign, we are perhaps caught in a great blazing light, so dazzling that instinctively we veil our eyes — *the sun is dark when this happens*, observes the Mother. Then it is necessary to let this Force within grow, grow, this Consciousness-Force which gropes towards the heights, to impel it by our needs for something else, for a truer life, a truer knowledge, a truer relationship with the world and beings — our *greatest progress [is] a deepened need;*[13] to refuse all mental constructions which at every moment try to grab the shining thread; to keep in a *state of openness*, be too great for ideas. For it is not ideas that we need but space. *We must not only cut asunder the snare of the mind and the senses, but flee also beyond the snare of the thinker, the snare of the theologian and the church-builder, the meshes of the Word and the bondage of the Idea. All these are within us waiting to wall in the spirit with forms; but we must always go beyond, always renounce the lesser for the greater, the finite for the Infinite; we must be prepared to proceed from illumination to illumination, from experience to experience, from soul-state to soul-state.... Nor must we attach ourselves even to the truths we hold most securely, for they are but forms and expressions of the Ineffable who refuses to limit itself to any form or expression; always we must keep ourselves open to the higher Word from above that does not confine itself to its own sense and the light of the Thought that carries in it its own opposites.*[14] Then one day, through our great need, through our being like a compressed mass, the doors will open: *The consciousness rises*, says the Mother, *it breaks this hard lid, there, at the top of the head, and one emerges into the light.*

Above was an ardent white tranquillity.[15]

This experience is the starting-point of Sri Aurobindo's yoga. It is the emergence into the Superconscient, the passage from a past which binds us hand and foot to a future which sees. Instead of being down below, always under a weight, one is up above and breathes freely: *The consciousness is no longer in the body or limited by it; it feels itself not only above it but extended in space; the body is below its high station and enveloped in its extended consciousness... it becomes only a circumstance in the largeness of the being, an instrumental part of it... in the definitive realisation of a higher station above there is really no more coming down except with a part of the consciousness which may descend to work in the body or on the lower levels while the permanently high-stationed being above presides over all that is experienced and done.*[16]

Ecstasy?

This taking-off once effected, it is a matter of proceeding slowly and systematically. The first movement of the consciousness, in fact, is to shoot forth straight towards the heights, with a sensation of infinite ascent, just like a rocket, then of stabilisation in a sort of luminous nirvana. The bliss that comes with this opening on the summit (at least on what appears to us to be the summit) or with this dissolution is so irresistible that it would seem altogether incongruous to come down again to intermediary levels to explore anything at all — it would be a falling off; there is but one longing, to remain as still as possible so as not to ruffle that unbroken Peace. Indeed, one has not even noticed that there may be intermediary levels between the going out from the top of the head and the fusion "far up above"; dazzled, somewhat like the new-born babe opening its eyes for the first time, the seeker does not recognise himself there, he mingles all in a sort of blank whiteness or a white-bluishness, and he loses hold, that is, he falls into a trance or an "ecstasy" as it is said in the West or into *samadhi* as they say in India. And when he returns from there, he is not more advanced than before. *In his haste to arrive... [the seeker] assumes that there is nothing between the thinking mind and the Highest, and, shutting his eyes in samadhi, tries to rush through all that actually intervenes without even seeing these great and luminous kingdoms of the Spirit. Perhaps he arrives at his object, but only to fall asleep in the Infinite.*[17]

Naturally, the seeker will say that it is a marvellous state, unutterable, supreme, and this is true, but as the Mother remarks, *One can say all one likes about it because precisely one remembers nothing.... Yes, you enter into samadhi when you go out of your conscious being and you enter a part of your being which is completely inconscient or rather a domain where you have no corresponding consciousness.... You are in an impersonal state, that is, a state where you are inconscient, and because of this you remember nothing, for you have not been conscious of anything.* Sri Aurobindo used to say quite simply that ecstasy was a higher form of inconscience. It may turn out that what we call Transcendent, Absolute, Supreme is not the ecstatic annihilation so often described to us but only the limit of our *present* consciousness; it is perhaps absurd to say: "Here ends the world and there begins the Transcendent," as though there were a gap between the two, for the Transcendent may begin at the a b c of reason for a pigmy and the world may vanish not higher than the intellect. There is no gap except in our consciousness. Perhaps the progress of evolution is precisely to explore zones of consciousness always farther into an inexhaustible Transcendent which is not truly located "on high" or elsewhere outside this world but everywhere down here, unveiling itself slowly to our vision — for if, one day in our prehistory, the Transcendent was situated a little above the protoplasm, it is not that it has left the world of protoplasm to take refuge higher up, above the batrachia, the chimpanzee, then man, in a sort of race where It is gradually outrun — it is that *we* have left the primitive inconscience to live a little ahead in a Transcendent present everywhere.*

* At this stage of our search, it is not possible to say more about this. We must await the supramental experience to have the key to this false opposition.

Thus, instead of fainting away at the summit or what he takes for the summit, and believing that his ecstasy is a sign of progress, the seeker must understand that it is a sign of inconscience, and work to discover the living existence concealed under his bedazzlement: *Try to develop your inner individuality*, says the Mother, *and you will be able to enter these very regions* in full consciousness, *and to have the joy of communion with the highest regions without losing consciousness for this and returning with a Zero instead of an experience.** And Sri Aurobindo insisted: *It is in the waking state that this realisation must come and endure in order to be a reality of life.... Experience and trance have their utility for opening the being and preparing it, but it is only when the realisation is constant in the waking state that it is truly possessed.*[18] The state of integral mastery, this is the goal we pursue, not the state of a spiritual marmot, and this mastery is possible only in a continuity of consciousness: when we go into an ecstasy, we lose the "someone" who would form the bridge between the powers above and the impotence below.

When he had broken through the lid at the top of the head, Sri Aurobindo began, in the Alipore jail, to explore methodically the planes of consciousness above the ordinary mind, as he had explored in Baroda the planes of consciousness down below. He took up again, where he had left off, the ascension of the great ladder of consciousness extending without gap or ecstatic break from Matter

---

* "Ecstasy", it is thought, is better defined as "enstasy". Must we then believe that one is "in oneself" only when being outside oneself? For "ecstasy" — *exstare* — by definition means to be outside one's body or outside the perception of the world. We would have an "in oneself" which is not outside oneself, to put things plainly. We cannot in truth speak of "enstasy" except after the supreme experiences are located in our body and in the very midst of our daily life. Otherwise it is an abuse of language, although this expresses perfectly, in its own way, the gulf we have dug between life and the Spirit.

to this X point which was to be the place of his discovery. For *the highest truth, the integral self-knowledge is not to be gained by this self-blinded leap into the Absolute but by a patient transit beyond the mind.*[19]

Beings and Forces

Everyone of us receives constantly, without noticing it, influences or inspirations from these higher superconscient planes, which translate themselves in us into ideas, ideals, aspirations, works of art; it is these that secretly mould our life and our future; similarly, we receive constantly without knowing it, vital or subtle physical vibrations which determine every minute our affective life and our exchanges with the world. We are shut up in an individual personal body only through a tenacious visual derangement; in fact we are porous everywhere and bathe in universal forces as the anemone in the sea: *Man twitters intellectually* (=*foolishly*) *about the surface results and attributes them all to his 'noble self', ignoring the fact that his noble self is hidden far away from his own vision behind the veil of his dimly sparkling intellect and the reeking fog of his vital feelings, emotions, impulses, sensations and impressions.*[20] Our sole freedom is to lift ourselves to ever higher planes by an individual evolution and our single role to transcribe and incarnate materially the truths of the plane to which we belong. Two important points then could be stressed, common to all these planes of consciousness, from top to bottom, if we wish to understand better the mechanism of the universe. First, these planes do not depend upon us and upon what we think of them, not more than the sea upon the anemone; they exist *independently of man*. Contemporary psychology which mixes up pell-mell all the degrees of being in a so-called "collective Unconscious" as if it were an enormous magician's hat whence could be drawn in a happy-go-lucky way archetypes or neuroses, shows in this an insufficiency of vision: on the one hand, because the forces of these planes are not at all inconscient, except for us; they are very conscious, infinitely more conscious than we; and on the other, because these forces are not "collective" in the sense that they are as little the product of a human secretion as the sea is the product of the anemone; it is the frontal man who is the product of this Immensity behind. *The gradations of consciousness are universal states not dependent on the outlook of the subjective personality; rather the outlook of the subjective personality is determined by the grade of consciousness in which it is organised according to its typal nature or its evolutionary stage.*[21] But naturally, it is just human to reverse the order of values and put oneself at the centre of the world. Besides, it is not a question of theory, always disputable, but of experience to which all are welcome: when one exteriorises oneself, that is, goes out of one's body and enters consciously these planes, one sees very well that they exist completely outside us, as the entire world exists completely outside Piccadilly, with forces and even beings, places, which have nothing in common with our terrestrial world — whole civilisations witness this and have conveyed it, engraved, painted on their walls or in their temples, civilisations which were perhaps less ingenious than ours but certainly not more stupid.

The second important point concerns the conscious forces and the beings which people these planes. Here must be shown clearly the side of superstition and even of deceit, which represents our "collective" contribution, and the side of truth. As always the two are closely mingled. This is why the integral seeker, more than any other, must be armed with that *clear austerity* upon which Sri Aurobindo insisted so much, and must not confuse the suprarational with the irrational. In practice, when one enters consciously these planes, whether in sleep or in meditation or by voluntary exteriorisation, one can see two kinds of things: impersonal currents of force, more or less luminous, or personal beings. But these are two ways of seeing *the same thing: The wall between consciousness and force, impersonality and personality becomes much thinner when one goes behind the veil of matter. If one looks at a working from the side of impersonal force one sees a force or energy at work acting for a purpose or with a result, if one looks from the side of being one sees a being possessing, guiding and using or else representative of and used by a conscious force as its instrument of specialised action and expression.... In modern science it has been found that if you look at the movement of energy, it appears on one side to be a wave and act as a wave, on the other as a mass of particles and to act as a mass of particles each acting in its own way. It is somewhat the same principle here.*[22]

Certain seekers will then never see beings but luminous forces; others will see only beings and never forces; all will depend on their inner attitude, their aspiration, their religious, spiritual and even cultural formation. It is here that subjectivity begins and with it the danger of error and superstition. But subjectivity is not a disqualification of the experience, it is simply the sign that the same thing can be viewed and transcribed in different ways according to our formation — we would very much like to know if two painters have ever seen the same landscape in the same way, to speak only of our "concrete" realities. The criterion of truth, to believe the jurists of the natural and the supernatural, should be an unchanging constant, but this is very likely the criterion of our numbness; the multiplicity of experiences proves only that we are before a *living* truth, not a hardened residue as of our mental and material truths. Moreover, these conscious forces — very conscious — can take all the forms they wish, not for deceit but to make themselves accessible to the consciousness of those who open to them and invoke them. A Christian saint who has the vision of the Virgin, for example, and an Indian who has the vision of Durga see perhaps the same thing, they have perhaps entered into contact with the same level of consciousness and the same forces; but it is quite obvious that Durga would signify nothing to the Christian and if, in another connection, this force manifested itself in its pure state, that is, in the form of a luminous impersonal vibration, it would not be accessible to the consciousness of the devotee either of the Virgin or of Durga, or in any case would not speak to their hearts. Devotion too has its rights; everybody is not sufficiently developed to understand the intensity of love there can be in a simple little golden light without form. But what is more interesting still is that if a poet, a Rimbaud or a Shelley, opens to these *same* planes of consciousness, he would see yet another thing, which however is always the same thing; it is quite evident that neither Durga nor the Virgin forms a part of the preoccupations of these poets; they would perceive perhaps a great vibration or shining pulsations or coloured lights which would be translated in them by an intense poetic emotion — consider, for instance, Spender:*

* The French original quotes here Rimbaud: "O bonheur, ô raison, j'écartai du ciel l'azur, qui est du noir, et je vécus, étincelle d'or de la lumière *nature.*"

> Terrible wave white with the seething word!
> Terrible flight through the revolving darkness!...
> My will behind my weakness silhouettes
> My territories of fear, with a great sun.

— and this emotion comes perhaps from the same level of consciousness or has the same frequency, if we may call it so, as that of the Indian or Christian mystic, although the poetic transcription of the vibration perceived may seem to be at the opposite pole of all religious belief. And the mathematician, too, who suddenly in a flash which transports him with joy, sees a new figuration of the world, has perhaps touched the same height of consciousness, the same revelatory vibration. For nothing takes place "in the air", all is *located* somewhere, on a plane, and each plane has its own wave-length, its own luminous intensity, its particular vibratory frequency, and one may touch the *same* plane of consciousness, the *same* illumination by a thousand different ways.

Those who have gone beyond or thought they have gone beyond the stage of religious forms come quickly to the conclusion that all personal forms are deceiving or of a lower kind and that only impersonal forces are true, but this is an abuse of human logic which would like to reduce everything to uniformity. The vision of Durga is not more false or imaginary than a poem of Shelley or than certain equations of Einstein which were verified ten years later. Error and superstition begin when one says that the Virgin alone is true in the whole world or Durga alone or Poetry alone. The reconciliatory truth would be to *see* that all these forms come forth in variable degrees from the same divine Light.

But it would be another error still to believe that the

forces said to be impersonal are improved mechanical forces; they have an intensity, a warmth, a luminous joy which have all the presence of a person without a face— for one who has once been invaded by a torrent of golden light, a sapphire-blue flowering, a sparkling of white light, there is no doubt left that with this gold comes a spontaneous knowledge full of delight; with this blue, a solid power; with this whiteness, an ineffable Presence. There are forces which descend upon us like a smile. Then truly one understands that the personal-impersonal, consciousness-force wall is a practical distinction made by human logic without any relation to the reality, and that it is not necessary to see personages to be in the presence of *the* Person.

Practically the only essential thing is to open to these higher planes; when there each one receives according to his capacity and his needs or his aspiration. All the quarrels between materialists and the religious, philosophers and poets and painters and musicians are the childishness of an inexperienced humanity where each one wishes to lodge the whole world under his own signboard. When one contacts the luminous Truth, one sees that It can contain everything without any quarrel and that every single being is its child — the mystic receives the joy of Him he loves, the poet the joy of poetry and the mathematician the joy of mathematics and the painter coloured revelations, and all these are spiritual joys.

However, a "clear austerity" is a powerful protection, for unhappily everybody has not the capacity to rise to high regions where the forces are pure; it is much easier to open to the vital level, which is the world of the great Force of Life, of desire and the passions (the one well known to mediums and occultists) and there the lower forces are quick to put on divine disguises under blazing colours or terrible forms. If the seeker is pure, he will easily look through the double deceit, fearful or marvellous, and his little psychic light will dissolve all the threats, all the garish mirages of the vital melodrama. But who can ever be sure of his purity? If then we do not pursue personal forms but only an ever higher truth which we leave free to manifest itself under the form It chooses, we shall be sheltered from error and superstition.

We may now try to give a glimpse of these superconscient gradations as they are discovered when one does not succumb to the ecstatic inconscience, and as Sri Aurobindo experienced them; and it is certain that what comes closest to the universal truth is not forms, which are always limited and relative to a tradition or an age — though these forms have their place and their truth — but luminous vibrations. And when we say "vibrations", we do not mean some wave-mechanics without contents but movements of light which inexpressibly contain joy, love, knowledge, beauty and all the qualities which variously clothe at different levels the high manifestations of human consciousness, whether religious or not:

> *A light not born of sun or moon or fire,*
> *A light that dwelt within and saw within*
> *Shedding an intimate visibility....*[23]

The Planes of the Mind

Before reaching the supramental plane which is the beginning of *the higher hemisphere* of existence, the seeker will cross various mental layers or worlds which Sri Aurobindo

has called respectively in their ascending order higher
mind, illumined mind, intuitive mind and overmind (not
to be confused with supermind). Naturally we may use different terms if we wish, but these four zones correspond to
facts of experience quite distinct, verifiable by all those who
have the capacity to undertake the ascension consciously.

Theoretically, these four zones of consciousness form
a part of the Superconscient; theoretically, because it is
quite obvious that the superconscient line will vary according to individuals; for some the higher mind or even the
illumined mind is not at all superconscient, it is a part
of their normal waking consciousness whilst for others the
simple reasoning mind is a yet far-off stage of inner development; in other words, the superconscient line tends to
withdraw as our evolution progresses. If the subconscient
is our evolutionary past, the Superconscient is our
evolutionary future. It is a Superconscient which gradually
becomes our normal waking consciousness.

We shall not say here what these higher planes of consciousness are in themselves, independently of man; each
of them is a whole world, vaster and more active than the
earth, and our mental language is inadequate to describe
them; we would need the language of the visionary and
poet — "another language". This is what Sri Aurobindo
has found in *Savitri*, his poetic epic to which we refer the
reader.

> *A million lotuses swaying on one stem,*
> *World after coloured and ecstatic world*
> *Climbs towards some far unseen epiphany.*[24]

But we may say what these planes bring to man and how
they change our vision of the world when we rise to them.

The ordinary mind which we all know sees things step by step, successively, linearly; it cannot take a jump, else this makes holes in its logic and it loses its bearings, it says this is incoherent, irrational, smoky. It cannot see more than one thing at a time, else it says this is contradictory; it cannot admit a truth or a fact in its field of consciousness without automatically rejecting all that is not this truth or this fact — it is like a camera-shutter which lets in one and only one image at a time. And all that does not appear on its momentary screen belongs to the limbo of error, falsehood and night. Everything goes then in an inexorable antinomic system: white-black, truth-error, God-Satan, and it proceeds like a donkey on the road seeing one tuft of grass after another. Briefly, the ordinary mind cuts out untiringly small pieces of time and space. The more one goes down the ladder of consciousness, the more accentuated becomes the cutting; for a scarab, let us suppose, all that crosses its own sweet little path comes out from the future at the right, cuts the line of its present and whisks away into the past at the left; the passer-by who bestrides it and finds himself at once to the right and the left is quite simply miraculous and irrational, unless he has one leg in the truth and the other in falsehood which is not possible; and therefore man does not exist, he is scarabically impossible! For us the shutter is a little wider, future and past are no longer to the right and left in space, they are yesterday and tomorrow in time — we have gained time on the scarab. But there is another consciousness, the supramental, which can widen the shutter yet more, gain yet more time and bestride yesterday and tomorrow; it sees simultaneously present, past and future, the white and the black, the truth and what is conventionally called error, the good and what is conventionally called evil, the yes and the no — for all opposites are the products of a cutting up of time. We speak of "error" because we do not yet see the good it is preparing or of which it is the sketchy half; we speak of "falsehood" because we have not had time to see the lotus blossom from the mud; we speak of "black", but our day is black for him who sees the Light! Our error was the necessary companion of good; the no, the indissoluble half of yes; the white and black and all the rainbow hues the various forms of a single light which gradually unfolds itself — there are no contraries, there are only complementaries. The whole story of the ascension of consciousness is the story of an "unshuttering" and the passage from a linear and contradictory consciousness to a *global consciousness*.

But Sri Aurobindo aptly uses the word "global", he aptly speaks of the higher *hemisphere* of consciousness when speaking of the Supermind, because the so-called higher truth is not a cripple of the earth, without its lower half it is not the whole truth. The high does not annul the low, it fulfils it; the timeless is not the contrary of the temporal, even as the two arms which embrace are not contraries for the being embraced. And the secret, precisely, is to discover the timeless at the heart of the temporal, the infinite in the finite and the round wholeness of things in the obscurest fraction, otherwise no one is embraced and no one embraces anything.

This ascension of consciousness is not only the story of the conquest of time, it is also the conquest of joy, love, vastness of being. The lower evolutionary levels are not satisfied with carving out little bits of time and space, they cut up everything. A *law of* increasing *fragmentation*[25] presides over the descent of consciousness, from the Spirit to the atom — fragmentation of joy, fragmentation of love and of power, and naturally fragmentation of knowledge and vision; all is finally decomposed into a swarming of minute tropisms, a hazy dust of *somnambulist consciousness*[26] which is already a quest of the Light or perhaps a memory of Joy. *The general sign of this descent is an always diminishing power of intensity, intensity of being, intensity of consciousness, intensity of force, intensity of the delight in things and the delight of existence. So too as we ascend towards the supreme level these intensities increase.*[27]

a) *The Ordinary Mind*

It is the quality of the light or the quality of vibrations which, essentially, distinguishes one plane of consciousness from another. If we start from our own evolutionary level and if we consider consciousness under its aspect of light from which all the others derive, the ordinary mind appears to the eye that sees as a sort of greyness with a number of small dark points or of minute, fairly obscure vibratory knots, like a cloud of flies whirling around the heads of people, which represent their thousand and one thoughts— they come, go, turn, circulate from one to another. Then, from time to time, a tiny burst of light descends from above, a tiny joy, a tiny flame of love dancing in this greyness. But this *ground of neutrality*, as Sri Aurobindo says, is so thick, so sticky, that it absorbs everything, discolours everything, pulls everything down into its obscure gravitation — we cannot for long contain joy or suffering, cannot bear much light; it is all too small, spasmodic, quickly extinguished. And all is subject to a thousand conditions.

b) The Higher Mind

This new level appears frequently in philosophers and thinkers; it is already less opaque, more free. The ground is no longer quite grey or the grey verges on blue and the little burstings of light which descend are less quickly engulfed; they are also more intense, more rich, more frequent. Joy tends to last longer, love to be wider, and they are less subject to the innumerable conditions of the lower stages — one begins to know what joy is in itself, love in itself, without cause. But it is yet a cold light, a little hard. It is yet a heavy mental substance which catches the light from above and dissolves it in its own substance, covers it up with a thinking layer without even noticing it and does not truly understand the light received until everything is over, when it has been diluted, logicised and fragmented into so many pages, words or ideas. Moreover, the pages or paragraphs of the higher mind are founded upon a single point of light or a small number of points it has seized (it is its conclusion before having begun, a small drop of intuition hurriedly swallowed up) and it takes a lot of trouble to eliminate on the way everything that would be contrary to its conclusion. Certainly it can open to higher planes and receive flashes but this is not its normal altitude; its mental substance is of the kind to decompose the light. It begins to understand when it has explained.

c) The Illumined Mind

The illumined mind is of another nature. As the higher mind gradually accepts the silence, it wins access to this domain, that is, its substance becomes clear and what came drop by drop comes in a stream: *The ground is no longer a general neutrality but pure spiritual ease and happiness upon which the special tones of the aesthetic consciousness come out or from which they arise. This is the first fundamental change.*[28] The consciousness fills with a flood of light, often golden, infused with varying colours according to the inner state; it is a *luminous invasion.* And simultaneously comes a state of "enthusiasm", as the Greeks understood the word, a sudden awakening, as if the entire being were on the *qui vive*, alerted, plunged all at once into a very rapid rhythm and a brand new world, with new values, new reliefs, unexpected correspondences; the world's curtain of smoke is raised, everything is linked in a great joyous vibration; life is vaster, more true, more vivid; small truths kindle everywhere, silently, as if each thing had a secret, a special meaning, a special life. One is in an unutterable *state of truth* without understanding anything about it — simply, *it is.* And marvellously. It is light, it is living, it loves.

For each one this luminous flood will be differently translated (one is always in too great a hurry to put it into form instead of letting it quietly impregnate the being and do its work of clarification of our substance), for some it will be a sudden poetic opening, others will see new architectural forms, others still will find themselves on the trail of new scientific discoveries and yet others will love their God. Generally the access to this new consciousness is accompanied by a spontaneous blossoming of creative capacities, particularly in the poetic field. It is strange to see a number of poets of all languages, Chinese, Indian, English, etc. among the disciples of Sri Aurobindo, as if poetry and the arts were the first practical result of his yoga: *I have seen both in myself and others a sudden flowering of capacities in every kind of activity come by the opening of consciousness, — so that one who laboured long without the least success to express himself in rhythm becomes a master of poetic language and cadences in a day. It is a question of the right silence in the mind and the right openness to the Word that is trying to express itself — for the Word is there ready formed in those inner planes where all artistic forms take birth, but it is the transmitting mind that must change and become a perfect channel and not an obstacle.*[29]

Poetry is the most convenient means of explaining what these higher planes of consciousness are, for in the rhythm of the poem the vibrations are easily caught. We shall have recourse to poetry then, here and later, although the Superconscient is not the sole privilege of poets! In his vast correspondence on poetry and in his *Future Poetry* Sri Aurobindo has given numerous examples of poetry from the illumined mind. It is naturally Shakespeare who would give us the most abundant illustrations of this, if we listen to something else, something that vibrates behind (for poetry and all the arts are finally only a means of catching a tiny ineffable note, which is nothing and yet is the truth of life)*:

> that his virtues
> Will plead like angels, trumpet-tongued...
> And, pity, like a naked new-born babe
> Striding the blast, or heaven's cherubin, horsed
> Upon the sightless couriers of the air

* In the French original, the following lines from Rimbaud's *Bateau Ivre* are quoted here:

> Je sais les cieux crèvent en éclairs, et les trombes
> Et les ressacs et les courants; je sais le soir
> L'Aube exaltée ainsi qu'un peuple de colombes,
> Et j'ai vu quelquefois ce que l'homme a cru voir.

Shall blow the horrid deed in every eye
That tears shall drown the wind.

Poetry is not called "illumined" because of its sense; it is
illumined because it carries a particular note from this
plane and we would find the same note in a certain picture
of Rembrandt, for example, a musical composition of
César Franck or even quite simply in the words of a friend
— it is the touch of truth behind, the little vibration that
goes straight to the heart and of which the poem, the can-
vas or the sonata are only more or less transparent thicken-
ings; and the higher one climbs, the purer is the vibration,
more luminous, vast, powerful. When Wordsworth says*:

And beauty born of murmuring sound
Shall pass into her face...

the vibration is almost visible, so palpably is it there.
But this is not an illumined vibration, one can feel that
clearly; it does not come from above the head but from
the heart-centre — and this has nothing to do with the
sense of the lines: the words are only the clothing of this
vibrating something. On the other hand, this line from
Francis Thompson comes directly from the illumined
mind†:

The abashless inquisition of each star.

What characterises essentially all the works which come

* And here, in the original, these lines also from Rimbaud:
    O saisons, ô châteaux,
    Quelle âme est sans défauts?
† In the original, Mallarmé's line:
    Le transparent glacier des vols qui n'ont pas fui!

from this plane is what Sri Aurobindo calls a *luminous sweep*, a sudden melting of light; the vibration is similar to no other; there is a shock, always, then the vibrating thing afterwards, like a diapason. But it does not for long remain pure in a work, for the rhythm of the work follows that of the consciousness, which constantly ascends and descends, for lack of a special discipline to stabilize it; the rest of the Shakespearean passage — the last three lines — falls away from the illumined overhead inspiration and contains a touch of the vital also and of the ordinary mind.*

Along with its beauty we find the limits of the illumined mind: illumined poetry translates itself into a flood of images and revelatory words (because often the vision opens at this stage and also one begins to hear), almost an avalanche of images, luxuriant, often disordered, as though the consciousness was hard put to it to contain the luminous wave and this additional intensity — there is too much of it, it overflows. Enthusiasm changes easily into excitement and, if the rest of the being is not sufficiently purified, any lower part whatever may get hold of the light and force which descend to use them for its own ends, — this is a frequent danger. When the lower parts of the being, specially the vital, seize the luminous flood, they harden it, dramatize it, torture it — the power is still there, but hardened — whilst the essence of the illumined mind is joy. Here we could cite the names of many poets and creative writers.† Besides, the substance of the illu-

---

* The original French continues here the reference to Rimbaud: "The *Bateau Ivre* contains the illumined mind, but also much of the vital and of the very simple mind and even an outburst of the overmind."

† Perhaps here must be stressed the great difference between the individual who receives occasional inspirations or illuminations, often unreliable, and

mined mind is not actually transparent, it is only translu-
cid; its light is diffused — somewhat as though it fingered
the truth everywhere without really touching it — whence
the frequent incoherences, the vagueness. It is only the
beginning of a birth. Before obtaining higher access, yet
another purification is necessary and above all, more
peace, equilibrium, silence. The higher one climbs in
consciousness, the more one needs an equilibrium of
granite.

d) *The Intuitive Mind*

The intuitive mind differs from the illumined mind by
its clear transparency — it is rapid, it runs barefooted from
rock to rock; it is no longer clogged like the higher mind,
by this thinking orthopaedy which glues us to the soil as
though knowledge depended on the ponderous volume of
our reflections. Knowledge is a lightning flashed from the
silence and all is there, not higher or deeper, in truth,
but just there, under our very eyes, awaiting our becoming
a little clear — it is a matter not so much of raising oneself as of clearing obstructions. The rice-fields of India in
spring-time stretch calm and green with their sweet fragrance, as far as the eye can reach, under a heavy sky; then,
at one go, with one cry, thousands of parrots fly out. And
a minute before we had seen nothing. All is so rapid, flash-
ing — terrible rapidities of the clearing consciousness. A
point, a sound, a drop of light, and a whole world, bursting, crowded, is contained therein — thousands of swift-

one who has systematically developed his consciousness, degree by degree, so
well that he can at will fix himself at any level of consciousness, remain there
as long as he wishes and receive from it without deformation the corresponding inspirations and illuminations. This is the work of the integral yoga.

winging elusive birds in the flash of a second. Intuition repeats at our level the original mystery of a great Gaze — a formidable glance which has seen all, known all, and which plays at seeing bit by bit, slowly, successively, temporally, from a myriad points of view, that which It had englobed alone in a fraction of eternity.

An eternal instant is the cause of the years.[30]

With the intuition comes a special joy, different apparently from the joy of illumination. It is no longer a wave that seems to invade from outside, it is a sort of recognition, as though we were always two, a brother of light who lives in the light and a brother of shadows, ourself, who lives down below and repeats gropingly, in the shadow, knocking himself about everywhere, the gestures of the brother of light, the movement, the knowledge, the great adventure of the brother of light, but it is all paltry down below, scraggy, clumsy; then suddenly there is a coincidence — we are one. We are one in a point of light. For once there is no difference and this is joy.

And when we shall be one at all points, this will be the Life Divine.

And this point of coincidence is cognition, knowledge, which may be translated in one way or another according to the preoccupation of the moment, but which is always, essentially, a shock of identity, a meeting — one knows because one recognises. Sri Aurobindo used to say that intuition is *a memory of the Truth.*[31] And one sees quite well, truly, in the intuitive flash, that knowledge is not a discovery of the unknown — one discovers only oneself! there is nothing else to discover — but a slow recognition in time of this second of Light which we have *all seen.* Who has not seen, even once? who has not that Memory in his life? Whatever be our beliefs or unbeliefs, our capacities or incapacities, our altitudes low or less low, there is always a moment which is *our* moment. There are lives which have lasted but one second, and all the rest belongs to oblivion.

The language of intuition gathers itself into a concise formula, without a word too much, in contrast with the opulent language of the illumined mind; but that also, by its very abundance, brings a luminous rhythm and a truth less clearly outlined perhaps but warmer. When Plotinus gathered the whole cycle of human effort into three terms: "A flight of the Alone to the Alone", he was using a highly intuitive language, as do also the Upanishads. But this quality marks also the limits of intuition; however crowded with life be our flashes, our formulae, they cannot contain the whole truth — a richer warmth is needed, such as would be brought by the illumined mind but in a high transparency. For *the Intuition ... sees things by flashes, point by point, not as a whole.*[32] The space unveiled by the flash is capturing, irrefutable, but it is only *a space of truth.*[33] Besides, the mind lays hold of the intuition and, as Sri Aurobindo observes, it *makes at once too little and too much of it*:[33] too much, because it generalises its intuition unduly and would wish to extend its discovery to all space; too little, because instead of letting the flash quietly do its work of illumination and clarification of our substance, it immediately grabs it, coats it with a layer of thought (or a picturesque, poetic, mathematical, religious layer) and understands its light only through the intellectual, artistic or religious form it has put upon it. It is very difficult to make the mind understand that a revelation can be all-powerful, even formidable, without one's understanding anything of it and, above all, that it is all-powerful as long as it is not brought down a few degrees, diluted, fragmented in order to be supposedly "understood". If one could remain quiet with this vibrating flash, as if suspended in its light, without leaping upon it in order to pull it to small intellectual pieces, one would find after a while that the *whole* being has changed its altitude and that there is a new vision in place of a little defunct formula. When one explains, three-fourths of the transforming power evaporates.

But if the seeker instead of hastening to his pen or his brush or plunging into a torrent of words to throw out the excess of light received takes care to preserve his silence and his transparency, if he is patient, he will see the lightning flashes gradually multiply, become more packed in a way, and another consciousness taking shape in him, which is at once the fulfilment and the source of the illumined mind and the intuitive mind, and of all human mental forms; we speak of the overmind.

e) The Overmind

The overmind is the rarely attained summit of human consciousness. It is a cosmic consciousness but without the loss of the individual. Instead of rejecting all to burst forth in mid-air, the seeker has patiently climbed every rung of the being, so well that the bottom one remains linked to the top, without any break of continuity. This is the world of the gods and the source of inspiration of the great founders of religion; it is here that all the religions we know have been born; they come from an overmind experience, as one of its thousand facets. For a religion or a revelation, a spiritual experience belongs to a certain plane, it does not spring up from the thunders of God or from nowhere; those who incarnate the revelation have not drawn it out of nothing: the overmind is their plane of origin. This is also the birth-place of high artistic creations. But it must be well emphasised that it is yet a plane of the mind, although its summit.

When the consciousness rises to this plane, it no longer sees "points by point," but *calmly, in great masses*.[34] It is no longer the diffuse light of the illumined mind nor the isolated flashes of the intuitive mind but, to cite the wonderful Vedic expression, "An ocean of stable lightnings." The consciousness is no longer limited to the brief present moment and the narrow space of its visual field, it is "unshuttered", it sees in a single glance *large extensions of space and time*.[34] The essential difference from the other planes lies in the equality or the almost complete uniformity of the light: in a particularly receptive illumined mind one would see, for example, a bluish expanse or ground with jets of sudden light, intuitive flashes, luminous outflowerings moving across, sometimes even great overmental cataracts, but this would be an intermittent luminous play, nothing stable — it is the usual condition of the greatest poets we know; they have reached a given level or a rhythm, a general poetic luminosity, then, from time to time, they push up into higher regions and bring from there those rare dazzling verses (or musical phrases) which are repeated generation after generation like an Open Sesame. The illumined mind is generally the base (a base already very high) and the overmind a divine kingdom to which one has access in hours of grace.

But for a complete and permanent overmind consciousness, such as was realised by the Vedic rishis, for instance, there are no longer luminous intermittences, the consciousness is *a mass of stable light*. From this comes a continu-

ous universal vision; one knows universal joy, universal
beauty, universal love, for all the contradictions of the
lower planes came from an insufficiency of light or from a
narrowness of light which lit up only a limited field; whilst
in this equal light the contradictions which are like spaces
of shadow between two flashes or like dark frontiers at the
end of our light, melt away into a unified visual mass. And
the moment light is everywhere, joy and harmony and
beauty are everywhere, necessarily, because all these
contraries are no longer seen as negations or as shadowy
gaps between two clicks of consciousness but as elements
of variable intensity in a continuous cosmic Harmony. Not
that the overmind consciousness is incapable of seeing
what we call ugliness or evil or suffering, but all is linked
in a great universal theme where each thing has its obvious place and utility. It is a unitary not a separatist consciousness. The capacity for unity gives exactly the measure
of overmind perfection. Moreover, having the vision of
this unity, necessarily divine (the Divine is no longer something supposed or conceived but seen, touched, *become*
ourself naturally, as our consciousness becomes the light),
the overmind being perceives everywhere the same light,
in all the things, in every being, as it perceives it in its own
self; there are no more separating voids, no more rifts of
strangeness, all is bathed continuously in a single substance; it knows universal love, universal comprehension,
universal compassion for all those other "itselfs" which too
travel towards their divinity or rather become slowly the
light they are.

One can then find access to this overmind consciousness
by all sorts of ways, by a religious intensity, a poetic, intellectual, artistic, heroic intensity, by all that helps man to
surpass himself. Sri Aurobindo assigned a particular place

to Art, which he considered one of the best means of spiritual progress; unhappily, artists and creators have generally a considerable ego which blocks their way; that is their big difficulty. The religious man, who has laboured to dissolve his ego, finds things easier, but it is rarely that he enters universality by the individual road of consciousness, he rather leaps outside the individual — kicking aside the ladder—without bothering to develop all the intermediary stages of the personal consciousness, and when he reaches the "summit" he has no longer the ladder to come down again or he does not wish to come down, or there is no longer any individual in him to translate what he sees, or it is his old former individual who tries as best he can to translate his new consciousness, if it be at all that he feels the need to translate anything. The Vedic rishis who give us probably the unique example of a systematic spiritual progression, continuous, from plane to plane, are perhaps among the greatest poets the earth has known — Sri Aurobindo has shown us this in his *Secret of the Veda*. The word *kavi* indicated inseparably the seer of the Truth and the poet. A man was a poet because he was a seer. Here is an obvious fact that has been quite forgotten. We could then say a few words here about Art as a means of the ascension of consciousness and particularly about the poetry of the overmind plane.

Mantric Poetry

The planes of consciousness are not distinguished only by the luminous vibrations of different intensities but by different auditory vibrations or rhythms which can be heard when one has that "ear of the ear" of which the

Veda speaks. Sounds or images, lights or forces, or beings are different aspects of the same Existence which manifests itself variously and with various intensities according to the planes. The more one descends the ladder of consciousness, the more do the auditory vibrations, like the lights, like the beings or the forces, get broken up. On the vital plane, for example, can be heard the disordered vibrations of Life, jarring, syncopated, like certain types of music which come from this plane or like a certain type of vital painting or poetry which, all of them, translate this broken, highly-coloured rhythm. The higher one rises, the more do the vibrations harmonise, unite, spin out like certain great notes of Beethoven's String Quartets, which seem to draw us vertiginously, with held breath, to the resplendent heights of pure light. The power is not characterized any longer by volume or coloured outburst but by a high inner tension. The vibratory rapidity turns the rainbow to a pure white, a high note so swift that it seems to be still, caught in eternity, a single sound-light-force which is perhaps the sacred syllable of the Indians, *OM* — [*the*] *Word concealed in the upper fire.*[35] "In the beginning was the Word", say the Scriptures.

There exists in India a secret knowledge based on the study of sounds and the differences of vibratory modality according to the planes of consciousness. If the sound *OM* is pronounced, for example, one can clearly feel that it envelops the head centres, whilst the sound *RAM* touches the navel centre; and as each of our centres of consciousness is in direct communication with a plane, one can thus, by the repetition (*japa*) of certain sounds put oneself in communication with the corresponding plane of consciousness.* An entire spiritual discipline called "tantric"

---

* If the diagram of the centres of consciousness is studied carefully, in the

because derived from certain sacred texts called *tantra*,
is founded on this fact. The basic or essential sounds
which have the power of establishing the communication
are called *mantra*. The mantras, always secret and given
to the disciple by the Guru,* are of all kinds (each plane of
consciousness has a crowd of degrees) and they may
serve the most contradictory ends. By the combination
of certain sounds one can, at lower levels of consciousness,
generally at the vital level, put oneself in relation with the
corresponding forces and obtain many strange powers:
there are mantras which kill (sometimes in five minutes,
— terrifying vomitings), mantras which attack with precision a particular part or organ of the body, mantras
which heal, mantras which kindle fire, which protect,
spell-bind. This kind of magic or vibratory chemistry
proceeds simply by the conscious manipulation of the
lower vibrations. But there is a higher magic which also
proceeds by the handling of vibrations but on higher
planes of consciousness; this is poetry, music, the spiritual
mantras of the Upanishads and the Vedas or the mantras
which the Guru gives his disciple to help him enter consciously into direct communication with such or such a
plane of consciousness, such or such a force, such or such
a divine being. Here the sound carries in itself the power
of experience and realisation — it is a sound that makes
one see.

Poetry and music which are an unconscious handling

---

middle of each centre will be found a Sanskrit letter: *Lam, Vam, Ram, Yam,
Ham, OM,* in the ascending order. These essential sounds represent the
particular vibration which commands the forces of each of the given planes.
(See A. Avalon. *The Serpent Power*).

* One may read mantras in a book and repeat them as much as one likes,
they will have no power or "active force" unless given by a Master or Guru.

of secret vibrations may then be considered powerful means of the opening of consciousness. If we could succeed in composing poetry or music which is the product of a conscious handling of higher vibrations, we would create great works having an initiatory power. Instead of a poetry which is a fantasy of the intellect and a *nautch-girl of the mind*[36] as Sri Aurobindo says, we would create a mantric music or poetry *to bring the gods into our life*.[37] For true poetry is an act, it makes holes in the consciousness — we are so walled in, barricaded! — through which the Real can enter: it is a *mantra of the Real*,[38] an initiation. This is what the Vedic rishis and the seers of the Upanishads have done in their mantras which have the power of communicating an illumination to one who is ready;* this is what Sri Aurobindo has explained in his *Future Poetry* and this is what he has done in *Savitri*.

The mantra or great poetry, great music, the sacred Word, come from the overmind. This is the source of all creative or spiritual activities (it is not possible to distinguish between the two: the categorical divisions of the intellect vanish in a clear air wherein all is sacred, even the profane). We may hence try to say in what lies the particular vibration or particular rhythm of the overmind. And, first, for any one who has the capacity to enter more and more consciously into relation with the higher planes — poet, writer, artist — it is quite evident, perceptible, that after a certain level of consciousness it is no longer ideas that one sees and tries to translate. One hears. There are literally vibrations or waves, rhythms which lay hold

---

* Unhappily, these texts come to us in translation; all the magic of sound has taken flight. The strange thing, however, is that if one hears the Sanskrit text chanted by someone who has the knowledge, one can receive an illumination without understanding anything of what has been said.

of the seeker, invade him, *then* clothe themselves with words and ideas or with music, colours, in their descent. But the word or the idea, the music, the colour, is the result, a secondary effect; they just give a body to that first terribly imperious vibration. And if the poet, the true one, corrects and re-corrects, it is not to improve upon the form as one says, or to express himself better, but to catch that vibrating thing — and if the true vibration is not there, all his magic crumbles, as that of the Vedic priest who has badly pronounced the mantra of the sacrifice. When the consciousness is transparent, the sound becomes clearly audible, and it is a seeing sound, a sound-image or a sound-idea, which links indissolubly in the same luminous body the audition to the vision and the thought. All is full, contained in a single vibration. On the intermediary planes (higher mind, illumined or intuitive mind) these vibrations are generally broken up — they are jets, impulsions, pulsations, — whilst in the overmind they are vast, sustained, self-luminous, like those great notes of Beethoven. They have neither beginning nor end, they seem *born out of the Infinite and disappear into the Infinite;*[39] they do not "begin" somewhere, they come into the consciousness with a sort of halo of eternity which vibrates ahead and continues to vibrate long after, like the track of *another* journey behind this one:

Sunt lacrimae rerum et mentem mortalia tangunt.

This line from Virgil which Sri Aurobindo has quoted as the very first among inspirations of overmind origin, owes its overmind quality not to the sense of the words but to this rhythm which precedes the line and follows it, as though it were carried on a background of eternity or rather *by* Eternity itself. So too this line of Leopardi which does not owe its grandeur to the sense but to that something so subtly more than the meaning, which quivers behind:

Insano indegno mistero delle cose.

Or this line of Wordsworth:

Voyaging through strange seas of thought, alone.

And Sri Aurobindo also quoted Rimbaud:

Million d'oiseaux d'or, ô future Vigueur!

Poetry has been restored to its true role, which is not to please but to make the world more real because more full of the Real.

Perhaps we shall yet see the gods who people this world, if we are religious-minded. Beings or forces, sounds, lights, rhythms are so many true aspects of the same Thing, indefinable but not unknowable, which is called God — we speak of God, make temples, laws, poems, to try and trap a single pulsation which fills us with sunlight, but which is free as the great wind on the foam-sprayed shores. Perhaps we shall also enter the world of music which in fact is not distinct from the others but a special translation of this same great unutterable Vibration. And if once, just once, be it a few minutes in a life-time, we hear that Music there, that Joy which sings above, we shall know what Beethoven and Bach used to hear; we shall know what God is because we shall have heard God. We shall not even say anything in capital letters; simply we shall know that *this exists* and all the suffering of the world is redeemed.

At the extreme frontiers of the overmind, there remain only *great waves of coloured light*, says the Mother, the play of spiritual forces which will be translated later — sometimes long afterwards — by new ideas, social changes, terrestrial events, after having crossed one by one all the layers of consciousness and been considerably darkened or deformed in the course of the journey. There are sages down here, rare and silent, who can handle, combine these forces, and who draw them to the earth, as others combine sounds for a poem. Perhaps these are truly *the* poets. Their existence is a living mantra which precipitates the Real upon the earth.

Thus were completed the degrees of ascension which Sri Aurobindo covered alone in his cell at Alipore. But we have only given a few human gleams of these heights, we have said nothing of their essence, nothing of these worlds as they are in their glory, independently of our poor translations. One must hear for oneself, one must *see*!

> *Calm heavens of imperishable Light,*
> *Illumined continents of violet peace,*
> *Oceans and rivers of the mirth of God*
> *And griefless countries under purple suns.*[40]

On the 5th May, 1909, after a year's imprisonment, Sri Aurobindo was acquitted. He owed his life to two unexpected incidents: one of the prisoners having betrayed him, denouncing him as the leader of the secret movement, his evidence in the case would have meant the death penalty for Sri Aurobindo, when, mysteriously, he was killed by a revolver-shot from a neighbouring cell. Then came the day of trial and as everyone sat expecting the verdict of capital punishment, his own advocate was seized by a sudden illumination which spread through the entire hall and shook the jury: "Long after he is dead and gone, his words will be echoed and re-echoed, not only in India, but across distant seas and lands. Therefore I say that the man in his position is not only standing before the bar of this court, but before the bar of the High Court of History." Sri Aurobindo was thirty-seven. His brother Barin, beside him in the cage, was sentenced to the gallows.*

But Sri Aurobindo heard all the time the Voice: *Remember never to fear, never to hesitate. Remember that it is I who am doing this, not you nor any other. Therefore whatever clouds may come, whatever dangers and sufferings, whatever difficulties, whatever impossibilities, there is nothing impossible, nothing difficult.*

It is I who am doing this.[41]

---

* His penalty was commuted into transportation for life to the Andaman Islands.

CHAPTER THIRTEEN

UNDER THE SIGN OF THE GODS

When he came out of the Alipore jail, Sri Aurobindo found a political scene emptied by the executions and mass deportations of the British government. He, however, took up his work again, started a Bengali weekly and another in English, the *Karmayogin*, which bore the very symbolic motto of the Gita, "Yoga is skill in works". Once again Sri Aurobindo declared the ideal of total independence and of non-cooperation with the British, at the risk of a new imprisonment, but it was not only the destiny of India which pre-occupied him but that of the whole of humanity. He had attained that overmind consciousness whence one sees at a single glance, "great extensions of space and time" and he questioned himself about the future of man. What *can* man do?

Now he was on the confines of human consciousness; higher up there seemed to be only a rarefied whiteness, fit for other beings or another mode of existence but not for lungs of the earthman. Whether one takes the mystic path, finally, or the slower one of the poet and artist and of all the great creators, the consciousness seems to vanish equally at a white frontier where everything is annulled. The "someone" who could build the bridge disappears, all pulsation dies out, all vibration ceases in a frost of light. A little sooner or a little later, the human is effaced in the Non-human, as though the goal of all this evolutionary ascension were only to leave behind the smallness of man and return to the Source whence we should never have come out. And even if we suppose a level of unknown consciousness beyond the overmind, would it not be also a more rarefied level, more evanescent? — one climbs higher and higher, more and more divinely, but farther and farther from the earth. The individual is transfigured, perhaps, but the world is where it was. What then is our terrestrial future, if there is nothing else, in truth, except this overmind consciousness?

We all hope that with the development of consciousness and science combined together we shall arrive at a better humanity and a more harmonious life. But life is not changed by miracles, it is changed by instruments. And we have only one instrument, the Mind; it is our ideas which organise our scientific discoveries. If then we wish to look clearly at our future, without being easily taken in by the circumstances of the moment or its apparent triumphs — others had triumphed before us, at Thebes, at Athens, at Ujjain — it is advisable to examine a little more closely our instrument, the Mind; for such as it is, such will be our future. Now, everything goes on, it seems, as though the most beautiful ideas, the highest creative schemes, the purest acts of love became disfigured, deformed, polluted, as soon as they descended into life. Nothing arrives pure. Mentally we have already invented the most marvellous recipes; Life has never wanted them. Twenty years after Lenin, to speak only of our present civilisation, what remains of pure communism? What remains even of the Christ under that heap of dogmas and interdicts? Socrates is poisoned and Rimbaud flees to the Abyssinian desert; we know the fate of Phalansterism, of non-violence; the Catharists end on the stake. And history turns like a Moloch; we are the triumph, perhaps, after many failures, but of what other triumph are we not the failure? A chronology of victories or failures? Life seems made of a subs-

tance unredeemably distorting, everything sinks into it as
in the sands of Egypt, everything is levelled down in an
irresistible *"gravitational pull"*. *It is clear*, remarks Sri
Aurobindo, *that Mind has not been able to change human
nature radically. You can go on changing human institutions infinitely and yet the imperfection will break through all your institutions.... It must be another power that can not only resist but overcome that downward pull.*[1]

But even if our ideas could arrive pure into life, they
would yet be incapable of creating anything other than a
disciplined barrack, perhaps even a holy barrack, comfortable and religious, but a barrack all the same, because the
Mind knows only how to make systems and it wants to en-
close everything within its systems. *The reason of man struggling with life becomes either an empiric or a doctrinaire;*[2] it gets
hold of one bit of truth, one drop of divine illumination,
and makes of it a law for everybody — it confuses unity
with uniformity, as we know. And even when it is capable
of understanding the need of diversity, it is practically incapable of manipulating it, because it knows how to manipulate only what is invariable and finite, whilst the world
teems with an infinite variety: *Ideas themselves are partial
and insufficient : not only have they a very partial triumph, but if
their success were complete, it would still disappoint, because they
are not the whole truth of life and therefore cannot securely govern
and perfect life. Life escapes from the formulas and systems which
our reason labours to impose on it ; it proclaims itself too complex,
too full of infinite potentialities to be tyrannised over by the arbitrary intellect of man.... The root of the difficulty is this that at
the very basis of all our life and existence, internal and external,
there is something on which the intellect can never lay a controlling
hold, the Absolute, the Infinite. Behind everything in life there is
an Absolute, which that thing is seeking after in its own way;*

*everything finite is striving to express an infinite which it feels to be
its real truth. Moreover, it is not only each class, each type, each
tendency in Nature that is thus impelled to strive after its own
secret truth in its own way, but each individual brings in his
own variation. Thus there is not only an Absolute, an Infinite
in itself which governs its own expression in many forms and
tendencies, but there is also a principle of infinite potentiality and
variation quite baffling to the reasoning intelligence; for the reason
deals successfully only with the settled and the finite. In man this
difficulty reaches its acme. For not only is mankind unlimited in
potentiality! not only is each of its powers and tendencies seeking
after its own absolute in its own way and therefore naturally restless under any rigid control by the reason; but in each man their
degrees, methods, combinations vary, each man belongs not only to
the common humanity, but to the Infinite in himself and is therefore
unique. It is because this is the reality of our existence that the intellectual reason and the intelligent will cannot deal with life as its
sovereign, even though they may be at present our supreme instruments and may have been in our evolution supremely important and
helpful.*[3]

But if the evolution, as Sri Aurobindo declares, is an evolution of consciousness, we may think that humanity will
not remain eternally at the present mental stage, that its
mind will be illumined, will become more and more intuitive and, finally perhaps will open to the overmind. An
overmind humanity, we would think, should be capable of
manipulating the complex diversity of life. The overmind
is a god-like consciousness, it is indeed the very consciousness of the greatest prophets humanity has known — a
mass of stable light; it would seem then that all must harmonise in this great light. Unhappily, two facts contradict
this hope: the first is due to the inequality of development
of individuals and the other to the very nature of the over-

mind. The overmind certainly may seem to have a fairly
formidable power compared with our mind, but this is a
superiority in degree of the *same kind*; one does not come
out of the mental principle, one is only at the acme of the
mind. It can enlarge the human circle, not change it; it can
divinise man, but also *colossalise*[4] him, says Sri Aurobindo,
for if man attaches this new power to his ego instead
of attaching it to his soul, he will make a Neitzschean
superman, not a god. It is not a more formidable consciousness we need but another consciousness. But even if
we suppose that man accepts to obey his soul, not his ego,
the overmind will not change life, for the very reasons
which have prevented Christ and all the great prophets
from changing it. Because the overmind is not a new principle of consciousness, it is this which right through has presided over our evolution since the appearance of man; it
is from this that have come the high ideas, the high creative forces — we have lived under the sign of the gods for
millenniums, sometimes through the voice of our prophets and our religions, sometimes through that of our
poets and our great creators, and it is evident that these
have not changed the world, neither the former nor the
latter, though they have bettered it. We cannot even say
that our life is more graceful than that of the Athenians,
can we?

The failure of the overmind is due to several reasons.
First of all, it is a principle of division. We had mentioned, however, that an overmind consciousness is a mass of
stable light, that it has the vision of a cosmic harmony, of
a cosmic unity, because it sees everywhere the light as in
itself. As such, it is not a principle of division in division,
as is the ordinary mind; it is a principle of division in
unity. The overmind sees clearly that all is one but, by the

very structure of its consciousness, in practice it cannot help dividing the unity: *It sees all but sees all from its own viewpoint.*[5] It is enough to listen to the voices so apparently contradictory of our prophets to note that each one sees the unity but that each one sees it *from his own viewpoint*; their consciousness is like a beacon-light which sweeps across the world and which can gather all in its beam, without a shadowy gap, but it is a beam that ends in a point. And thus we find ourselves before a series of experiences or divine visions apparently irreconcilable: some see everywhere the cosmic Divine, others everywhere the Transcendent beyond the cosmos and others everywhere the immanent Divine; or they proclaim the truth of the personal God, the truth of the impersonal God, the truth of Nirvana, the truth of Love, the truth of Force, of Beauty, of the Intellect — the truths of the innumerable sages, sects, churches or visionaries who have transmitted the Word. And all are divine truths, all the experiences wholly true, wholly authentic, but each one is a single ray of the full light. Naturally, these great prophets are wise enough to see the truth of the other divine expressions — they are wiser than their Churches, wiser than their devotees — but they are tied down to a fundamental incapacity of consciousness which cannot help dividing as the prism divides light. Mental or overmental, the consciousness can experience but one truth and one only at a time. This is what all the mythologies, past or present, express: each god is the incarnation of *one* cosmic power and one alone — love, wisdom, destruction, preservation.... Buddha expresses the transcendent Nought and he sees only his Nought; Christ expresses loving Charity and he sees only this Charity, and so with the others; yet, however high may be each of these truths, it is only *one* truth. And the more the overmind truth, already fragmented, descends from plane to plane to translate itself into life, the more will it be fragmented — starting from division it ends in a superdivision, inevitably; from the Buddha to the "vehicles" and from Christ to all the Christian sects, the mechanism is visible. And not only in the spiritual or religious field but in all the fields of life, because the very function of the overmind is to bring out to the utmost *one* possibility and only one: *It gives to each [possibility] its full separate development and satisfaction.... It can give to intellect its austerest intellectuality and to logic its most sheer unsparing logicality. It can give to beauty its most splendid passion of luminous form and the consciousness that receives it a supreme height and depth of ecstasy.*[6] And it is thus that millions of idea-forces divide the world: communism, individualism; non-violence, force of battle; epicurism, asceticism, etc.; and each is a facet of the divine Truth, each a ray of God; there is no absolute error anywhere, there are only divisions of the Truth. Of course we can see the Oneness, the truth of the others, and make a synthesis, but all our syntheses will not re-establish the Oneness, because this will still be a mental synthesis, *a potpourri, not the unity*, says the Mother — this will be the prism playing at telling itself that all the colours come from a single Light, but meanwhile, *practically*, all the colours will be divided in the world; all the forces emanated by the overmind plane will be the result of its original division. And it must be emphasised that it is not here a problem of thought or a philosophical question that is to be solved but a matter of *cosmic fact*, of an organic phenomenon, like the spines on the back of the hedgehog. For the division to cease, the prism must go. And this is why the world is divided and will be so ineluctably, as long as the principle of mental consciousness, high or low, ordinary or extraordinary, remains the master of the world.

One may conceive, however, that in a more or less near evolutionary future, one perfect overmind being or even several simultaneously may succeed in incarnating on the earth. The less evolved fraction of humanity which rallies round these luminous centres will be able to live a harmonious life and, to this extent, life will be changed, there will be a sort of unity. But this will be a unity in the midst of a single luminous beam; some will be in the ray of pure Beauty, for example, others perhaps in the beam of integral Communism founded on fraternal love (it would seem more probable, unfortunately, from the evolutionary trend, that these beams would be of a hard light, centred around some economic or titanic ideology). But allowing that the divine hearth-fires are lit in the world, not only would their unity work to the detriment of the elusive diversity of life, but they would also be menaced by the surrounding darkness — men are unequally developed, this is what we seem always to forget, this is the eternal rift in all our grand citadels; our hearths of grace would be like *islands of light*[7] in the midst of a less evolved humanity which naturally would tend constantly to re-invade, obscure or level down the privileged light. We all know the fate of Greece and Rome in the midst of the barbarian world. It would seem that, by a very wise evolutionary law, the evolution of the world is linked to the totality of the world and that nothing can be saved if all is not saved — excommunications and hells are puerile ignorances; and our land of milk and honey on this earth or up above; there can be no paradise so long as a single man is in hell! — because there is but one Man. Besides, supposing that one of these islands of light, by the Power of its centre, can resist the outer incursions, nothing indicates that this protection will outlast the Power at the centre. The history of all the religious movements occult, initiatory, chivalrous or others, throughout the world, shows us sufficiently that after the death of the Master and of his direct initiates, everything is scattered, vulgarised, levelled down, or gets deformed or dies. The law of downward gravitation has seemed till today unsurmountable. Life must therefore be transformed entirely, not a fragment of life, not a privileged beam, a happy isle, if we want the evolution to triumph, and for this another Power is necessary, a Power capable of resisting the downward gravitation; another principle of consciousness, undivided or global, which can hold, without mutilating it, the innumerable diversity of life.

If, instead of looking at the evolutionary future from the collective viewpoint, we look at it from the individual viewpoint, even the overmind does not bring us the living plenitude to which we aspire. If the goal of evolution truly is to produce more Beethovens or Shelleys, perhaps even some super-Platos, we cannot help thinking that this is a poor ending for so many thousand millions of individuals consumed on the way. Beethoven and Shelley or even St. John cannot be evolutionary ends, or else life has no sense, for who cannot see that their works are admirable by a deficiency of life? They all tell us that it is so much more beautiful up there than here, with "millions of golden birds" and divine music. Everything goes on up above, but what happens here? Here life continues as before. We may be told that these high thoughts, these poems, these quartets, these divine moments in which we have seen, are more precious than all the hours of our life put end to end, and this is true, but precisely this is an admission that life is formidably poor or that the goal

of life is not in life. We need a truth of the body and of
the earth also, not only a truth above the head. We do
not want recreations but a re-creation.

Everything has gone on till today as if the individual's
progress in evolution consisted in discovering the higher
planes of consciousness, then, once there, in building up
each one a world apart, yet another private island of
light in the midst of the economic philistinism, one man in
music, one in poetry, others in mathematics or religion
and others on a fine sailing-boat for the holidays or in a
monk's cell each with his own skylight or his distractions,
as if life and the body served only to help escape from life
and the body. But it is sufficient to look at our own life,
one is never within! One is before or after, in remembrance or in hope — the here-now is miserable or neutral,
we do not even know if it exists, except precisely in those
moments which belong no longer to life. We can blame
nothing on the Churches, we all live in the beyond, constantly; they preach only a more considerable beyond.
Rimbaud also said it: "The true life is elsewhere".

Sri Aurobindo was in quest of a true life down here:
*Life, not a remote silent or high-uplifted ecstatic Beyond-Life
alone, is the field of our Yoga*[8] and he came to see that the
summits of consciousness did not suffice to make of life
a true life. We may have touched the overmind, found its
joy, its singing vastness, but not that of life which continues
to grate: *When one is far up above in the consciousness,* says
the Mother, *one sees things, one knows, but in fact, when one
comes down again into Matter, it is like water entering into sand.*
We have sent our rocket very high in the spiritual heavens,
sung what is best in man without preoccupying ourselves
with the lower stages, satisfied if the brute in us was
sufficiently asleep not to trouble our divine dreams, and

this is why life remains brutish, like us: *To hope for a true change of human life without a change of human nature is an irrational and unspiritual proposition; it is to ask for something unnatural and unreal, an impossible miracle.*[9] And this is why our islands of light are invaded every time by our intimate barbarity and hidden cancers, as were other islands called Athens or Thebes; this is why they die and die, as if the Lord of evolution stuck our nose in the earth each time to remind us that we have not found all the light when finding it only up above. Life does not die because it gets worn out, it dies because it has not found itself. For centuries we have made the voyage of ascension, conquered island after island, and we have found only half the Secret, and each time we have been ruined; but this is perhaps not because history is vain nor to punish us for our "sins" nor to expiate an improbable Fault, it is perhaps to find down here, in Matter, the other half of the Secret. Pursued by Death and Inconscience, harassed by suffering and evil, there is but one solution and this is not to escape but to find in the depths of Death and Inconscience, in the heart of Evil, the key of the divine life. It is to transform this barbarity and our night, not to banish it from our island. After the ascension of consciousness, the descent. After the illuminations above, the joy below and the transformation of Matter. *One may say that it is truly when the circle will be complete and the two extremities have touched, when the highest will manifest itself in the most material, — the supreme Reality at the heart of the atom — that the experience will be in truth conclusive. It seems*, says the Mother, *that one never truly understands anything till one understands with the body.*

For the Secret, which Sri Aurobindo has called the Supermind, is not a further degree above the overmind, it is not a super-mind nor a super-ascension, it is a new

Sign, which is no longer that of the gods and the religions, and on which depends the very future of our evolution.

In February 1910, less than a year after his coming out of Alipore, one evening in the office of the *Karmayogin* Sri Aurobindo was warned that he was to be arrested again and transported to the Andaman Islands. He heard the Voice, suddenly, which spoke distinctly three words: *Go to Chandernagore.* Ten minutes later Sri Aurobindo took the first boat down the Ganges and was gone. This was the end of his political life, the end of the integral yoga and beginning of the supramental yoga.

CHAPTER FOURTEEN

THE SECRET

We may attempt to speak of this Secret, but keeping in mind that the experience is in the making. Sri Aurobindo found the Secret at Chandernagore in 1910 and worked on it for forty years; he gave up his life for this. The Mother continues.

Sri Aurobindo has never told us the circumstances of his discovery; he was extraordinarily silent about himself, not through reserve, but simply because the "I" did not exist. "One felt," reports his host at Chandernagore with a naive surprise, "one felt when he spoke as if somebody else was speaking through him. I placed the plate of food before him, — he simply gazed at it, then ate a little, just mechanically! He appeared to be absorbed even when he was eating; he used to meditate with open eyes."[1] It is only later, from his works and the fragments of his conversation, that we find again the thread of his experience. The first clue we get is from a chance remark of his to a disciple and it shows that from Alipore onwards he was on the trail: *I was mentally subjected to all sorts of torture for fifteen days. I had to look upon pictures of all sorts of suffering.*[2] Now in these worlds vision is synonymous with experience, if one understands what that means. At the very moment Sri Aurobindo began his ascension towards the overmind, his consciousness descended, simultaneously, into what is conventionally called hell.

This is also one of the first things that the seeker discovers in various degrees. *This is not a yoga for the weak*, says the Mother, and it is true. For if the first tangible result of the

yoga of Sri Aurobindo is to bring out new poetic and artistic faculties, the second, perhaps even the immediate
consequence is to show up in a ruthless light all the shady
places of the consciousness, personal first, then universal.
This close — and strange — relatedness between the
superconscient and the subconscient was undoubtedly the
starting-point of Sri Aurobindo's discovery.

The Subconscient Grades

The subconscious of which modern psychology speaks
is only the outer fringe of a world almost as vast as the
Superconscient, with its grades, its forces, its beings (or
its being-forces if one prefers to call them so). It is our evolutionary past, immediate and remote, with all the imprints of our present life and all those of our past lives, even
as the Superconscient is our evolutionary future. All the
residues and all the forces which have presided over our
ascension, from Matter to the animal and from the animal
to man, are not only engraved there, but continue to live
and influence us — if we are diviner than we think through
the superconscient future which draws us, we are still more
of animals than we imagine through the subconscient
and inconscient which drag us back. This double mystery
holds the key of the total Secret. *None can reach heaven who
has not passed through hell.*[3]

It is true that one may reach the spiritual beatitudes
without knowing these bad places except by accident;
but there are heavens and heavens, even as there are hells
and hells (each level of our being has its "heaven" and
its "hell"). Generally, religious men go out of the individual range, and at the same time they go out of the sub-

conscient; they have only one passage to cross, with the "guardians of the threshold" sufficiently unpleasant to justify all the "nights" and "temptations" of which the lives of saints speak. But this is only *one* passage. Even so, the heaven they contemplate consists of leaving the outer existence and plunging into ecstasy. The end of this yoga, as we have said, is not to lose consciousness, any more down below than above. And specially not to close the eyes below. The integral seeker is not made either for the obscure night or for the blinding light. Everywhere he goes, he must see; this is the first stage of the mastery. For it is not a question of "passing on" to a better existence but of transforming the present existence.

As there are several superconscient degrees, so there are several subconscient layers or worlds, several "dark caverns" as the Rig Veda says. In fact there is one subconscient behind each of the degrees of our being — a mental subconscient, a vital subconscient and a physical subconscient ending in the material Inconscient.* We shall find here, in their order, all the dwarfish and brutal mental forms or forces which were the first to appear in the world of Matter and Life; all the aggressive impulsions of the

---

* For Sri Aurobindo, the psychological divisions follow the evolutionary ascension, which appears logical, for it is in Matter and beginning from it that higher and higher degrees of consciousness have been manifested. The Inconscient then represents our material, corporal base (Sri Aurobindo prefers to call it "Nescience", this Inconscient not being really inconscient) whilst the Subconscient contains our terrestrial past and the Superconscient our future. In the midst of these three zones rise in tiers the various universal planes of consciousness (which Sri Aurobindo sometimes groups under the name "subliminal" in order to distinguish them clearly from the subconscient which is very little or very badly conscious — sub-conscious — whilst the subliminal planes are filled with extremely conscious forces). The "personal" fraction of these various zones is a thin strip: our own body and what we have individualised or colonised in the course of this life and all our lives.

beginnings of Life, all its sacred and suffering reflexes; and finally the forces of illness and disintegration and Death which preside subconsciently over physical life. One understands then that it is not possible to have a true life on the earth so long as these worlds are the masters of our material destiny. Now, we are the place where the battle is fought — in us all the worlds meet, from the highest to the lowest. It is not a matter of fleeing away, holding one's nose or crossing oneself but of entering in and conquering:

> *He too must carry the yoke he came to unloose;*
> *He too must bear the pang that he would heal...*[4]

Limits of Psychoanalysis

Contemporary psychology has also become aware of the importance of the subconscious and the necessity of cleaning; but it has seen one half of the picture, the sub-conscient without the Superconscient, and it has believed that with its little mental gleams it would be able to light up this cavern of thieves; as well go deep into the jungles armed with a flash-lamp. In fact, most often it sees of the subconscient only the reverse of the little frontal fellow; for there is a fundamental psychological law which no one escapes, the law that the descent is proportional to the ascension: one cannot descend lower than one has climbed. Because the force necessary for the descent is the very one necessary for climbing; if by some chance we were to descend lower than our capacity for the heights, this would automatically bring about an accident, a possession or madness, because we would not have the corresponding force. The more we draw near a beginning of Truth down here, the more we discover an unfathomable wisdom. The mysterious complexes of Mr. Smith are found some few centimeters underneath, even as his conscious existence is found some centimeters above. Unless then our psychologists are particularly luminous, they cannot truly go down into the subconscient and hence they cannot truly heal, except some subcutaneous anomalies, and even then they are in constant danger of seeing their illnesses sprout up elsewhere under another form. One cannot heal unless one heals the very depths, and one cannot go to the depths unless one goes to the heights. The further one wants to descend, the more one needs a powerful light, otherwise one gets eaten up.

If psychoanalysis remained within its superficial limits, there would be nothing to say about it, it would in the long run undoubtedly find out its own limitations and, meanwhile, would cure usefully some itchings. Unhappily, it has become a sort of new gospel for many and has contributed powerfully to the perverting of men's minds by fixing them unhealthily on their filthy possibilities rather than on their divine ones. No doubt, in the course of evolution our "errors" always end up by finding their place and their utility; it was well that our moral and bourgeois complacencies were shaken; but the method chosen is dangerous, because it calls up the disease without having the power to cure it: *it tends*, says Sri Aurobindo, *to make the mind and vital more and not less fundamentally impure than before*[5]. *...Modern psychology is an infant science, at once rash, fumbling and crude. As in all infant sciences, the universal habit of the human mind — to take a partial or local truth, generalise it unduly and try to explain a whole field of Nature in its narrow terms — runs riot here....The psychoanalysis [specially] of Freud....*

takes up a certain part, the darkest, the most perilous, the unhealthiest part of the nature, the lower vital subconscious layer,* isolates some of its most morbid phenomena and attributes to it and them an action out of all proportion to its true role in the nature.... To raise it up prematurely or improperly for experience is to risk suffusing the conscious parts also with its dark and dirty stuff and thus poisoning the whole vital and even the mental nature. Always therefore one should begin by a positive, not a negative experience, by bringing down something of the divine nature, calm, light, equanimity, purity, divine strength into the parts of the conscious being that have to be changed; only when that has been sufficiently done and there is a firm positive basis, is it safe to raise up the concealed subconscious adverse elements in order to destroy and eliminate them by the strength of the divine calm, light, force and knowledge.[6]

But there is another drawback of psychoanalysis, yet more serious. For if by chance the psychoanalysts had truly the power to descend into the subconscious, not only would they not heal, not only would they risk setting in motion forces they cannot control, like the Sorcerer's apprentice, but even if they had the power to master and destroy them, they would risk destroying at the same time the good with the evil and mutilating irreparably our nature. Because they do not have the knowledge. Because from the height of their mind they cannot see sufficiently far into the future to understand the good that this evil is preparing and the dynamic Force under the play of contraries; to

---

* We have said there are numerous grades and sub-grades in the subconscient. It is deliberately that we have not dwelt upon the description of these lower worlds; the seeker will experience them for himself when his moment comes. To give a precise mental form to these lower forces is not truly to exorcise them as some imagine, but to give them a greater hold upon our consciousness. It is not by the mind that one heals.

separate this dark marriage another power is needed and above all another vision: *You must know the whole before you can know the part and the highest before you can truly understand the lowest. That is the promise of the greater psychology awaiting its hour before which these poor gropings will disappear and come to nothing.*[6]

And here we put our finger upon the fundamental error of our psychology. It is incapable of understanding because it seeks down below in the evolutionary past. Certainly half the Secret is there, but it is the force above which opens the door below. We are not made to look ever behind us but in front and above into the superconscient light because that is our future and only the future explains and heals the past: *I find it difficult,* wrote Sri Aurobindo to a disciple, *to take these psychoanalysts at all seriously — yet perhaps one ought to, for half-knowledge is a powerful thing and can be a great obstacle to the coming in front of the true Truth.... They look from down up and explain the higher lights by the lower obscurities; but the foundation of these things is above and not below. The superconscient, not the subconscient, is the true foundation of things. The significance of the lotus is not to be found by analysing the secrets of the mud from which it grows here; its secret is to be found in the heavenly archetype of the lotus that blooms for ever in the Light above.*[6]

We appear to progress from below upwards or from the past towards the future or from night towards conscious light, but this is our small momentary vision which cuts off the totality of the picture, otherwise we would see that it is the future which draws, not the past which pushes, and the light above that gradually enters our night—else how would the night be ever able to create all that light? If we started from the night, we would end up only in the night. "This is the eternal Tree with its roots above and its branches

downward," says the Katha Upanishad (VI.I). We have
the impression of making great efforts of growth to understand and know and of a tension towards the future, but
this is our small point of view; there is perhaps another
viewpoint whence we would see this superconscient Future
pushing to enter our present. And we would perhaps see
that our great efforts were only the *resistance* of our grossness and our obscurity. The future does not move only
from below above, otherwise there would be no hope for
the earth, it would finish by bursting into mid-air in a supreme psychic tension or by falling back into its night; it
moves from above downwards; it descends more and more
into our mental fog, our vital confusions, into the subconscient and inconscient night until it has lit up everything, revealed everything, healed everything — and finally fulfilled everything. And the more it descends, the more
the resistance increases — it is the Iron Age, the time of
the great Revolt and the Peril. The time of Hope. At the
supreme point where this Future will touch the depth of
the past, where this Light will split the rock-bottom of the
Night, God willing, we shall find the secret of Death
and of immortal Life. But if we look down below and only
down below, we shall find mud and nothing but mud.

The Dark Half of the Truth

Now we are getting to it. It is with a positive experience
that the seeker has begun. He started on his way because
he needed something else. He has made efforts at mental
silence and he has found that the single fact of his making
the effort has brought an Answer; he has felt a descending
Force, a new vibration in him, which made life clearer,

more living; perhaps he has even had the experience of a
sudden tearing of the limits and an emergence on another
altitude. In a thousand ways the sign may come indica-
ting that a new rhythm has been established. Then suddenly, after this arrow-like start, all was veiled, as though
he had dreamed or had let himself be dragged away by a
puerile enthusiasm after all — something is busy avenging
itself on him by raising up scepticism, disgust, revolt. And
this will be the second sign, perhaps *the true sign* that he is
progressing and has come to grips with the realities of his
nature or rather that the descending Force has begun its
work of churning. The progress, after all, does not consist
so much in rising up as in decanting all that encumbers —
when one is clear, all is *there*. And the seeker discovers his
multiple encumbrances. One has often the impression,
on the path of integral yoga, of setting out to find the best
and of discovering the worst, of having searched for peace
and light and of finding war. In fact, it is a battle, we must
not hide that from ourselves. So long as one swims with the
current, one can believe oneself quite gentle, proper, well-
intentioned; as soon as one reverses the stroke, all resists.
Then one understands quite tangibly the enormous forces
of stupefaction which weigh upon men — one must have
tried to come out of it to see. And when the seeker has had
a first decisive opening above, when he has seen the Light,
he will feel almost simultaneously a return-shock from below, as if something in him was aching; he will then know
what Sri Aurobindo meant by *the wounded gloom complaining
against light*.[7] And he will have learnt his first lesson: one
cannot take a step upwards without taking a step downwards.

Instead of taking these brutal incurvations as a sort of
fatality, the seeker will make them the basis of his work.

This double movement of ascension and descent constitutes the fundamental process of the integral yoga: *On each height we conquer we have to turn to bring down its power and its illumination into the lower mortal movement*;[8] it is at this price alone that life is transformed, else we keep on poeticising and spiritualising on the summits whilst down below the old life goes jolting along. Actually the movement of descent is not accomplished by an arbitrary decision of the mind — the less it interferes there, the better — and besides, one may well question how the Mind could "descend", seated there behind its small office desk? ... It is the consciousness-force, awakened and individualised in us, which does the whole work, spontaneously. As soon as we have touched a certain intensity of consciousness or light, automatically it exercises a pressure on the rest of the nature and brings up swiftly the corresponding obscurities or resistances. Everything happens as though an overdose of oxygen had been forcibly introduced into the ocean underworld: some muraena and various sprats anxiously struggle or even blow up. It is a strange reversal of consciousness, as though one had passed from an illumined room to the *same* dark room, from a joyous room to the *same* dolorous room — all is the same and all has changed. As though it were the same force, the same vibratory intensity — perhaps even an *identical vibration* — but affected suddenly by a negative coefficient. One sees then, almost closely, how love for example changes into hatred and the pure into the impure — all is the same, but the wrong way up. And so long as our psychological states are simply one the inverse of the other, and our good the wrong side of evil (perhaps we should say the *right side* of evil?) there is no hope that life will be transformed. Something radically different is necessary — another consciousness. All our poets and creative minds have particularly known these vagaries of consciousness; at the same time as his *Illuminations* Rimbaud had access to strange domains which made him start back with terror; he too obeyed the law of the dark reversal. But the integral seeker instead of being tossed from one end to the other unconsciously, and climbing up without knowing how or descending without his wish, will work methodically, consciously, without losing his balance and above all giving himself up with a growing confidence to that Consciousness-Force which *never* raises more resistances than he can meet and never unveils more light than he can bear. After having lived sufficiently long between two crises, we shall finally perceive a method in the action of the Force, and that each time we seem to leave the ascending curve or even to lose a realisation we have had, it is to find again at the end the same realisation but a step just further up, enlarged, enriched with all the rest of our domain which, precisely by our "fall", has come to be integrated in the new light — if we had not "fallen", this depth would have never come to join itself to our height. Perhaps, collectively it was an identical process which brought about the fall of Athens so that the former barbarians also could one day understand Plato. The progress of the integral yoga does not describe a straight line which moves to lose itself ever higher up, in a finer and finer point, but a *spiral*, says Sri Aurobindo, which slowly, methodically, annexes all the levels of our being in an ever vaster opening and on a *deeper and deeper* basis. And not only shall we distinguish a method behind this Force or this Consciousness-Force rather, but regular cycles and a rhythm as sure as that of the tides and the moons; the more one progresses, the vaster become the cycles, the more linked to a cosmic movement, till the day

we are able to see in our own descents the periodical descents of the terrestrial consciousness and in our own difficulties all the whirlpools of the earth which resists and revolts. All will be so intimately linked, finally, that we shall
be able to read in the tiniest things, the most insignificant
happenings of daily life and the objects we touch, the sign
of vaster depressions which will pass over all men and make
them descend and climb up, these also, in the same evolutionary Spiral. Then we shall see that we are infallibly led
towards a Goal, that everything has a meaning, even the
minutest things — not a detail stirs without the whole
stirring — and that we are on our way to a grander adventure than we had thought.

Soon a second contradiction will strike us, which is perhaps yet the same. Not only is there a law of climbing and
of descent, but, it seems, a central contradiction. We have
all a goal to reach in this life and through all our lives,
something unique to express, because every man is unique
— this is our central truth, our special evolutionary tension.
This goal appears only slowly, after many experiences and
successive awakenings when we begin to become persons
formed from within; then we find that a kind of thread
links our life — and all our lives if we have become aware of
them — in a particular direction, as if everything flung us
always in the same way — a way more and more precise
and sharp as we advance further. And at the same time as
we become aware of our goal, we discover a particular
difficulty which seems the inverse or the contradiction of
our goal. It is a strange phenomenon, as if we had exactly
the shadow of our light — a particular shadow, a particular difficulty, a particular problem which presents and represents itself to us with a disconcerting insistence, always
the same under different faces and in the most distant cir-

cumstances, and which returns after every battle won with an increased strength, proportionate to our new intensity of consciousness, as though we must again and again fight the same battle on each newly conquered plane of consciousness. The clearer the goal becomes, the stronger becomes the shadow. Then we have become acquainted with the Foe:

> *This hidden foe lodged in the human breast*
> *Man must overcome or miss his higher fate.*
> *This is the inner war without escape.*[9]

Sri Aurobindo calls it also the Evil Persona. Sometimes even we begin by guessing negatively what may be our goal, before understanding it positively, through a repetition of the same contrary circumstances or the same failures which all seem to point in a single direction, as if we were turning round and round in an ever closer and more oppressing circle about a central point at once the goal and the opposite of the goal. *A person greatly endowed for the work,* says Sri Aurobindo, *has always or almost always, — perhaps one ought not to make a too rigid universal rule about these things — a being attached to him, sometimes appearing like a part of him, which is just the contradiction of the thing he centrally represents in the work to be done. Or if it is not there at first, not bound to his personality, a force of this kind enters into his environment as soon as he begins his movement to realise. Its business seems to be to oppose, to create stumblings and wrong conditions, in a word, to set before him the whole problem of the work he has started to do. It would seem that the problem could not, in the occult economy of things, be solved otherwise than by the predestined instrument making the difficulty his own. That would explain many things that seem very disconcerting on the surface.*[10]

The Mother in her "Conversations" with the disciples stresses the same phenomenon: *When you represent the possibility of a victory, you have always in you the thing opposed to this victory, which is your perpetual torment. When you see a very black shadow somewhere, something that is truly painful, you may be sure that you have the possibility of the corresponding light.* And she adds this: *You have a special aim, a special mission, a special realisation which is your own and you carry in yourself all the obstacles needed for this realisation to be perfect. Always you will find that within you the shadow and the light go together : you have a capacity, you have also the negation of that capacity. But if you discover a very thick and very deep shadow, be sure, somewhere in in you, of a great light. It is up to you to know how to utilise the one to realise the other.*

It is possible, finally, that the secret of existence has escaped us because we have imperfectly understood this dual law of shadow and light and the enigma of our double nature, animal and divine. Brought up on a Manichean conception of existence, we have seen there, in deference to our ethics and our religions, only a relentless struggle between Good and Evil, Truth and Falsehood, in which it was important to be on the good side, on the right hand of the Lord. And we have cut everything into two, the kingdom of God and the kingdom of the Devil, the lower life of this world and the real life in heaven. We have wanted to suppress the contrary of the goal and at the same time we have suppressed the goal. For the goal is not a mutilation, either at the bottom or the top. And so long as we reject the one for the other, we shall fail miserably and miss the aim of existence; for all is of a single piece, nothing can be removed without demolishing everything. And how could we truly deliver ourselves from the "evil" without blowing up the whole world? If a single man should liberate himself from the "evil", the world would crumble down, because all is *one*; the world is made of a single substance, not of two, a good and a bad. Nothing can be removed and nothing can be added. This is why there is no miracle, either, to save the world; the miracle is *already* in the world, all the possible lights are *already* in the world, all the imaginable heavens are *already* there; nothing can enter in without breaking the formula — all is there, we live amidst the miracle, without the key. For it is not perhaps something to suppress or something to add, perhaps not even "something else" to discover, but *the same thing*, in another way.

If we want to reach the Goal, we must then finish with our Manichaeism and come to a realistic understanding of what Sri Aurobindo called "the dark half of truth"[11]. *Human knowledge*, says Sri Aurobindo, *throws a shadow that conceals half the globe of truth from its own sunlight.... The rejection of falsehood by the mind seeking utter truth is one of the chief causes why mind cannot attain to the settled, rounded and perfect truth*[12]. If we eliminate everything that goes the wrong way — and God knows this world is full of errors and impurities — we may arrive at a truth, perhaps, but it will be an empty truth. The practical beginning of the Secret is to find first, then to *see* that each thing in this world, *even the most grotesque or far-wandering error*,[13] contains a spark of truth under the mask, because down here all is God who goes forward to meet Himself; there is nothing outside Him. *For error is really a half truth that stumbles because of its limitations; often it is Truth that wears a disguise in order to arrive unobserved near to its goal.*[13] If a single thing in this world were totally false, the whole world would be totally false. Hence if the seeker starts with this working hypothesis, a positive hypothesis, and if he climbs step by step accepting each

time to cover the corresponding step below, without
cutting off anything, in order to liberate from it the *same
light*[14] which is hidden under every mask, in every element,
even in the darkest mud, even in the most grotesque error,
the most sordid evil, he will see gradually everything clearing up under his eyes, not in theory but tangibly, and he
will discover not only the summits but *the abysses of Truth.*[15]
He will see that his Adversary was a most diligent collabora-
tor, most attentive to the perfect solidity of his realisation,
first because each battle increased his strength, then because each fall obliged him to liberate the truth down
below instead of taking flight all alone to vacant summits
— and that his Burden was the very burden of our mother
the Earth who also wants her share of the light. The
Princes of Darkness are already saved! they are at the
Work, they are the scrupulous exactors of a Truth which
contains rather than excludes all things:

> *Not only is there hope for godheads pure;*
> *The violent and darkened deities*
> *Leaped down from the one breast in rage to find*
> *What the white gods had missed; they too are safe.*[16]

And he will see that each thing has its inevitable place,
not only that *nothing can be cut off but that perhaps nothing is
more important or less important,* as if the totality of the
problem was in the smallest incident, the minutest daily
gesture, as much as in the cosmic upheavals, and that
perhaps also the totality of Light and Joy was there in the
least atom as much as in the superconscient infinitudes.
And slowly the dark half of the truth is illumined. Each
stumbling kindles a flame of suffering and makes a gap of
light below; each weakness is a call to strength, as if the

force of the fall was the very force of the rise, each imperfection a hollow for a fuller plenitude — there are no sins, there are no errors, there are only infinite miseries which oblige us to lean over the whole range of our kingdom and to embrace all so as to heal all and accomplish all. By this gap in our armour a love and pity for the world have entered, which all the radiant purities will never understand — purity is impregnable, it is barricaded, closed like concrete; a hole is needed for the Truth to enter!

[He] made error a door by which Truth could enter in.[17]

There is a truth of love behind evil. The lower one descends towards the infernal circles, the clearer becomes the immense *need* in the depths of Evil and one finds that nothing can be healed without a similar intensity: a flame lights up within, more and more powerful and warm under the suffocating pressure — there is nothing but That, nothing but That, that is all — as if Love alone could confront the Night and convince it of its half of light, as though all that Shadow was necessary that Love may be born. In truth, at the heart of all shadows, at the heart of all our evils, there is an inverse mystery. And if each one of us has a particular difficulty, at once the contradiction and the sign of our destiny, it is possible in the same way that the great "faults" of the earth, vulnerable, sinning, sorrowful, its thousand and one holes of poverty are the sign of its destiny and that one day it must incarnate perfect Love and Joy because it will have suffered all and understood all.

As one advances, the superconscient line withdraws towards the top, the subconscient line withdraws simultaneously towards the bottom; all is enlarged, all is illumined, but all closes in also, everything is accentuated around a single dark point, sharper and sharper, more and more crucial, pressing, as though one had turned for years and years, for lives, around the same Problem without ever truly touching it, and then it is there clinging to the bottom of the hole and struggling under the Light — all the evil of the world in one point. The hour of the Secret is near. For the law of the descent is not an iron law nor a law of sin and fall any more than a law of repentance and celestial escape, but a golden Law in truth, an unfathomable Premeditation which draws us below at the same time as above, right down to the depths of the subconscient and Inconscient, to the *central point*,[18] that knot of life and of death, of shadow and light, where the Secret waits. The more one approaches the Summits, the more one touches the Depth.

The Great Passage

The last steps of the descent are in the depths of our evolutionary past, beyond the Subconscient which was the former consciousness in our prehistory, at that level where for the first time in the world something living came forth from what seemed a Death, that is on the borders of the material Inconscient and the physical consciousness, in our body, witness and residue of this first birth in the world. The organs, the cells of the body have their own consciousness, very well organised and highly awakened, which knows what to choose, receive, reject, and which one can manipulate as soon as one has reached a sufficient yogic development. If it were only a question of bettering the conditions of the present life, the ordinary yogic consciousness would suffice: prolongation of life, immunity from diseases and even youthfulness are among the frequent acquisitions of this discipline. But as we have said, we seek to transform life, not only to plaster the façade. Now, under this physical consciousness, there is a physical subconsciousness which is the result of the evolution of life in Matter and wherein are engraved all the old habits of life, of which the worst is that of dying — its reflexes, its fears, its defences, and above all its habits of hardening, as though it had kept the memory of innumerable shells under which it had to protect itself in order to grow. And at the very bottom of this physical subconscient, at a place where every form of consciousness or of memory seems to be extinguished, one touches a bedrock, a first Carapace, which is the fundamental Death from which life has torn itself free. It is something very hard and very vast, so vast and so hard that the Vedic rishis spoke of it as "the infinite rock". This is the Inconscient. It is a wall — or perhaps a door. It is the bottom — or a crust perhaps. And perhaps it is not totally dead nor totally inconscient, for it is not something negatively immobile one meets, but something positively negative, if we may say so, something that refuses, that says No to life:

The stubborn mute rejection in Life's depths,
The ignorant No in the origin of things.[19]

If the very bottom was a Nothingness of inexistence, there would be no hope and, besides, nothing could have ever been born of nothing, but this very bottom is *something*; if there is a No, it is that there is a Yes within; if there is a Death, there is a Life within. And finally, if there is an end, there is a beginning on the other side. All negatives are necessarily one half of a positive. All our depths are the surface of something else. The very meaning of Sri Aurobindo's yoga is to find the positive of all these negatives, in each element and at all the levels of consciousness and, God willing, the supreme Positive (which however is neither positive nor negative, it just *is*) where all our dualities will be resolved, including those down below, that of life which dies or of Death which lives.

At Chandernagore Sri Aurobindo had reached the last steps of the physical subconscient; he was before a wall: *No, it is not with the Empyrean that I am busy, I wish it were. It is rather with the opposite end of things.*[20] One can conceive the difficulty of this descent if one already knows what resistances and return-shocks are met with when one barely arrives at the mental and vital subconscient — in the hole of vipers. And the more one goes down, the more one needs a high consciousness, the more one needs a powerful light, because one cannot go lower than one has climbed; and if one has understood that consciousness is a force as concrete as can be an electric current, one can imagine what traumatisms and lacerations an overmind power and light, for instance, represent — this *assault of ether and of fire*[21] — which descend like a cataract into the wallow of the physical subconscient. Here there are huge difficulties, even dangers, to which we shall come back when speaking of Transformation. So long as it is a question of mental and vital resistances, of our moral falsehoods, it is enough to train one's will and one's patience, but when one descends lower one must face *the falsehoods of the body*, as the Mother says, that is, disease and death. This is why Sri Aurobindo and the Mother insisted so much with their disciples on the imperious necessity of an all-proof physical basis: *Work from both ends, do not let go the one for the other.*

At the same time that he reached the extreme overmind border where the "great coloured waves" lose themselves across a white frontier, Sri Aurobindo touched correspondingly the black rock down below:

> *I have been digging deep and long*
> *Mid a horror of filth and mire....*
>
> *A voice cried, "Go where none have gone!*
> *Dig deeper, deeper yet*
> *Till thou reach the grim foundation stone*
> *And knock at the keyless gate."*[22]

Then it was that a strange thing happened, one day in 1910 at Chandernagore.... But before going further and reconstructing the experience which changes the whole face and course of our evolution, let us stop a brief moment to take the bearings and trace the co-ordinates of our human condition. And this is quite simple: we are shut up in Matter, there in the Black Egg which presses us in on all sides, at every second, and here is but one way of getting out of it, or perhaps two: to sleep (dream, go into an ecstasy, meditate, but all are grades of sleep, more or less noble, more or less conscious, more or less divine) or to die. Sri Aurobindo's experience brings the third key which allows the getting out without ecstasy, without dying, and in brief without getting out, and reverses the course of man's spiritual evolution because the end is no longer only above or outside but in the very midst, within; and this key, besides, opens the gate of wakefulness to all dreams, all ecstasies, and specially to the powers which will let us incarnate our dreams and transform this Black Egg into

a place open, clear and living.... That day of 1910 at Chandernagore Sri Aurobindo reached the bottom of the hole, he had crossed all the layers of dirt on which Life had sprung up, inexplicable flower; there was now only this Light above shining more and more intensely as he descended, throwing up all the impurities one by one under its keen ray as though all this Night called ever a greater Light, as though the line of the subconscient was withdrawing, withdrawing towards the depth in an ever more solid concentration in the inverse image of the concentration above, leaving this single wall of Shadow under this one Light; when, at one bound, without transition, at the bottom of this "inconscient" Matter and in the dark cells of this body, without falling into ecstatic trance, without the loss of the individual, without cosmic dissolution, and with eyes wide open, Sri Aurobindo found himself precipitated into the supreme Light:

> *He broke into another Space and Time.*[23]

Night, Evil, Death are a mask. The supreme Opposition awakens the supreme Intensity and the similar changes into Itself — there is only that One, *tad ekam.* The solar world, the supreme divine consciousness, the supermind, of which all the other levels are as separate rays, was there at the very heart of Matter. The step above the overmind is not "above", it is here and in all things — the door below opens the door above and everywhere:

> *A fathomless sealed astonishment of Light.*[24]

> *A grand reversal of the Night and Day*
> *All the world's values changed....*[25]

. . .

> *The high meets the low, all is a single plan.*[26]

The extreme limit of the Past touches the heart of the Future which conceived it, God-Spirit meets God-Matter and this is the divine life in a body. *Sat-Chit-Ananda* up above is *Sat-Chit-Ananda* down below, Existence-Consciousness-Power-Joy. Evolution does not end up in a white or a black sleep, nothing is engulfed in the Night, nothing bursts forth in mid-air, all is complete in a perfect circle. The Joy high up above is the Joy deep down below:

> *An exultation in the depths of sleep,*
> *A heart of bliss within a world of pain.*[27]

A joy which can act, a powerful illumination in our veins, instead of a barren bliss on the top of our heads:

> *Almighty powers are shut in Nature's cells.*[28]

For the Supermind is not a more ethereal consciousness but a denser consciousness, it is the very Vibration which composes and recomposes endlessly Matter and the worlds, it is this which can change the Earth:

> *At the very bottom of the inconscience*
> *most hard and rigid and narrow and stifling,*
> says the Mother, *I struck upon an almighty spring*
> *that cast me up forthwith into a formless*
> *limitless Vast vibrating with the seeds*
> *of a new world.*

And this is the key of the Transformation, the key of victory over the laws of Matter by the Consciousness in Matter — the Consciousness above is the Consciousness below; it is the door of the future world and the new earth which the Scriptures announced two thousand years ago: "A new earth wherein the Truth shall dwell" (II Peter III. 13). For surely the earth is our salvation, the earth is the place of the Victory and the perfect accomplishment, nothing needs to escape into the heavens, all is there and totally there in a body — the superme Joy, Consciousness, Power, if we have the courage to open our eyes and go down and have a living dream instead of a sleeping one:

> They must enter into the last finite if they want to reach the last infinite.[29]

And at the same time, Sri Aurobindo found the lost Secret, that of the Vedas and of all the more or less deformed traditions which have been transmitted down the centuries from Iran to Central America and the banks of the Rhine, from Eleusis to the Catharists and from the Round Table to the Alchemists, the Secret of all the seekers after perfection. It is the quest of the Treasure in the depths of the cavern, the struggle with the subconscious forces, ogres, dwarfs and serpents; this is Apollo and the Python, Indra and the serpent *Vritra*, Thor and the giants, Sigurd and Fafner. This is the solar myth of the Mayas, the Descent of Orpheus, the Transmutation. This is the serpent which bites its own tail. And this above all is the secret of the Vedic rishis who were no doubt the first to discover what they called "the great passage", *mahas pathah*, the world of "the unbroken Light," *Swar*, at the bottom of the rock of the Inconscient: "Our fathers by their words broke

the strong and stubborn places, the Angiras* seers shatter-
ed the mountain rock with their cry; they made in us a
path to the Great Heaven, they discovered the Day and the
sun-world" (Rig Veda I. 71.2), they discovered "the Sun
dwelling in the darkness" (III. 39. 5). They found "the
treasure of heaven hidden in the secret cavern like the
young of the Bird, within the infinite rock" (I. 130. 3).

The Shadow and the Light, Good and Evil prepared a
divine birth in Matter: "Day and Night both suckle the
divine Child".[30] Nothing is accursed, nothing is in vain,
Night and Day are "two sisters, immortal, with a common
lover (the sun)... common they, though different their
forms" (I. 113-2, 3). At the end of the "pilgrimage" of
ascension and descent, the seeker is "a son of the two
Mothers" (III. 55.7), he is the son of *Aditi*, the white
Mother† of the super-conscient infinite, and the son of
Diti, the terrestrial Mother of "the tenebrous infinite";
and he possesses "the two births," human and divine,
"eternal and in one nest ... as the Enjoyer of his two
wives" (I. 62.7): "The contents of the pregnant hill§ (came
forth) for the supreme birth ... a god opened the human
doors" (V. 45). "Then, indeed, they awoke and saw all
behind and wide around them, then, indeed, they held the
ecstasy that is enjoyed in heaven. In all gated houses‡
were all the gods" (Rig Veda IV. 1.18).

The hope of man is fulfilled and the prayer of the rishi:
"May Heaven and Earth be equal and one"[31]; the great
Equilibrium is found again.

* The first rishis.

† It is this ancient tradition, known also to the Hebrews, which
Christianity seems to have revived, quite literally, with the immaculate
conception of the Virgin Mary.

§ The material Inconscient.

‡ On all the planes of our being or in all the centres of consciousness.

Heaven in its rapture dreams of perfect earth,
Earth in its sorrow dreams of perfect heaven ...
They are kept from their oneness by enchanted fears.[32]

And this is joy — *Ananda*. It is at the beginning of things
and at the end and everywhere if we dig deep enough; it
is "the well of honey covered by the rock" (Rig Veda
II. 24. 4.)

CHAPTER FIFTEEN

THE SUPRAMENTAL CONSCIOUSNESS

It is quite difficult to define in mental terms the supramental consciousness, for it is non-mental by definition and escapes all our tri-dimensional laws and perspectives. Perhaps it is the word which misleads us; it does not signify the summit of human consciousness but another consciousness. We may attempt a few approximations and distinguish two aspects, of consciousness or vision and of power, but already we are falling into the mental trap, for these are two inseparable aspects — it is a consciousness that has power, an active vision. So often when Sri Aurobindo and the Mother try to express their experience, one can hear their reflections echo each other in English and in French: We need another language, *une autre langue*.

Supramental Vision

The supramental vision is a global vision. The mind cuts off little bits which it puts up against one another; the overmind regathers everything in a single beam, but its beam ends in only one point, and it sees all from its own point of view; it is unitary and universal through exclusion of other angles or through annexing them. The Supermind sees not only the whole world of things and beings in a single vision, which gathers up all the beams without opposing anything, but it sees the viewpoint of each thing, each being, each force — it is a rounded view which does not end in a central point but in myriads of points:

A   single   innumerable   look[1] ...

*The supramental being sees things not as one on the levels surround-
ed by a jungle of present facts and phenomena but from above, not
from outside and judged by their surfaces, but from within and
viewed from the truth of their centre.*[2] One can hence understand nothing of the Supermind if one does not constantly
refer to another dimension. But one can understand that it
is the very vision of Wisdom because each thing, each being, each force down here, tends towards its absolute which
it expresses more or less badly and often in an altogether
perverted way but through all its errors and perversions it
obeys an inner law which pushes it towards this *unique* truth
of its being — there is not a leaf of the same tree which is
not unique. If there were not this absolute at the centre of
each one of us, we would crumble to pieces. This is also
why we are so very attached to our pettinesses and our
mistakes because we feel clearly the truth which is behind
and grows behind them, as if *protected*,[3] says Sri Aurobindo,
by this very pettiness and all these stumblings. If we were
to catch the whole truth at the first go, we would make of
it a gnome in our own present image! The truth is not a
matter of thought or of good conduct — though these may
be stages on the way — but a matter of wideness of being,
and our growth is slow and difficult. *Errors, falsehoods,
stumblings! they cry. How bright and beautiful are Thy errors,
O Lord! Thy falsehoods save Truth alive; by Thy stumblings the
world is perfected.*[4] But the mind which sees only the bare
present surface of things would like to clip all that is exces-
sive, purify through emptiness and reduce its world to a
uniform truth, seemly and quite proper. It decrees: "This
is good, that is bad; this one is a friend, that one a foe,"
and perhaps it would want to eliminate all the Nazis from

the world, all the Chinese, for instance, thinking that here is quite a useless calamity. And it is right, by definition, because the mind is made to be reasonable and because it too tends towards a mental or moral absolute which has its place, its role. But this is not the whole truth, it is *one* point of view.* And this is why we do not have power, for if we had power we would make a gentleman's terrible mess of it, through ignorance and short-sightedness. Our infirmities are necessary infirmities. The supramental consciousness lays hold not only of all the points of view but the deep forces which are at work behind each thing and the truth of each thing — it is a *Truth-Consciousness* — and because it sees all, it has Power; here there is an automatic concordance. If we are powerless, it is that we do not see. Seeing and seeing totally, this is necessarily power. But the supramental power does not obey our logic and our morality, it sees far into space and time; it does not seek to chop off the evil to save the good, it does not work by startling miracles; it disengages the good which is in the evil and applies its force and light on the shadowy half so that this may consent to its luminous counterpart. Its first immediate effect, wherever it applies itself, is to spring a crisis, that is, put the shadow in the face of its own light. It is a formidable evolutionary ferment.

The written work of Sri Aurobindo offers a practical illustration of this global vision, though this may be a mental translation of a supramental fact. It is baffling

---

* We may be told that our partialities, our mind, our morality are instruments quite indispensable for managing the present world, and this is very evident. We need to be partial. But it is also because of this that the world remains "partial". Only, one must never lose sight of the fact that these are instruments of *transition* and that we ought to aim at replacing these *stop-gaps*⁵ as Sri Aurobindo calls them, by a consciousness which is vision, which is power.

for many, because it lacks all the angles which make a thought easily understandable — it is so easy to be doctrinaire. Sri Aurobindo turns literally around all the points of view to draw from them the deep truth and he never imposes his own viewpoint (perhaps because he has none — or he has all!), he points out only how each truth is incomplete and in what direction it can be enlarged. The Supermind does not set *truth against truth to see which will stand and survive, but completes truth by truth in the light of the one Truth of which all are the aspects.*[6] He spoke of *the light of the Thought that carries in it its own opposites.*[7] This is what the Mother calls *thinking spherically.* One always gets the feeling of being frightfully dogmatic and systematic when speaking of Sri Aurobindo, due undoubtedly to the drawback of our language which levels its searchlight at one point rather than another and casts shadows, whilst Sri Aurobindo embraces everything, not by a sort of "tolerrance", which is a mental substitute for Oneness, but by an undivided vision which is really *one* with each thing, at the heart of the thing. Perhaps this is the very vision of Love?

This undivided vision is so real that even the appearance of the physical world is changed for the supramental consciousness or rather the appearance has not changed, it is the physical world appearing as it really is; the separatist optical illusion in which we live disappears; the stick is no longer broken, everything holds together—the world is not as we see it: *Nothing to the supramental sense is really finite: it is founded on a feeling of all in each and of each in all: its sense definition... creates no walls of limitation; it is an oceanic and ethereal sense in which all particular sense knowledge and sensation is a wave or movement or spray or drop that is yet a concentration of the whole ocean and inseparable from the ocean.... It is as if the eye of the poet and artist had replaced the vague or trivial unseeing normal vision, but singularly spiritualised and glorified,—as if indeed it were the sight of the supreme divine Poet and Artist in which we were participating and there were given to us the full seeing of his truth and intention in his design of the universe and of each thing in the universe. There is an un-limited intensity which makes all that is seen a revelation of the glory of quality and idea and form and colour. The physical eye seems then to carry in itself a spirit and a consciousness which sees not only the physical aspect of the object but the soul of quality in it, the vibration of energy, the light and force and spiritual substance of which it is made.... There is at the same time a subtle change which makes the sight see in a sort of fourth dimension, the character of which is a certain internality, the seeing not only of the superficies and the outward form but of that which informs it and subtly extends around it. The material object becomes to this sight something different from what we now see, not a separate object on the background or in the environment of the rest of Nature but an indivisible part and even in a subtle way an expression of the unity of all that we see. And this unity...is that of the iden-tity of the eternal, the unity of the Spirit. For to the supramen-talised seeing the material world and space and material objects cease to be material in the sense in which we now on the strength of the sole evidence of our limited physical organs...receive [them] ; ...they appear and are seen as Spirit itself in a form of itself and a conscious extension.*[8]

Global vision, undivided vision, and also eternal vision. It is the conquest of time. If the overmind consciousness saw "large extensions of space and time", the supramen-tal envelops the three times; it *links past, present and future in their indivisible connections, in a single continuous map of know-ledge, side by side.*[9]*

---

* Quite an interesting comparison may be made with the theory of relativity. According to Einstein, the more one approaches the speed of

All time is one body, Space a single book.[10]

The consciousness is no longer the camera-shutter which needed to be narrow because without this narrowness it would have burst; it is a great tranquil Gaze: "Like an eye extended in heaven," says the Rig Veda (1.17.21). *The ordinary individual consciousness,* says the Mother, *is like an axis and everything turns around the axis. If it moves one feels lost. It is like a big axis (it is more or less big, it can be quite small) fixed in time, and everything turns around. It extends more or less far, it is more or less high, more or less strong, but all turns around the axis. And then there is no longer an axis—gone, fled! It can go to the north, it can go south, and to the east and to the west; it can go in front, can go behind, it can go no matter where. There is no longer an axis.*

It is difficult for us to imagine what the vision of this universal individual could be and we would be tempted to think from our mental viewpoint that a total knowledge of the three times takes away immediately all the surprise of existence. But this is to apply to the supramental consciousness the norms and reactions which belong only to the mind. The way of seeing and of *living* the world is quite different. The supramental consciousness is not anxiously bent over the future as we are; all is there under its eyes, but it lives divinely in time: *each second* of time is an absolute, a plenitude as complete as the millenniums put end to end; it is on the contrary the perfect perfection of time — in the ordinary life we are

---

light the more does time tend to slow down and the lengths to shorten. At the speed of light our clocks would stop and our metres shrink in. The supramental consciousness which is Light itself is also the conquest of time. Between the light of the physicists and that of the seer, there is perhaps less difference than one thinks.

never in the moment, we are either projected in front or drawn behind, by hope or by regret, because the moment is never what it is, because it always lacks something, it is terribly hollow, whilst for the supramental consciousness each thing is at each moment fully what it ought to be, as it ought to be. It is a beatitude, constant, inalterable. Each sequence, each image of the great cosmic Film is loaded with all the preceding images and all those that follow, it falls short neither through the absence of the future nor through the vanishing of the past — "That bliss which is most large and full and without a gap," says the Rig Veda (V.62.9), that *unwounded Delight*,[11] says Sri Aurobindo. And also, it is the perfect perfection of space; we are perpetually in quest of new things, new objects, because everything lacks all the other things which are not itself; our objects like our moments are hollow; whilst for the supramental consciousness each object, each thing it touches, is as full of totality and infinity as the vision of the immensities or the sum of all possible objects: *The Absolute is everywhere...every finite is an infinite.*[12] And it is an ever-renewed wonder which does not go by surprises but by the discovery of this eternal infinitude, this timeless Absolute in each thing in space and each fraction of time. And this is the perfect plenitude of life, for our finite, temporal life is not full, it is terribly wanting; we are obliged either to renounce the temporal to discover the timeless or to renounce our need of infinitude to enjoy the finitude, whilst the supramental plenitude discovers the infinite in the finite and the timeless in the temporal. It lives spontaneously from minute to minute each second, each object, and the immensity which contains all the minutes and all the objects; and these are two *simultaneous* ways of living and seeing the same thing.

The supramental consciousness does not occupy only a cosmic position but a transcendent position, and the two do not contradict each other. And not only are they not contradictory, but their simultaneity is the key of the true life. For life does not suffer only from its hollow objects and its minced moments but by its lack of repose and of solidity; all the religions, all the spiritualities have sprung up from this fundamental need in man: to find a Basis of permanence, a place of refuge and peace outside all the chaos of this world, this impermanence of the world, this suffering of the world — infinitely outside and protected. And suddenly, in the course of our quest we have emerged into a formidable silence, a vastness outside the world, and we have spoken of God, of the Absolute, Nirvana — little do the words matter, we have touched the great Deliverance. This is the basic experience. However little we draw near that great Silence, everything changes, this is the Certitude, the Peace, as of one shipwrecked who has touched a rock. In life everything runs through our fingers; it is only this Rock which never fails. This is why it is said that the kingdom of God is not of this world. The experience of Sri Aurobindo also began with Nirvana but it finishes with the plenitude of the world; there is here a central contradiction which it is important to catch if we want to know the practical secret of the true life.

The mind, even the overmind of our prophets, is un-redeemably linked to the dualities (dualities in Unity): if God is above, He is not below, if this is white, it is not black. For the supramental experience all is round, *it is all the time yes and no at the same time*, observes the Mother, the two poles of all things are constantly spanned in an-other "dimension" (the Vedic rishis spoke of "the secret inner spaces" — II.4.9). Thus, the Transcendent is not elsewhere outside the world; It is everywhere down here, at once totally inside and totally outside. The supramental consciousness in the same way is totally in the world and totally outside the world; it is in the eternal silence and in the midst of all tumults; it is seated on the unshakable Rock and is in the heart of the stream. And hence it can truly enjoy life and be the master of life, for if we are exclusively in the current there is neither peace nor mastery for us; we are carried away like a straw. It is possible to guess a little what this supramental experience may be if one just goes back to the very small first experiences at the beginning of the yoga. One finds quite quickly, in fact, that it is enough to step back into one's consciousness, make just a small movement of withdrawal, and one enters an expanse of silence behind — as though there were a corner of our being with eyes fixed forever on a great all-white North. The tumult is there without, the suffering, the problems, and one makes a slight inward movement as of crossing a threshold and immediately one is outside (or inside) a thousand leagues away and nothing is of importance any longer, one is on velvety snows. The experience ends up by acquiring so much agility, if we may say so, that in the full run of the most absorbing activities, in the street, when discussing things, when working, one plunges within (or without?) and nothing exists any more, except a smile — a fraction of a second suffices. Then one begins to know Peace; one has an impregnable Refuge everywhere, in all circumstances. And one perceives more and more tangibly that this Silence is not only within, in oneself; it is everywhere, it is as the deep substance of the universe, as though each thing stood out against this background, came from there, returned there. It is like a well of sweetness in the heart of things, like a velvet coat wrapping them around. And this Silence is not empty, it is an absolute Fullness but a Fullness with nothing inside or a Fullness which contains the essence of all that may be, just the second before the things are going to be born — they are not there, and yet they are all there, like an unsung song within. And one is marvellously Safe in there (or out there?). This is the first gleam of the Transcendent. At the extreme point one slides into Nirvana. Nothing exists any more except this Silence. And for the Supermind there is no more a "passage", no more a "threshold" to cross; one *does not pass* from one state to another, from the Silence to the tumult, from Inside outside, from the Divine to the non-divine — the two are fused in one single experience: the Silence which is outside all and the Becoming which flows everywhere; the one does not deny the other, the one *cannot be without the other*. For if the supreme Silence could not contain the contrary of the Silence, it would not be an Infinity. And if the Silence could not be totally outside that which seems its contrary, it would be a prisoner of its contrary. The kingdom of God is of this world and it is not of this world. The whole secret is to reunite the two experiences into one, the infinite in the finite, the timeless in the temporal and the transcendent in the immanent. Then one has Peace in action and Joy in every way.

> *A still deep sea, he laughs in rolling waves:*
> *Universal, he is all, — transcendent, none.*[13]

The supramental consciousness repeats the mystery of a great calm light which, "one day" outside time, wished to see itself temporally, successively, from a myriad points of view, and which yet does not cease being one and round, totally contained in itself in an eternal moment. The one goal of evolution is to rediscover down below this totality up above, it is to find here on earth, in the very midst of the dualities and the most poignant contradictions, the supreme Unity, the supreme Infinitude, the supreme Joy — *Ananda*. It is to find this secret that we have been drawn down each time we took a step up.

Supramental Power

The spiritualists reject power as a weapon unworthy of the seeker of truth; this is not Sri Aurobindo's view; on the contrary, the concept of Power — *Shakti* — is a key to his yoga, because without power nothing can be transformed. *I cherish God the Fire, not God the Dream!* exclaims Savitri.[14]

> *A fire to call eternity into Time,*
> *Make body's joy as vivid as the soul's.*[15]

It is a mistake of the ethical or religious mind to condemn Power as in itself a thing not to be accepted or sought after because naturally corrupting and evil; in spite of its apparent justification by a majority of instances, this is at its core a blind and irrational prejudice. However corrupted and misused, as Love and Knowledge too are corrupted and misused, Power is divine and put here for a divine use. Shakti, will, Power is the driver of the worlds and whether it be Knowledge-Force or Love-Force or Life-Force or Action-Force or Body-Force, is always spiritual in its origin and divine in its character. It is the use made of it in the Ignorance by brute, man or Titan that has to be cast aside and replaced by its greater natural — even if to us supernormal — action led by an inner consciousness which is in tune with the Infinite and the Eternal. The integral Yoga cannot reject the works of Life and be satisfied with an inward experience only; it has to go inward in order to change the outward.[16] It is this "force" or "power" aspect of the consciousness which India has represented under the face of the eternal Mother. Without consciousness there is no Force and without Force there is no creation — He and She, two in one, inseparable. *This whole wide world is only he and she.*[17] And the entire evolution is the story of Her who rediscovers Him and who wants to incarnate Him everywhere. One has not to reject the one for the other — without Him we are prisoners of a blind Force, without Her prisoners of a dazzled Void — but to unite both in a fulfilled world. "Into a blind darkness they enter who follow after the Ignorance, they as if into a greater darkness who devote themselves to the Knowledge alone," says the Isha Upanishad (9).

The Supermind is before all things a power—a formidable power. It is the direct power of the Spirit in Matter. All consciousness is power and the more one rises, the more forceful is the power, but the further does one go away from the earth at the same time; consequently when we want to apply our overmind power, for example, to the affairs of this world, we have to bring it down from plane to plane and it must overcome the determinisms of all the intermediary levels before reaching the bottom, in Matter. At the end of the trip, there remains only a gleam of the overmind, dulled and darkened, which must fight against more and more thick and rebellious determinisms. This is why the spiritualists have never been able to transform life. The Supermind is the supreme Consciousness-Force at the very heart of Matter, without any intermediary. It is the "sun in the darkness" of which the Veda speaks, the place where the Top and the Bottom directly meet. It can hence change everything. Let us recall the words of the Mother: "The true change of consciousness is that which will change the physical conditions of the world and make of it an entirely new creation."

The supramental power, we hasten to say, does not work by miracles or by violence — the notion of miracle is absurd, Sri Aurobindo has repeated this very often: *There is really no such thing as miracle*[18], there are only phenomena of whose process we are ignorant, and for him who sees there is only the intervention of the determinism of a higher plane in the determinism of a lower. Mind may appear as a miracle for the determinism of the caterpillar but we know well that our mental miracles obey a certain process. It is the same for the Supermind, it does not upset laws, simply it passes above (or within?) to a level where they exist no longer, not any longer than the laws of the caterpillar exist for man. Let us explain. The habitual repetition of a certain number of vibrations which are, so to say, coagulated around an individual, ends up by giving him an apparently stable structure; he says he obeys the "law" of his nature but this so-called law is not more ineluctable than the fact of going by one way rather than another in order to get home; these are only habits. The same holds for the entire cosmos; all our physical laws, supposedly ineluctable, are similarly coagulated habits which have nothing of the ineluctable and can be broken off if ever one wants to change the circuit, that is, change the consciousness. *An ordinary law*, says Sri Aurobindo, *merely means an equilibrium established by Nature; it means a balance of forces. It is merely a groove in* *which Nature is accustomed to work in order to produce certain results. But if you change the consciousness, then the groove also is bound to change.*[19] These "changes of grooves" have land-marked all our evolutionary story beginning from the appearance of Life in Matter, which modified the material groove, till the appearance of Mind in Life, which modified the vital and material groove. The Supermind is a third changing of grooves, which will modify Mind, Life and Matter. It has already started, the experience is on its way. Fundamentally, the supramental process consists in liberating the consciousness contained in each element. It does not upset the order of the universe, it commits no violence, it applies its power only to the fission of the darkness that it may give up its own light. "He has cloven wide away the darkness, as one that cleaves away a skin, that he may spread out our earth* under his illumining sun," says the Rig Veda (V.85.1). Because the divine solar consciousness is everywhere, the world and every atom of the world are divine — the Lord of all the universes is also "the One conscious in incon-scient things" of whom the Rig Veda speaks. Matter is not a crude substance incapable of change except through the violence of our hands or our heads, which have scarcely brought forth anything but monsters, it is a divine subs-tance which can "respond" instead of resisting and be transformed instead of dragging us down into its old habit of downward gravitation and disintegration. But it is a darkened or sleeping divinity, "somnambulist", as Sri Aurobindo calls it, a "lost sun", buried, as the Veda says. *The Inconscient is the Superconscient's sleep*[20] .... *The apparent Inconscience of the material universe holds in itself darkly all that*

* "The earth" in the Vedas is also the symbol of our own flesh.

is eternally self-revealed in the luminous Superconscient.[21] The Supermind then will use its light to awaken the corresponding light — *the same light* — in Matter:

> *The truth above shall wake a nether truth,*[22]

for the law is eternally the same: only the similar can act upon the similar; the power above is needed to liberate the power below.

What then is this Power? All concentration releases a subtle warmth, well known to those who have even slightly practised the yogic disciplines (the *tapasya* or yogic discipline is "that which produces heat"); the supramental power is a heat of this kind, but infinitely more intense, in the cells of the body. It is a heat released by the awakening of the consciousness-force in Matter: *Everything happens,* says the Mother, *as though our spiritual life were made of silver, whilst the supramental life is made of gold; as though the whole spiritual life down here were a silvery vibration, not cold but simply a light, a light which goes to the very summit, a light that is quite pure, pure and intense, but there is in the other, the supramental, a richness and a strength, a warmth, which makes all the difference.* This warmth is the basis of all supramental transmutation. In fact the heat released by combustions and other chemical reactions, not to speak of the incomparably greater energy liberated by fusions or nuclear fissions, is only the physical translation of a fundamental spiritual phenomenon which the Vedic rishis knew quite well and which they called *Agni,* the spiritual Fire in Matter: "Other flames are only branches of thy stock, O Fire.... O *Agni,* O universal Godhead, thou art the navel-knot of the earths and their inhabitants; all men born thou controllest and supportest like a pillar.... Thou

art the head of heaven and the navel of the earth.... Thou
art the power that moves at work in the two worlds"
(Rig Veda 1.59). "That splendour of thee, O Fire, which
is in heaven and in the earth and in the plants and in the
waters and by which thou hast spread out the wide mid-
air, is a vivid ocean of light which sees with a divine
seeing."[23]

"*Agni* has entered earth and heaven as if they were
one."* It is this supreme *Agni* which Sri Aurobindo and
the Mother have discovered in Matter and the cells
of the body — this is the lever of the transformation of
the body and the physical changing of the world. Henceforth, instead of acting on Matter through the deforming
and dulling agency of all the intermediary mental and
vital determinisms, it is Matter itself, awakened to the
consciousness of its force, which operates directly its own
transmutation. Instead of an evolution which seems to
be divided between two poles, of consciousness without
force ending in the bliss of the sage or of force without
consciousness ending in the brute joy of the atom, the
Supermind re-establishes the Equilibrium in the *total
being*: the highest consciousness in the most powerful
force, the fire of the Spirit in Matter — "O Flame with
the hundred treasures," exclaims the Rig Veda (1.59).

It is perhaps not useless to emphasise that Sri Aurobindo
made his spiritual discovery in 1910, even before having
read the Vedas and at a time when nuclear physics was
a matter of theoretical conjecture. Our science goes ahead
of our "conscience", whence the hazardous course of our
destiny.

The similarity with the nuclear force is yet more stri-

---

* Rig Veda III.7.4.

king if we come to the description of the supramental power as it appears to the seer. We have said that the more one rises in consciousness, the more does the luminosity tend to become steady, continuous: from the intuitive sparks to the "stable lightnings" of the overmind, the light becomes homogeneous. One would then think that the supramental light is a sort of luminous totality, perfectly immobile, continuous, without interstices. Now, it is remarkable that the Supermind is of a luminous quality quite different from the other grades of consciousness; it unites at a time complete immobility and the most rapid movement possible — here too, experimentally, the two poles are spanned. We can only quote the fact without being able to interpret it; this is how the Mother describes her first experience of the supramental light: *There was this impression of power, of warmth, of gold: it was not fluid, it was like a glow of dust. And each one of these things (they cannot be called particles nor fragments, not even points, unless one takes 'point' in the mathematical sense, a point which does not take up space) it was like vivid gold, a warm gold dust — one cannot say it was brilliant, one cannot say it was dark; nor was it made of light as we understand it: a crowd of tiny little points of gold, nothing but that. I would have said that they touched my eyes, my face. And with a formidable power! At the same time, a feeling of plenitude, the peace of all-power. It was rich, it was full. It was movement at its fastest, infinitely more rapid than anything one can imagine and at the same time it was absolute peace, perfect tranquillity.** Years later, when this experience had grown quite familiar, the Mother spoke of it in these terms: *It is a movement which is a kind of eternal*

---

* At the speed of light also we can find perfect immobility in supreme movement — immobility, if one sees the phenomenon from within, movement if one sees from without.

Vibration, with neither beginning nor end. It is something that is from all eternity, for all eternity, and there is no division of time; it is only when it is projected on a screen that it begins to take on the division of time; but one cannot speak of a second, one cannot speak of a moment... it is very difficult to explain. One has not even the time to perceive it when it is already not there — something without limits, without beginning, without end, which is a Movement so complete — total and constant, constant — that to any perception, it gives the feeling of a perfect immobility. It is absolutely indescribable, but it is this which is the Origin and the Support of the whole terrestrial evolution.... And I have noticed that in that state of consciousness the Movement exceeds the force or the power which concentrates the cells to make of them an individual form. When we shall get to know how to apply this Vibration or this "Movement" to our matter, we shall possess the practical secret of the passage from brute Matter to a more subtle Matter and we shall have the first supramental or glorious body on the earth.

This immobility in movement is the foundation of all the activities of the supramental being. This is the practical a b c of all discipline which tends towards the Supermind, perhaps even the a b c of all efficient action in this world. We have already said that immobility — inner immobility, of course — has the power of dissolving vibrations; that if we know how to remain perfectly still within, without the least vibration of response, we can master any attack of animal or man. This power of immobility is truly acquired only when one has begun to become aware of the great Silence behind and when one is able, at every moment, to step back and plunge deep, very far from external circumstances, thousands of leagues away. One needs the capacity to be altogether outside so as to master the inside of life. But what is strange, and natural after all, is that this supramental Power cannot be obtained except when one is completely outside, completely on the eternal Basis, out of time, out of space — as though the supreme Dynamism could come forth only from the supreme Immobility. The fact may seem paradoxical but it is practically comprehensible; one can understand that if the ordinary consciousness which stirs with the least quivering breath of wind, entered into contact with this "warm vibrating gold dust", it would be instantaneously swept off, disintegrated. Complete Immobility alone can support this Movement. And this is what struck so much those who saw Sri Aurobindo; it was not so much the light of his eyes (as it is with the Mother), but this immobile immensity one felt, so compact, so dense, as if one were entering a solid infinite. One understood then spontaneously, without proof, how the cyclone could not enter his room. One understood the whole meaning of this little phrase of his: *the strong immobility* of an immortal spirit.[24] It was through the strength of this immobility that he worked for forty years and could write twelve hours every night, walk eight hours every day (in order "to bring down light into Matter", as he said) and engage in the most strenuous battles in the Inconscient without incurring fatigue. *If when thou art doing great actions and moving giant results, thou canst perceive that THOU art doing nothing, then know that God has removed the seal on thy eyelids....* *If when thou sittest alone, still and voiceless on the mountain-top, thou canst perceive the revolutions thou art conducting, then hast thou the divine vision and art freed from appearances.*[25]

Immobility is the basis of the supramental power but silence is the condition of its perfect functioning. The supramental consciousness does not follow mental or moral criteria when deciding its actions — there are no

longer any "problems" for it — it acts naturally and spontaneously. This spontaneity is the distinctive mark of the
Supermind : spontaneity of life, spontaneity of knowledge,
spontaneity of power. In the ordinary life we seek to know
what is good or right and when we believe we have found
it we try somehow to materialise our thought. The supramental consciousness does not seek to know, it does not
seek to learn what it must do or not do, it is perfectly silent,
immobile, and lives spontaneously each second of time
without any straining towards the future; but at every
second, in the silence of the consciousness, the required
knowledge falls like a drop of light : what must be done,
must be said, what seen, what understood. The supramental Truth *is an arrow from the Light, not a bridge to reach
it*.[26] "In the level wideness they meet together and know
perfectly," says the Rig Veda (VII.76.5). And each time
a thought or a vision passes in the consciousness, it is not
a speculation on the future, it is an immediate action :

> *There every thought and feeling is an act*.[27]

Knowledge is automatically endowed with power. For it
is a true knowledge, which sees everything, and a true
knowledge is a powerful knowledge. We do not have
power because we do not see everything. But this total
vision escapes completely our momentary considerations,
it sees the prolongation of each thing in time; it is not an
arbitrary fiat which is going to upset the trajectory, it is
simply like a luminous pressure which will *accelerate* the
movement and put each thing, each force, each event, each
being in direct communication with its own content of light,
its own divine possibility and the very Goal which had put
it on its way. As we have said, it is a formidable evolution-

ary ferment. Perhaps one would be expected to say something here about how, in practice, this power translates itself in the life and acts of those who incarnate it: Sri Aurobindo and the Mother for the time being; but knowing well that no explanation is satisfying unless one has seen for oneself and that the experience will only begin to be convincing the day it becomes a collective possibility, it is best to keep silent; moreover, their action escaped very often even those who have benefited by it, for the simple reason that one cannot understand a thing unless one is on the same plane and also because we see only the moment, not the miracle prepared by that simple gaze, that second of light which will ripen in twenty years or in three centuries under our obscurities before becoming "natural" — *Neither you nor anyone else knows anything at all of my life*, wrote Sri Aurobindo to one of his biographer disciples; *it has not been on the surface for men to see*.[28] Our difficulty in speaking of this power comes from the fact that we have a false notion of power. When we speak of "powers", we immediately understand by them some fantastic things but this is not the true Power, this is not even the true fantasy of the universe; when the Supermind acts, it does not bring about wonderful changes, throwing dust in the eyes, it is an action tranquil, as of eternity, which pushes the world and each thing in the world towards its own perfection through all the masks of imperfection. The true miracle is not to coerce things but to precipitate them secretly and on the quiet towards their own centre, so that from their own depths they may recognise this Face which is their own face — there is but one miracle: this moment of recognition, when nothing is other any longer.

And the key of the supramental power is the individual.

The supramental being occupies not only a transcendent and a cosmic position, but an individual position — the triple hiatus of experience which divided the monist, the pantheist and the individualist is healed; its transcendent position does not abolish the world and the individual or its cosmic position deprive it of the Transcendent and the individual, and its individual position does not separate it either from the Transcendent and the universe; it has not thrown away the ladder to attain the goal, it has traversed all the evolutionary rungs from top to bottom — there is no gap anywhere, not a joint missing — and because it has kept its individuality instead of bursting forth into a luminous no man's land, it can not only climb but *descend* the great Stairway of existence and utilise its individual being as a bridge or a joint in Matter between the highest-above and the lowest-below. Its work on the earth is to put into direct contact the supreme Force and the individual, the supreme Consciousness and Matter — *to join the two Ends*, as the Mother puts it. It is a precipitator of the Real upon the earth. This is why we hope that the blind determinisms which at present govern the world — Death, Suffering, War — can be changed by this supreme Determinism and will give place to a new evolution in the Light: *It is a spiritual revolution we foresee and the material is only its shadow and reflex.*[29]

Two months after his arrival at Chandernagore, Sri Aurobindo heard once again the Voice: *Go to Pondicherry.* A few days later he set sail secretly on board the *Dupleix*, outwitting the British police, and he left North India for ever. *I had accepted the rule of... moving only as I was moved by the Divine.*[30] The last forty years of his life, with the Mother, were to be consecrated to transforming this individual realisation into a terrestrial realisation: *We want to bring down the supermind as a new faculty. Just as the mind is now a permanent state of consciousness in humanity, so also we want to create a race in which the supermind will be a permanent state of consciousness.*[31] And in order that his purpose might not be mistaken, Sri Aurobindo stressed this point — he has stressed it often: *It is far from my purpose to propagate any religion, new or old, for humanity in the future. A way to be opened that is still blocked, not a religion to be founded, is my conception of the matter.*[32] We do not yet know if the supramental adventure will succeed. The Vedic rishis could not "unblock the way", they could not open "the great passage" for everyone and transform their personal realisation into a permanent collective realisation: there was a reason why. We have to see if that reason yet holds good.

CHAPTER SIXTEEN

MAN, A TRANSITIONAL BEING

Sri Aurobindo lived in great difficulty during these first years in Pondicherry; he was far away from those who could have helped him, under suspicion, his mail censored, his least movements watched by the British spies who tried to obtain his extradition by all sorts of manoeuvres, including the hiding of compromising documents in his house and then denouncing him to the French police. They attempted even to kidnap him. Sri Aurobindo had no rest until one day the French police superintendent came to make a search and found in his drawers the works of Homer. After having inquired whether this was "really Greek", he was filled with admiration for this gentleman-yogi who read scholarly books and spoke French, and he went away. Thenceforth the exile could receive whomsoever he wished and move about as he pleased. A few comrades-in-arms had followed him, awaiting the hour their "chief" would resume the political struggle, but as "the Voice" gave no order, he did not stir. Besides, Sri Aurobindo saw that the machinery was working now; the spirit of independence had been awakened in his compatriots and events would follow their inevitable course until the liberation, as he had foreseen. He had something else to do.

The Works

A discovery marks the first years of exile: the reading

of the Vedas in the original. Till then Sri Aurobindo had read only the English or Indian translations and had seen there, with the scholars, only a ritualistic mass, rather obscure, *of small value or importance for the history of thought or for a living spiritual experience.*[1] And suddenly now in the original he discovered *a constant vein of the richest gold of thought and spiritual experience*[2].... *I found that the mantras of the Veda illuminated with a clear and exact light psychological experiences of my own for which I had found no sufficient explanation either in European psychology or in the teachings of Yoga or of Vedanta.*[3] One may imagine, in fact, that Sri Aurobindo was the first to be baffled by his own experience and that it took him some years to understand exactly what had happened. We have described the supramental experience at Chandernagore as though the stages had been linked very carefully, each with its explanatory label, but the explanations came long afterwards, at that moment he had no guiding landmarks. And here was the most ancient of the four Vedas,* the Rig Veda, bringing him unexpectedly the sign that he was not quite alone and astray on this planet. That the western or even Indian scholars have not grasped the extraordinary vision of these texts is not surprising if one knows that Sanskrit roots lend themselves to a double or triple meaning which in its turn envelops itself in a double symbolism, esoteric and exoteric. One can read these hymns on two or three planes of superimposed meanings and even when one has come to the exact sense one believes for example that the "Fire in the water" or "the mountain pregnant with the supreme birth" and all that quest for the "lost Sun" followed by the discovery of the "Sun in the darkness"

---

* Rig Veda, Sama Veda, Yajur Veda, Atharva Veda.

have a symbolism that is at the very least bizarre, if one does not have the experimental key to the spiritual Fire in Matter, the blasting of the rock of the Inconscient and the illumination in the cells of the body. But did not the rishis themselves speak of "secret words, seer-wisdoms that utter their inner meaning to the seer" (IV.3.16)? Because he had seen, Sri Aurobindo recognised immediately, and he began to translate an important part of the Rig Veda, particularly the admirable *Hymns to the Mystic Fire*. One cannot help being left wondering and questioning, when one thinks that the rishis of five or six thousand years ago transmitted not only their own experience but that of their "ancestors" or "the fathers of men" as they called them—how many millenniums ago?—which was repeated generation after generation without a mistake, without omitting the least diaeresis, because the efficacy of the mantra depended precisely on the exactness of the repetition. We are before the most ancient tradition of the world, intact. That Sri Aurobindo rediscovered the Secret of the beginning of our human cycle (perhaps there were others before?) in an age which the Indians call "black", *Kali-yuga*, is not without significance. If it is true that the Bottom touches a new surface, we are drawing close.*

It would be wrong, however, to identify Sri Aurobindo with the Vedic revelation; striking as it is for us, for him it

---

* According to Indian tradition, each cycle unrolls itself in four periods: *Satya-yuga*, the age of truth (or golden age), then the age when there does not remain more than "three-fourths of the truth", *Treta-yuga*, then a "half of the truth", *Dwapara-yuga*, and finally the age in which most of the truth has disappeared, *Kali-yuga*, and the pass-word has been lost. The Kali-yuga is followed by a new Satya-yuga, but between the two there occurs a complete destruction, *pralaya*, and the universe is "swallowed up again". According to Sri Aurobindo, the discovery of the Supermind opens other horizons.

was only a sign of recognition on the way, a confirmation after the event; to want to resuscitate the Veda in the twentieth century, as though the summit of the Truth therein were definitively attained, is a futile endeavour because the Truth never repeats itself twice. Did he not write in a humorous vein: *Truly this shocked reverence for the past is a wonderful and fearful thing! After all, the Divine is infinite and the unrolling of the Truth may be an infinite process...not a thing in a nutshell cracked and its contents exhausted once and for all by the first seer or sage, while the others must religiously crack the same nutshell all over again.*[4] Sri Aurobindo was not going to work at an individual realisation like the rishis but at a collective realisation, in conditions which are no longer those of the prehistoric shepherds. And first of all he was to devote a good deal of time to a written work which is undoubtedly, for the moment, the most visible sign of his collective action. In 1910 there came to Pondicherry a French writer, Paul Richard, who met Sri Aurobindo and was so impressed by the breadth of his views that he made a second trip in 1914 specially to see him, and this time urged him to write. A bilingual review was started, Richard undertaking the French part. Thus was born the *Arya*, or *Review of the Great Synthesis*. But the war broke out, Richard was called back to France and Sri Aurobindo found himself alone with 64 pages of philosophy to bring out every month, he who had nothing of the philosopher in him: *And philosophy! Let me tell you in confidence that I never, never, never was a philosopher — although I have written philosophy which is another story altogether. I knew precious little about philosophy before I did the Yoga and came to Pondicherry — I was a poet and a politician, not a philosopher. How I managed to do it and why? First, because Paul Richard proposed to me to cooperate in a philosophical review — and as my theory was that a*

Yogi ought to be able to turn his hand to anything, I could not very well refuse; and then he had to go to the war and left me in the lurch with sixty-four pages a month of philosophy all to write by my lonely self. *Secondly, because I had only to write down in the terms of the intellect all that I had observed and come to know in practising Yoga daily and the philosophy was there automatically. But that is not being a philosopher!*[5] It was thus that Sri Aurobindo became an established writer. He was forty-two. Typically, he had decided nothing for himself; it was "outer" circumstances that had launched him on this path.

For six years without interruption, right up to 1920, Sri Aurobindo published in one breath almost the whole of his written work, nearly five thousand pages. But he wrote in a strange way; it was not one book after another, but four and even six books at a time that he wrote, on the most varied subjects, like *The Life Divine*, his fundamental "philosophic" work and his spiritual vision of evolution; *The Synthesis of Yoga*, where he describes the stages and experiences of the integral yoga with a survey of all the yogic disciplines, past or present; the *Essays on the Gita* expounding his philosophy of action, *The Secret of the Veda* with a study on the origins of language, *The Ideal of Human Unity* and *The Human Cycle*, which envisage evolution under its sociological and psychological aspect and examine the future possibilities of human societies. He had found

The single sign interpreting every sign.[6]

Day after day, quietly, Sri Aurobindo filled his pages; any one else would have been fagged out but he did not "think" out what he was writing: *I have made no endeavour in writing*, he explains to a disciple, *I have simply left the higher Power to work and when it did not work, I made no effort at all. It was*

*in the old intellectual days that I had sometimes tried to force things
and not after I started development of poetry and prose by Yoga. Let
me remind you also that when I was writing the* Arya *and also
whenever I write these letters or replies, I never think... it is out of
a silent mind that I write whatever comes ready-shaped from above.*[7]
Often his disciples, writers and poets, used to ask him for
explanations of the yogic process of creation, and he did
not fail to explain to them fully the method, knowing that
creative activities are a powerful means of pushing back
the superconscient line and precipitating into Matter the
luminous possibilities of the future. Some of his letters are
very instructive: *The best relief for the brain,* he writes to
one of them, *is when the thinking takes place outside the body and
above the head (or in space or at other levels but still outside the
body). At any rate it was so in my case ; for as soon as that happened there was an immense relief ; I have felt body strain since then
but never any kind of brain fatigue.*[8] We must understand
that "thinking outside the body" is not at all a supramental phenomenon but a very simple experience which can
occur from the beginning of mental silence. The true process, according to Sri Aurobindo, is to reach an effortless-
ness, to efface oneself as completely as possible and let the
current pass: *There are two ways of arriving at the Grand Trunk
Road. One is to climb and struggle and effortise (like the pilgrim
who traverses India prostrating and measuring the way with his
body : that is the way of effort). One day you suddenly find yourself
on the G.T.R. when you least expect it. The other is to quiet the
mind to such a point that a greater Mind can speak through it (I
am not here talking of the Supramental).*[9] But, asked a disciple,
if it is not our mind which thinks, if thoughts come from
outside, how is it there is such a great difference between
the thought of one person and another? — *First of all,* replied Sri Aurobindo, *these thought-waves, thought-seeds or*

*thought-forms or whatever they are, are of different values and come
from different planes of consciousness. And the same thought substance can take higher or lower vibrations according to the plane of
consciousness through which the thoughts come in (e.g. thinking mind,
vital mind, physical mind, subconscient mind) or the power of consciousness which catches them and pushes them into one man or another. Moreover there is a stuff of mind in each man and the incom-
ing thought uses that for shaping itself or translating itself (transcribing we usually call it), but the stuff is finer or coarser, stronger
or weaker, etc., etc., in one mind than in another. Also there is a
mind-energy actual or potential in each which differs and this mind-
energy in its recipience of the thought can be luminous or obscure,
sattwic (serene), rajasic (impassioned) or tamasic (inert) with consequences which vary in each case.*[10] And Sri Aurobindo added:
*The intellect is an absurdly overactive part of the nature; it always
thinks that nothing can be well done unless it puts its finger into the
pie and therefore it instinctively interferes with the inspiration,
blocks half or more than half of it and labours to substitute its own
inferior and toilsome productions for the true speech and rhythm that
ought to have come. The poet labours in anguish to get the one true
word, the authentic rhythm, the real divine substance of what he has
to say, while all the time it is waiting complete and ready behind.*[11]
But the effort exists, protested the disciple again, and by
dint of beating one's brains, the inspiration comes: *Exactly!
When any real effect is produced, it is not because of the beating
and the hammering, but because an inspiration slips down between
the raising of the hammer and the falling and gets in under cover of
the beastly noise.*[12] After having written so many books for
his disciples, Sri Aurobindo said that the only utility of
books and philosophies was not truly to enlighten the mind
but to bring it to silence so that, calmed, it could pass to
the experience and receive the direct inspiration. And he
summed up the place of the mind on the evolutionary lad-

der thus: *Mind is a clumsy interlude between Nature's vast and precise subconscient action and the vaster infallible superconscient action of the Godhead. There is nothing mind can do that cannot be better done in the mind's immobility and thought-free stillness.*[13]

At the end of six years, in 1920, Sri Aurobindo felt that he had said enough for the moment. It was the end of the *Arya*. The rest of his life as a writer was to be almost exclusively devoted to his enormous correspondence — thousands and thousands of letters containing all kinds of practical hints on yogic experiences, difficulties, progress — and, above all, he was to write and rewrite for thirty years that prodigious epic of 23,813 lines, *Savitri*, like a fifth Veda, his most vivid message, where he speaks of the experience of the higher and lower worlds, his battles in the Subconscient and Inconscient and of the whole occult history of terrestrial and universal evolution including his vision of the future:

> *Interpreting the universe by soul signs*
> *He read from within the text of the without.*[14]

The Mother

Sri Aurobindo had not come only to write, he had something to do. It was in 1920 that he stopped the *Arya*, the year the Mother came to stay in Pondicherry. *When I came to Pondicherry*, Sri Aurobindo once told his early disciples, *a programme was dictated to me from within for my sadhana (discipline). I followed it and progressed for myself but could not do much by way of helping others. Then came the Mother and with her help I found the necessary method.*[15]

We can scarcely speak of the Mother, undoubtedly be-

cause a personality like hers suffers ill that it be enclosed in a small story — she is a Force in movement. All that has happened but yesterday, all that has been said, done, experimented only the previous evening, is already old for her, uninteresting. She is always ahead, always in front. She has been born to *break the limits*, like Savitri. It would then be hardly fair to imprison her in a record. Just let us say simply that she was born in Paris on the 21st February, 1878 and that she also had, on her side, the supramental vision. It is not surprising that with this consciousness she knew of the existence of Sri Aurobindo long before meeting him physically and her coming to join him. *Between eleven and thirteen*, she says, *a series of psychic and spiritual experiences revealed to me not only the existence of God but man's possibility of meeting with Him or revealing Him integrally in consciousness and action, of manifesting Him upon earth in a life divine. This along with a practical discipline for its fulfilment was given to me, during my body's sleep, by several teachers some of whom I met afterwards on the physical plane. Later on, as the interior and exterior development proceeded, the spiritual and psychic relation with one of these beings became more and more clear and pregnant.... The moment I saw Sri Aurobindo, I knew that it was he who had come to do the work on earth and that it was with him I had to work.* The "transformation" was to begin. It was the Mother who took up the charge of the Ashram when Sri Aurobindo retired into solitude in 1926, it is she who continues the Work since his departure in 1950. *The Mother's consciousness and mine are the same.*[16] It is very symbolic that the living synthesis between East and West, which Sri Aurobindo already represented, is completed by this new meeting of West and East, as though the world indeed could only be fulfilled by the junction of these two poles of existence, Consciousness and Force, the Spirit and the Earth, He and She always.

An Outline of Evolution

We are all, one day or another, called to join the work of transformation to which Sri Aurobindo and the Mother have devoted themselves, because this is our evolutionary future. If we wish to understand the process exactly, the difficulties, the possibilities of failure or success, we must first understand the meaning of our own evolution, so as to be able to participate actively in it, instead of letting the centuries and millenniums do the work for us through interminable meanders. Sri Aurobindo is not interested in theories, his vision of evolution rests essentially upon an experience, and if he has attempted to formulate it in terms which may seem to us theoretical because we do not have the experience (not yet), it is not to make us share in one more idea among the millions of current idea-forces but to help us get hold of the lever of our *own* dynamism and precipitate the course of evolution. No doubt the present state of humanity is scarcely worth one's lingering there.

This lever is *Agni*, the consciousness-force, and the whole of evolution may be described as a voyage of *Agni* in four movements — involution, devolution, involution, evolution — starting from the eternal Centre and in Him. In fact, the fourfold movement is He. All is He. *Himself the play, Himself the player, Himself the playground.*[17] He outside time, outside space, pure Being, pure Consciousness, the great white Silence where all is in a state of *involution*, contained, yet formless. And He who becomes: the Force separates from the Consciousness, She from Him, the voyage of *Agni* begins:

> ...*scattered on sealed depths, her luminous smile*
> *Kindled to fire the silence of the worlds.*[18]

She flings herself forth from Him in an outburst of joy, to play at finding Him again in Time — He and She, two in one. *What then was the commencement of the whole matter? Existence that multiplied itself for sheer delight of being and plunged into numberless trillions of forms so that it might find itself innumerably.*[19] But it is a perpetual beginning, which is not anywhere in Time; when we say "first" the Eternal, "then" the Becoming, we fall into the illusion of spatio-temporal language, as even when we say "high" and "low"; our language is false, like our vision of the world. In reality, Being and Becoming, He and She are two *simultaneous* faces of the same eternal FACT — the universe is a perpetual phenomenon, as perpetual as the Silence beyond time: *In the beginning, it is said, was the Eternal, the Infinite, the One. In the middle, it is said, is the finite, the transient, the Many. In the end, it is said, shall be the One, the Infinite, the Eternal. For when was the beginning? At no moment in Time, for the beginning is at every moment; the beginning always was, always is and always shall be. The divine beginning is before Time, in Time and beyond Time for ever. The Eternal, Infinite and One is an endless beginning. And where is the middle? There is no middle; for there is only the junction of the perpetual end and the eternal beginning; it is the sign of a creation which is new at every moment. The creation was for ever, shall be for ever. The Eternal, Infinite and One is the magical middle-term of his own existence; it is he that is the beginningless and endless creation. And when is the end? There is no end. At no conceivable moment can there be a cessation. For all end of things is the beginning of new things which are still the same One in an ever developing and ever recurring figure. Nothing can be destroyed, for all is He who is forever. The Eternal, Infinite and One is the unimaginable end that is never closing upon new interminable vistas of his glory.*[20] And Sri Aurobindo said again: *The experiment of human life on an earth is not now for the first time enacted. It has been conducted a million times before and the long drama will again a million times be repeated. In all that we do now, our dreams, our discoveries, our swift or difficult attainments, we profit subconsciously by the experience of innumerable precursors and our labour will be fecund in planets unknown to us and in worlds yet uncreated. The plan, the peripetia, the dénouement differ continually, yet are always governed by the conventions of an eternal Art. God, Man, Nature are the three perpetual symbols. The idea of eternal recurrence affects with a shudder of alarm the mind entrenched in the minute, the hour, the years, the centuries, all the finite's unreal defences. But the strong soul conscious of its own immortal stuff and the inexhaustible ocean of its ever-flowing energies is seized by it with the thrill of an inconceivable rapture. It hears behind the thought the childlike laughter and ecstasy of the Infinite.*[21]

This perpetual passage from Being to Becoming is what Sri Aurobindo calls *devolution*. It is a gradual passage. The supreme Consciousness does not at one go become Matter. Matter is the final precipitate, the ultimate product of an incessant fragmentation or "densification" of consciousness, which is worked out slowly through successive planes. At the "summit" of this devolutive curve — but it is not a summit, it is a supreme Point which is everywhere — the supramental Consciousness-Force contains gathered together all the infinite possibilities of the Becoming, in a single Gaze, as the solar Fire contains all the rays gathered in its centre: "They unyoked the horses of the Sun," says the Rig Veda, "the ten hundreds stood together, there was that One, *tad ekam*" (V.62.1). Then the Overmind opens, the "great cleavage" of consciousness begins: the rays of the Sun separate, the single Consciousness-Force is henceforth loosed in trillions of forces each of which will seek to realise itself absolutely. Once started off, the Play will not stop until all the possibilities have been realised, including those which seem the very opposite of the eternal Player. The Force is thrown out in an ever more rapid passion as though She wished to burst forth up to her utmost confines to seize herself ever farther and replace the One by an impossible number. And the consciousness scatters itself. It will go on fragmenting itself more and more, thickening, obscuring itself, depositing itself in successive strata or in worlds, with their beings and forces, their particular mode of life; all the traditions witness this; we too may see in our sleep or with eyes wide open, when the eye of vision is unsealed in us. From the gods to the symbolic gnomes, the consciousness dwindles, crumbles, is pulverised — overmind, intuitive mind, illumined mind, higher mind, then the mind, vital and subtle physical — more and more does it get glued down in its force, captured, dispersed, confused in small instincts moment by moment, in little tropisms so as to live, right up to its final scattering in Matter where all is fragmented: "In the beginning," says the Veda, "darkness was hidden by darkness, all this was one ocean of inconscience. Universal being was concealed by fragmentation" (X.129.1-5). The devolution is complete, it is the *plunge of Light into its own shadow*,[22] Matter.

And here we are before two poles. At the summit, a supreme Negative (or Positive, as we please), where the Force is as if swallowed up in a Nought of Light, a gulf of unruffled peace, where all is contained in itself, already there, without its needing the least quiver in order to be — IT IS. At the other pole, a supreme Positive (or Negative if we like), where the Consciousness is as though engulfed in a shadowy Nothingness, an abyss of blind

Force for ever imprisoned in its own dark whirling — it becomes, inexorably, unceasingly. The first duality arises, whence all the others derive: the One and the Innumerable, the Infinite and the Finite, Consciousness and Force, Spirit and Matter, the Formless and a delirium of forms — He and She. And all our existence ebbs and flows between the one pole and the other, some wanting to see only the Transcendent which they call the supreme Positive, and rejecting Matter as a sort of provisional falsehood whilst awaiting the Great Return (but where is the place of the Return? the return is at every point! above and below, to the right and the left); others swearing only by Matter which they call the supreme Positive and rejecting Spirit as a definite and negative falsehood, because in accordance with the logic of man the more cannot be the less or the less the more. But this is an illusion. Consciousness does not abolish Force, nor Matter the Spirit, nor the Infinite the finite, any more than the top annuls the bottom — it *is* the bottom, which is down below only for us, and each extreme conceals its eternal Companion: *In the world as we see it, for our mental consciousness however high we carry it, we find that to every positive there is a negative. But the negative is not a zero, — indeed whatever appears to us a zero is packed with force, teeming with power of existence.... Neither does the existence of the negative make its corresponding positive non-existent or an unreality; it only makes the positive an incomplete statement of the truth of things and even, we may say, of the positive's own truth. For the positive and the negative exist not only side by side, but in relation to each other and by each other; they complete and would to the all-view, which a limited mind cannot reach, explain one another. Each by itself is not really known; we only begin to know it in its deeper truth when we can read into it the suggestions of its apparent opposite.*[23] On the summits

She is as if asleep in Him, in the depths He is as if asleep in Her, Force dissolved in Consciousness or Consciousness in Force, the Infinite contained in the finite as the tree and all its branches are in the seed. This is what Sri Aurobindo calls "the involution": *The nescience of Matter is a veiled, an involved or somnambulist consciousness which contains all the latent powers of the Spirit. In every particle, atom, molecule, cell of Matter there lives hidden and works unknown all the omniscience of the Eternal and all the omnipotence of the Infinite.*[24] The involution above is completed by a new involution below where in everything is contained, latent in the Night, as all was contained latent in the Light above. *Agni* is there "like a warm golden dust", "*Agni* has entered earth and heaven as if they were one," says the Rig Veda (III.7.4). *In a sense, the whole of creation may be said to be a movement between two involutions, Spirit in which all is involved and out of which all evolves downward (or devolves) to the other pole of Matter, Matter in which also all is involved and out of which all evolves upwards to the other pole of Spirit.*[25]

Without this involution, no evolution would be possible, and how could something come out of nothing? For an evolution to take place, there must be something within pushing up! *Nothing can evolve out of Matter which is not therein already contained.*[26] But at the depth of this dumb stupor which awakens, behind the evolutionary explosion of forms, it is *Agni* which pushes and goads, the Force in quest of the Consciousness, She is in search of Him and of forms more and more capable of manifesting Him, She who comes out of her inconscient Night and gropes with her millions of works and millions of species as if to rediscover everywhere the beauty of the one lost Form, innumerably the Joy which was one — *a million-bodied beati-*

tude[27] instead of a white ecstasy. And if we have that "ear of ears" of which the Veda speaks, perhaps we shall hear everywhere this cry of the Night towards the Light, of the walled-in Consciousness towards Joy, *the deep spiritual cry in all that is*[28] — it is this that pushes up from the depths, it is a Fire within, a flame in Matter, a flame in Life, a flame in our Mind, a flame in our soul. It is this Fire which must be seized, it is this the thread and the lever, the secret evolutionary tension, the soul and the flame of the world. If this world were only made of lifeless and inert stone, it would never become anything but a lifeless and inert stone; if the soul were not already in Matter, it could never emerge in man: *But what after all, behind appearances, is this seeming mystery? we can see that it is the Consciousness which had lost itself returning to itself, emerging out of its giant self-forgetfulness, slowly, painfully, as a Life that is would-be sentient, half-sentient, dimly sentient, wholly sentient and finally struggles to be more than sentient, to be again divinely self-conscious, free, infinite, immortal.*[29]

Until the day She arrives at man, her conscious instrument in whom, through whom She is going to be able to find Him: *Our humanity is the conscious meeting-place of the finite and the infinite and to grow more and more towards the Infinite even in this physical birth is our privilege.*[30] But a special phenomenon occurs at the human stage of the journey of *Agni*. At the preceding stages the evolutionary flame seems to subside of itself as soon as the stability of the new emergence is assured; the profusion of plant-life seems to subside when the animal type is solidly fixed in Life, as the teeming of animal species seems to subside when the human type is definitively fixed in the evolution — it does not seem that Nature has created any new animal or vegetable species since man has occupied the evolutionary crest. In other words, the species have become stationary; they have attained a certain perfection, each in its order, and do not move from there. Now, with man, the evolutionary tension has not subsided, though his type has been solidly established in evolution; he is not complete, not satisfied as are the other species, he has not the harmony, the joy of the acquired equilibrium: *Man is an abnormal who has not found his own normality, — he may imagine he has, he may appear to be normal in his own kind, but that normality is only a sort of provisional order ; therefore, though man is infinitely greater than the plant or animal, he is not perfect in his own nature like the plant and the animal.*[31]

This imperfection must not at all be deplored, says Sri Aurobindo, it is on the contrary *a privilege and a promise ;*[31] if we were perfect and harmonious in our kind, without sin and without error, we would be already a stationary species, like the batrachians and the molluscs. But in us who reproduce the great cosmic Play, the force has not yet found its consciousness, nor our nature its spirit, She has not found Him — was there ever a Plato satisfied, a Michael Angelo pacified? "One night I took Beauty upon my knees and I found her bitter!" cried out Rimbaud. And this is also a sign that the summit of mental intelligence or of aesthetic refinement is not the end of the journey, not the plenitude, not the great Equilibrium of Her who has found Him again. That spirit within which awakens and grows — He in Her, — that little flame at the centre clings at first to minute fragments, to molecules, to genes, to the protoplasm; it organises itself psychologically around a separate and fragmentary ego; it sees dimly and gropes; it too is doubly "involved", and sees only through a thin mental slit between an enormous subconscience and a formidable superconscience. It is this childish fragmen-

tation, for it belongs to our human childhood, which is the
cause of all our errors, all our suffering — there is no
other "sin"; all our evil comes of this narrowness of vision,
which is a false vision of ourselves and the world. For in
truth the world and each cell of our body is *Sat-chit-ananda*,
is Existence-Consciousness-Beatitude — we are light and
joy. *Our sense by its incapacity has invented darkness. In truth
there is nothing but Light, only it is a power of light either above or
below our poor human vision's limited range.*[32] And all is joy:
"For who could live or breathe if there were not this delight of existence as the ether in which we dwell?" says
the Upanishad.* It is our weakness of vision which hides
from us *the happiness absolute in the heart of things,*[33] it is *our
pallid sense,*[34] too immature, which does not yet know how to
contain all that immensity — the Spirit in us has not yet
finished discovering itself, the journey of *Agni* is not over.
Man, says Sri Aurobindo, is not the last term of the evolution, he is *a transitional being.*[35] *We speak of the evolution of
Life in Matter, the evolution of Mind in Matter; but evolution
is a word which merely states the phenomenon without explaining
it. For there seems to be no reason why Life should evolve out of
material elements or Mind out of living form, unless we accept...
that Life is already involved in Matter and Mind in Life because
in essence Matter is a form of veiled Life, Life a form of veiled
Consciousness. And then there seems to be little objection to a farther step in the series and the admission that mental consciousness
may itself be only a form and a veil of higher states which are beyond Mind. In that case, the unconquerable impulse of man towards
God, Light, Bliss, Freedom, Immortality presents itself in its right
place in the chain as simply the imperative impulse by which Nature
is seeking to evolve beyond Mind, and appears to be as natural, true*

* Taittiriya Upanishad II.7.

and just as the impulse towards Life which she has planted in forms of Matter or the impulse towards Mind which she has planted in certain forms of Life.... The animal is a living laboratory in which Nature has, it is said, worked out man. Man himself may well be a thinking and living laboratory in whom and with whose conscious cooperation she wills to work out the superman, the god. Or shall we not say, rather, to manifest God?[36] If evolution manages this difficult passage, the great Equilibrium will be reached, we shall enter "the vast home" (Rig Veda V. 68.5); the Force will have found again all its Consciousness instead of turning round without knowledge and the Consciousness all its Force instead of understanding and loving without power.

But the rishis also knew that the journey was not over; they said that *Agni* "conceals his two extremities", that he is "without head and without feet" (Rig Veda IV.1.7,11); we are a little brief flame between the superconscient *Agni* of the heavens and the subconscient *Agni* of the earth, and we suffer, we turn and toss upon our bed of misery, one in search of his heaven, another in search of his earth, without ever joining the two ends; another race is to be born among us, a complete Man, if only we would give our consent: "Weave an inviolate work, become the human being, create the divine race.... Seers of Truth are you, sharpen the shining spears with which you cut the way to that which is Immortal; knowers of the secret planes, form them, the steps by which the gods attained to immortality" (X.53). Then we shall find again our solar wholeness, our two hidden extremities, our two Mothers in one alone: "O Flame, O *Agni*, thou goest to the ocean of Heaven, towards the gods; thou makest to meet together the godheads of the planes, the waters that are in the realm of light above the sun and the waters that abide below"

(III.22.3). Then shall we have the joy of the two worlds and of all the worlds, *Ananda*, of the earth and the heavens as though they were One: "O Flame, thou foundest the mortal in a supreme immortality... for the seer who has thirst for the dual birth, thou createst divine bliss and human joy" (1.31.7). For this is the goal of our evolution, finally — joy. One speaks of love, but is there a word more faked — by our sentimentalities, our sects, our Churches? — whilst that joy, nobody can imitate that! it is a child laughing in the sun, and it loves, it would whirl along everything in its dance. Joy, yes, if we have the courage to want it: *The laurel and not the cross should be the aim of the conquering human soul*[37] — but *men are still in love with grief.... Therefore Christ still hangs on the cross in Jerusalem.*[38] The joy of being and being fully, in all that is, has been, will be, down here, elsewhere, everywhere, *as if honey could taste itself and all its drops together and all its drops could taste each other and each the whole honeycomb.*[39] Then the evolution will emerge from the Night to enter the cycle of the Sun; we shall live under the sign of the One; the god crucified in us will descend from his cross and man will at last be Himself, normal. For to be normal is to be divine. *There are only two spontaneous harmonic movements, that of the life, inconscient or largely subconscient, the harmony that we find in the animal creation and in the lower Nature, and that of the spirit. The human condition is a stage of transition, effort and imperfection between the one and the other, between the natural and the ideal or spiritual life.*[40]*

---

* It is interesting to note that the serpent of the earthly paradise, according to the Mother, would be the symbol of the evolutionary force which impelled men to come out of the state of animal happiness and to find the state of divine happiness by eating the fruit of knowledge and developing their mental capacity right up to its point of reversal. In Greece also it is the plumed serpents which draw the chariot of Demeter. The serpent is not only a symbol of cosmic evolution but also the symbol of the individual

CHAPTER SEVENTEEN

THE TRANSFORMATION

The emergence of the Spirit in a supramental consciousness and a new body, a new race, is a phenomenon as
inevitable as the appearance of homo sapiens after that of
the primates. The only question in truth is to know if this
new evolution will come about with or without us. This
is how Sri Aurobindo formulates the dilemma: *If a spiritual
unfolding on earth is the hidden truth of our birth into Matter, if it
is fundamentally an evolution of consciousness that has been taking
place in Nature, then man as he is cannot be the last term of that
evolution: he is too imperfect an expression of the spirit, mind itself
a too limited form and instrumentation; mind is only a middle term
of consciousness, the mental being can only be a transitional being.
If, then, man is incapable of exceeding mentality, he must be surpassed and supermind and superman must manifest and take the lead of
the creation. But if his mind is capable of opening to what exceeds
it, then there is no reason why man himself should not arrive at
supermind and supermanhood or at least lend his mentality, life
and body to an evolution of that greater term of the Spirit manifesting in Nature.*[1] We have reached, says Sri Aurobindo,

evolutionary force: when the ascending force (*kundalini*) awakes at the
base of the vertebral column and comes out of our physical consciousness
where it was asleep, coiled like a serpent in its hole (*kundalini* means "the
coiled one") and when it rises from centre to centre, the evolved man
emerges from the ordinary inconscience and enters a cosmic consciousness,
then with the opening at the top of the head, the divine solar consciousness. For Sri Aurobindo and the rishis and probably other wisdoms
which have disappeared, the discovery of this solar consciousness above
was only a first evolutionary stage which had to be followed by the
discovery of the same solar consciousness down here, in Matter. This is the
serpent that bites its own tail or what Sri Aurobindo calls the *transformation*.

a new *crisis of transformation*[2] as crucial as must have been the crisis which marked the appearance of Life in Matter or the crisis which marked the appearance of Mind in Life. And our choice is crucial also, for this time, instead of letting Nature work out her transmutations without caring much for living contingencies, we can be the "conscious collaborators of our own evolution", accept the challenge or, as Sri Aurobindo says, let ourselves be surpassed.

Future Prospects

What will this new race be like? To understand the aim is already a great stage on the way of transformation, for however faintly we understand and aspire for this Future, we open an invisible door through which forces greater than ours can enter and we begin to collaborate. In truth, it is not our human forces which will work out this passage to the supermind but a more and more conscious surrender to the Force from above.

We have already said in what the consciousness of the supramental being lies, but it would not be too much to repeat with Sri Aurobindo that *supermanhood is not man climbed to his own natural zenith, not a superior degree of human greatness, knowledge, power, intelligence, will, character, genius, dynamic force, saintliness, love, purity or perfection. Supermind is something beyond mental man and his limits.*[3] Pushed to the extreme, Mind can only harden man, not divinise him or even simply give him joy, for it is an instrument of division and all its hierarchies rest inevitably on force, whether they be religious, moral, political, economic or sentimental, for it is constitutionally incapable of admitting the totality of

human truths. And even when it is capable of admitting this, it is incapable of realising it. And if truly collective evolution has nothing better to offer us than an agreeable mixture of human and social "greatness," Saint Vincent de Paul and Mahatma Gandhi, with a smattering of Marxism-Leninism and of organised leisures, we cannot help thinking that it is an end more insipid than the "millions of golden birds" or the String Quartets of the summits of individual mental evolution. *Pralaya* or the cosmic dissolution the old traditions have promised us would perhaps not be so bad after all, if so many millenniums of suffering and effort have for their sole outcome this sort of kermess on the earth.

If our mental conditions are insufficient, even at their zenith, our vital and physical conditions are still more so. It is doubtful whether the Spirit, when it manifests itself in a supramental consciousness, will be satisfied with a body subject to our physical laws of disintegration and gravity and whether it will accept as its only means of expression the limited possibilities of mental language, of pen or burin or brush. In other words, Matter will have to change. This is the object of the "Transformation". And first of all our first matter, the body: *In the spiritual tradition the body has been regarded as an obstacle, incapable of spiritualisation or transmutation and a heavy weight holding the soul to earthly nature and preventing its ascent either to spiritual fulfilment in the Supreme or to the dissolution of its individual being in the Supreme. But while this conception of the role of the body in our destiny is suitable enough for a sadhana [discipline] that sees earth only as a field of the ignorance and earth-life as a preparation for a saving withdrawal... it is insufficient for a sadhana which conceives of a divine life upon earth and liberation of earth-nature itself as part of a total purpose of the embodiment of the spirit here. If a*

total transformation of the being is our aim, a transformation of the
body must be an indispensable part of it ; without that no full divine
life on earth is possible.[4]

According to Sri Aurobindo the essential characteristic
of supramentalised Matter is receptivity; it will be capable
of responding to the conscious will and modelling itself at
its order as clay responds to the fingers of the potter. Matter, releasing the spiritual power it contains involved and
becoming openly conscious, will be capable of answering
corresponding vibrations of the supramental consciousness,
just as we answer a vibration of anger by anger or a vibration of love with a warmth of the heart. Conscious mallea-
bility will be the fundamental property of supramentalised
Matter. All the other qualities derive from this fundamental
property: immortality or at least the power to modify
the form and even to change the form at will, lightness,
beauty, luminosity. These will be the natural attributes
of supramental Matter. *The body could become a revealing*
vessel of a supreme beauty and bliss, — casting the beauty of
the light of the spirit suffusing and radiating from it as a lamp
reflects and diffuses the luminosity of its indwelling flame, carrying
in itself the beatitude of the spirit, its joy of the seeing mind, its
joy of life and spiritual happiness, the joy of Matter released into a
spiritual consciousness and thrilled with a constant ecstasy.[5] But
have not the Vedas already said: "Then shall thy humanity become as if the workings of the gods; it is as if the
visible heaven of light were founded in thee"(Rig Veda
V.66.2)?

Before these spectacular changes which probably will
be the last to be manifested, Sri Aurobindo envisages a
considerable change in our physiology; we shall come
back to this when speaking of the practical work of transformation; for the moment it is enough to mention some

functional modifications as Sri Aurobindo observed them in his own body: *There would have to be a change in the operative processes of the material organs themselves and, it may well be, in their very constitution and their importance; they could not be allowed to impose their limitations imperatively on the new physical life.... The brain would be a channel of communication of the form of the thoughts and a battery of their insistence on the body and the outside world where they could then become effective directly, communicating themselves without physical means from mind to mind, producing with a similar directness effects on the thoughts, actions and lives of others or even upon material things. The heart would equally be a direct communicant and medium of interchange for the feelings and emotions thrown outward upon the world by the forces of the psychic centre. Heart could reply directly to heart, the life-force come to the help of other lives and answer their call in spite of strangeness and distance, many beings without any external communication thrill with the message and meet in the secret light from one divine centre. The will might control the organs that deal with food, safeguard automatically the health, eliminate greed and desire, substitute subtler processes or draw in strength and substance from the universal life-force so that the body could maintain for a long time its own strength and substance without loss or waste, remaining thus with no need of sustenance by material aliments, and yet continue a strenuous action with no fatigue or pause for sleep or repose. ...Conceivably, one might rediscover and re-establish at the summit of the evolution of life the phenomenon we see at its base, the power to draw from all around it the means of sustenance and self-renewal.*[6] Beyond the Mind the complete man consciously finds once again what Matter already represents unconsciously: Energy and Peace; so true is it that Matter is only a sleep of the Spirit.

At a later stage of the transformation, Sri Aurobindo envisages the replacing of the organs by a dynamic func-

tioning of our centres of consciousness or *chakras*. Herein
is the true passage from the animal-man as conceived by
the lower evolution to the human-man of the new evolution. This is one of the tasks undertaken by Sri Aurobindo
and the Mother. From the earliest stages of the yoga we
have found that each one of our activities, from the highest
to the most material, was nourished or set going by a current of consciousness-force which seemed to branch off at
different levels, to different centres, with different vibrations according to the kind of activity and, if we have tried
ever so little to manipulate this current, we have found that
it is a source of formidable energy, limited only by the
smallness of our capacity. It is then not inconceivable that
our organs which are only the physical translation or the
material concentration of this current behind may in the
course of the evolution give place to the direct action of
the centres of consciousness which will irradiate their energies through the new body, as today the heart, the blood,
the nerves radiate through our body. This is how, one day,
the Mother explained the future body to the children of
the Ashram: *Transformation implies that all this purely material
arrangement will be replaced by concentrations of force, each having
a different mode of vibration; instead of organs there will be centres
of conscious energy moved by the conscious will. No stomach, no
heart any longer, no circulation, no lungs; all this disappears and
gives place to a play of vibrations representing what these organs
are symbolically. For the organs are only the material symbols of
centres of energy; they are not the essential reality: simply, they
give it a form or a support in certain given circumstances.
The transformed body will then function through its* real
*centres of energy and not any longer through their symbolic
representatives such as were developed in the animal body. First
then you must know what your heart represents in the cosmic energy,*

what your circulation, your brain, your lungs represent in the cosmic energy, then you must be able to have at your disposal the original vibrations of which the organs are the symbols, and you must slowly gather together all these energies in your body and change each organ into a centre of conscious energy which will replace the symbolic movement by the real one. For example, behind the symbolic movement of the lungs, there is a true movement which gives you the capacity of lightness and you escape the laws of gravitation.* And so for each organ. There is a true movement behind every symbolic one. This does not mean that there will no longer be any recognisable forms; the form will be built by qualities rather than by solid particles. It will be, if one may say so, a practical or pragmatic form: it will be supple, mobile, light at will in contrast to the present fixity of the gross material form.... And Matter will become a divine expression; the supramental Will shall translate the whole gamut of its inner life into corresponding modifications of its own substance, even as today our face changes (however slightly and however badly) under the impact of our emotions: the body will be made of *concentrated energy which obeys the will.* Instead of being "a little soul carrying a corpse"† in the powerful words of Epictetus, we shall be living souls in a living body.

Not only will the body and mind have to change with the supramental consciousness but the very substance of life. If there is one characteristic sign of our mental civilisation it is artifice; nothing happens there naturally, we are prisoners of a formidable trickery — aeroplane,

---

* This true movement behind respiration is the same as the one which governs the electric and magnetic fields, according to Sri Aurobindo; it is what the ancient yogis called *vayu,* the Life-Energy. The well-known respiratory exercises (*pranayama*) are simply one system (among others) to acquire the mastery of *vayu,* which eventually allows one to escape gravitation.

† Quoted by Sri Aurobindo.

telephone, television and all the plethora of instruments
which paint our poverty — and we relinquish even all our
natural capacities which get atrophied from generation to
generation through laziness or ignorance. We forget a
very simple fundamental truth, that our marvellous
inventions are only the material projections of powers
which exist in us — if they were not already there in us
we would never be able to invent them. We are this
thaumaturge sceptic of miracles[7] of whom Sri Aurobindo
speaks. Having delegated to the machine the business
of seeing for us, hearing for us, travelling for us, we can
no longer do without it; our human civilisation, made for
the joy of life, has become the slave of the means needed to
enjoy life — sixty per cent of our lifetime passes in the
acquisition of the means and thirty per cent in sleeping.
The absurdity here, says the Mother, *is all the artificial means
to which one must have recourse. Any idiot you know has more
power if he has the means of acquiring the necessary devices.
But in the true world, a supramental world, the more conscious
one is and in harmony with the truth of things, the more authority
has the will over the substance, and the substance obeys the will.
There authority is a true authority. If you want a dress you must
have the power to make it, a real power. If you do not have this
power, well, you go naked! There is no artifice there to make
up for the want of power. Here, not once in a million times
is authority the expression of something true. Everything is utterly
stupid.* This supramental "authority" is not a sort of
super-prestidigitation, far from it; it is an extremely
exact process, as exact and detailed as may be a chemical
experiment; only instead of manipulating external bodies,
the supramental being manipulates the true vibration that
is at the centre of each thing and links it with other
vibrations to obtain the required result, somewhat as the

artist mixes colours to make a picture or as the poet strings together sounds for a poem. And he is truly a poet, for he creates what he names; the real name of an object is the vibration constituting it: to name an object means the power to evoke it or destroy it.

The spontaneity, the naturalness of the supramental life — for, finally, Truth alone is natural — will be expressed also in a supramental art, which will be the direct and unveiled representation of our particular spiritual tonality; an art where one cannot cheat because only our inner light will be able to play upon the same involved lights in Matter and draw out thence the corresponding forms. If our vibration is grey, our world will be grey and all we touch will be grey; our physical, external milieu will resemble our inner milieu, we shall be able to manifest only what we are. And life itself will be a work of art, our outer estates the changing scenes of our inner states. The word also will have power only through the true spiritual force in us, it will be a living *mantra*, a visible language like the tint of emotions on a face. And this will be the end of all the shams, political, religious, literary, artistic or sentimental. A sceptical disciple having once stated that the Supermind was an impossible invention, first because it had never been seen or "done", Sri Aurobindo replied with his characteristic humour: *What a wonderful argument! Since it has not been done, it can't be done! At that rate the whole history of the earth must have stopped long before the protoplasm. When it was a mass of gases, no life had been born,* ergo, *life could not be born — when only life was there, mind was not born, so mind could not be born. Since mind is there but nothing beyond, as there is no Supermind manifested in anybody, so Supermind can never be born.* Sobhanallah! *Glory, Glory, Glory to the human reason! Luckily the Divine or the Cosmic Spirit or Nature or whatever is there cares a damn for the human reason. He or She or It does what He or She or It has to do, whether it can or can't be done.*[8] Millenniums ago, the rishis spoke of the poverty of sceptics: "In these there is not the Wonder and the Might" (Rig Veda VII. 61.5).

The Work (First Phase)

Striking as the results will be, the work is modest, humble, patient, like that of the scientist before his culture test-tubes: *a microscopic work*, says the Mother. For it is not a matter of working fugitive miracles but of establishing a new physical basis by freeing from each atom, each cell the consciousness-force it contains. One would then think that this work on the body implies the use of psychophysical methods somewhat like those of hatha-yoga, but it is nothing of the kind. It is the consciousness which remains the central lever: *The change of consciousness will be the chief factor, the initial movement, the physical modification will be a subordinate factor, a consequence.*[9] And Śri Aurobindo puts us before the simple truth with his usual clarity: *In the previous stages of the evolution Nature's first care and effort had to be directed towards a change in the physical organisation, for only so could there be a change of consciousness; this was a necessity imposed by the insufficiency of the force of consciousness already in formation to effect a change in the body. But in man a reversal is possible, indeed inevitable; for it is through his consciousness, through its transmutation and no longer through a new bodily organism as a first instrumentation that the evolution can and must be effected. In the inner reality of things a change of consciousness was always a major fact, the evolution has always had a spirit-*

ual significance and the physical change was only instrumental ; but this relation was concealed by the first abnormal balance of the two factors, the body of the external Inconscience outweighing and obscuring in importance the spiritual element, the conscious being. But once the balance has been righted, it is no longer the change of body that must precede the change of consciousness ; the consciousness itself by its mutation will necessitate and operate whatever mutation is needed for the body.[10]

Three phases may be distinguished in the work of Sri Aurobindo and the Mother, corresponding to the progress of their discoveries, — three phases which seem to pass from the most brilliant to the most obscure, from the miraculous to a sober commonplaceness, from the individual cell to the earth. During the first phase we witness a verification of the powers of the consciousness; this is what some disciples have called "the bright period"; it was between 1920 and 1926, the year Sri Aurobindo retired into complete solitude for twenty-four years to concentrate exclusively on the Work. With the new power, the supramental, which they had discovered, Sri Aurobindo and the Mother tried out first of all a series of experiences on their own body — "testing" is one of the important words of Sri Aurobindo's vocabulary, as also the word "experiment": *I have been testing day and night for years upon years more scrupulously than any scientist his theory or his method on the physical plane.*[11] From this enormous mass of experiments, traces of which are found everywhere in the correspondence and the works of Sri Aurobindo, we may choose four symbolic facts illustrating the power of the consciousness and the "verifications" of Sri Aurobindo, keeping in mind that it is a question here of only a few details among hundreds of others and that neither Sri Aurobindo nor the Mother attached any particular importance to these; it is only from chance conversations or letters that we have ever known anything about them. First, hardly had he arrived in Pondicherry, when Sri Aurobido undertook a prolonged fast, "in order to see"; some years later, when a disciple happened to ask him whether it was possible to do without food, this is what he was told: *Yes, it is. When I once fasted for about 23 days or more.... I very nearly solved the problem. I could walk eight hours a day as usual. I continued my mental work and sadhana [discipline] as usual and I found that I was not in the least weak at the end of 23 days. But the flesh began to waste away and I did not find a clue to replacing the very material reduced in the body. When I broke the fast, I also did not observe the usual rule of people who observe long fasts, — by beginning with little food. I began with the same quantity I used to take before.... I tried fasting once in jail but that was for ten days when I used to sleep also once in three nights. I lost ten pounds in weight but I felt stronger at the end of ten days than I was before I began the fast... I was able to raise a pail of water above my head, a thing I could not do ordinarily.*[12] Another event goes back to the Alipore jail: *I was concentrated. And my mind was questioning : Were such siddhis [capacities] possible? when I suddenly found myself raised up... I could not have held my body like that normally even if I had wanted to and I found that the body remained suspended like that without any exertion on my part.*[13] Another time Sri Aurobindo had a considerable quantity of opium bought from the Pondicherry bazaar, enough to flatten out several people, and swallowed it all up at once without suffering any consequences, — to verify the control of the consciousness. We owe the fourth fact to the impatience of a disciple who complained that he had not received a quick enough answer to his letters: *You do not realise*, Sri Aurobindo replied, *that I have to spend 12 hours over the ordinary correspondence. I work 3 hours in the afternoon and the whole night up to*

6 in the morning over this... even the rocky heart of a disciple would be touched.[14]

Sleep, food, gravity, causes and effects, Sri Aurobindo verified one by one all the so-called laws of nature to find that they held only to the extent we believed they had a hold over us; if one changed the consciousness, the "groove" changed also. All our laws are only "habits": *Her firm and changeless habits aping Law,*[15] says *Savitri* of Nature, for there is but one true Law, that of the Spirit, which can modify all the lower habits of Nature: *The Spirit made it and the Spirit can exceed it, but we must first open the doors of our prison-house and learn to live less in Nature than in the Spirit.*[16] Sri Aurobindo has no miraculous recipes, no fantastic tricks; all along his yoga rests upon a double certitude which is very simple, the certitude of the Spirit which is in us and the certitude of the terrestrial manifestation of the Spirit — this is the only lever, the true lever of his work: *In each man there is a God and to make him manifest is the aim of the divine life. That we can all do.*[17] A certain disciple having argued that it was quite easy for exceptional beings like Sri Aurobindo and the Mother to defy the natural laws whilst poor common mortals had only their ordinary means, Sri Aurobindo protested very forcefully: *My sadhana [discipline] is not a freak or a monstrosity or a miracle done outside the laws of Nature and the conditions of life and consciousness on earth. If I could do these things or if they could happen in my Yoga, it means that they can be done and that therefore these developments and transformations are possible in the terrestrial consciousness.... I had no urge towards spirituality in me, I developed spirituality. I was incapable of understanding metaphysics, I developed into a philosopher. I had no eye for painting — I developed it by Yoga. I transformed my nature from what it was to what it was not. I did it by a special manner, not by a miracle and I did it to show what could be done and how it could be done. I did not do it out of any personal necessity of my own or by a miracle without any process. I say that if it is not so, then my Yoga is useless and my life was a mistake — a mere absurd freak of Nature without meaning or consequence.*[18] For Sri Aurobindo, the true key is to understand that Spirit is not the contrary of life but the plenitude of life, that *the inner realisation is the secret of an outer realisation*:

Heaven's touch fulfils but cancels not our earth.[19]

When humanity will have grasped this simple lever, when it has given up its age-old habit of confining the Spirit to the heavens and believing in death, believing in its laws, believing in its own smallness, we shall be safe and ready for the divine life. It is this that Sri Aurobindo has come to show us before everything else, — the *fact* that it is not necessary to run to the heavens to find the Spirit, the *fact* that we are free, the *fact* that we are stronger than all the laws, for God is in us. To believe, simply this. For it is faith that precipitates the fairyland of the world. *That was the thing that saved me all through, I mean a perfect balance. First of all I believed that nothing was impossible and at the same time I could question everything.*[20] When urged one day to resume his political struggle, Sri Aurobindo promptly replied that what was wanted was *not a revolt against the British Government, which anyone could easily manage... [but] a revolt against the whole universal Nature.*[21]

During this first phase, the few disciples — there were about fifteen — all agree in saying the prevailing atmosphere was very special, highly concentrated. They had marvellous experiences as if almost in play, there were divine manifestations, the natural laws seemed to yield a little; that is, the veil between the physical world and the other planes of consciousness had become very thin and beings called gods or forces of the overmind could manifest, act on the laws and bring about what are called miracles. If things had continued at this rate, Sri Aurobindo and the Mother would have been well on their way to founding a new religion and the Ashram to becoming one of those new "high places" where spiritual perfumes overlay more modest odours. One day, whilst the Mother was narrating to Sri Aurobindo one of the last unusual incidents, he remarked humorously: *Yes, it is very interesting, you will work miracles which will make us famous throughout the whole world, you will be able to turn earthly events topsyturvy, indeed* (Sri Aurobindo smiled) *it will be a grand success.* And he added: *But this is an overmind creation, it is not the highest truth. It is not success we want; we want to establish the supermind on the earth, to create a new world.* Half an hour later, everything was stopped: *I said nothing, not a word*, relates the Mother, *in half an hour I had undone everything, cut the connection between the gods and these disciples, demolished everything. For I knew that as long as this was there, it was so attractive (one saw astonishing things all the time) one would have been tempted to continue...I undid everything. And since that moment, we set out once again on other bases.*

This was the end of the first phase. Sri Aurobindo and the Mother had verified the power of consciousness and they had found that these "miracles with a method," or the intervention of higher powers of consciousness, only sugar the pill without affecting the essence. They are futile from the point of view of transformation of the world. The real problem, *the real thing*, as the Mother says, is not to modify Matter from outside by fugitive so-called supernatural interventions but to modify it from within, lastingly; to establish a new physical basis. Already in the past we have known many high places which have all failed; we have lived long enough under the sign of the gods and religions: *I have no intention of giving my sanction to a new edition of the old fiasco,* said Sri Aurobindo, *a partial and transient spiritual opening within with no true and radical change in the law of the external nature.*[22] Levitation, the conquest of sleep and hunger and even of illness only touch the surface of the problem, it is a negative work *against* an order of things, it means still recognising, though negatively, the old law, whilst it is the order itself which must change, good or bad as it may be, for that good goes necessarily with that bad. All miracles are only the wrong side or rather the "right" of our poverty. What is needed is not a better world but a new world, not a "highly concentrated" atmosphere but one concentrated "lowly", down below. And that everything down here may be the High Place.

Suddenly, on the 24th November, 1926 Sri Aurobindo announced that he would retire into a complete solitude; the Ashram was officially founded under the guidance of the Mother. The disciples had no need to be told that the yoga would henceforth be done "in the subconscient and Inconscient": all their splendid experiences came crashing down to make them try their strength against much harder realities. Thus opened the second phase of the work of transformation.

The Fundamental Agni

At the threshold of the second phase we find a rather strange conversation which Sri Aurobindo had in 1926, a little before his retirement, with a French scientist. The remarks made by Sri Aurobindo, which could then have appeared enigmatic, throw a very curious light on the orientation of his experiences. It was a question of "modern" science:

There are two statements of modern science that would stir up deeper ranges in an occultist:

˙1) Atoms are whirling systems like the solar system.

2) The atoms of all the elements are made out of the same cons-tituents. A different arrangement is the only cause of different properties.

If these statements were considered under their true aspect, they could lead science to new discoveries of which it has no idea at present and in comparison with which the present knowledge is poor. This was in 1926.

And Sri Aurobindo continued: *According to the experience of ancient Yogis... Agni is threefold:*

1) *ordinary fire,* jada Agni
2) *electric fire,* vaïdyuta Agni
3) *solar fire,* saura Agni

Science has only entered upon the first and second of these fires. The fact that the atom is like the solar system could lead it to the knowledge of the third.[23]

What was Sri Aurobindo hinting at, and first, how was it that he had been able to know before all our laboratories (not to consider the rishis of six thousand years ago) that the solar heat — Saura Agni — had a different origin from what we call fire or electricity, that it is produced by nuclear fusion and the power of solar energy resembles that enclosed in our atoms? Here is something perhaps disconcerting for science which judges only from "concrete realities", this fact that all our physical realities, of whatever kind, are lined with an inner reality which is their cause and foundation; there is not the least material element which has not its inner lining, beginning from our own physical organs which are only the material counter-part or the support of the centres of consciousness. Every-thing down here is the projected shadow or the symbolic translation of a light or a force which is behind, on another plane. This whole world is a vast symbol. Science analyses phenomena, finds the equation of gravitation, weight, fis-sion of atoms, etc. but it only touches the effect, never the real cause. The yogi sees the cause before the effect. The scientist may be able to deduce the cause from the effect; the yogi deduces the effects from the cause; he may even deduce effects yet inexistent from the cause which already exists, the accident that will occur tomorrow from the force of the accident which is already there behind. The scientist manipulates the effect and sometimes brings about catastrophes, the yogi manipulates the cause or rather identifies himself with the Cause and he can change the effects or, as Sri Aurobindo says, the "habits" which we call laws. For indeed all our physical effects which we have codified under the form of laws are nothing more than a convenient *support* for the manifestation of forces which are behind, exactly as in a magic operation where one needs certain ritualistic diagrams, certain ingredients, certain formulae to enable the invoked forces to manifest. The whole world is a tremendous magical process, a continu-ous magic. But the terrestrial diagram and all the ingre-dients we have carefully and unchangeably codified, our infallible formulae are simply a convention — the terres-trial ritual can change if, instead of being hypnotised by the effects we pass to the cause which is behind, to the side of the Magician. There is the story of that Hindu Brahmin who, every day at the time of worship had the house cat tied up so as not to be disturbed. The Brahmin died, the cat died. And the son having become the officiating priest had a cat brought and carefully tied up during the sacrifice! From father to son the cat had become an instrument indispensable to the efficacy of the rites. There are surely a few little cats in our ineluctable laws. If one goes back to the force hidden behind the physical support, to the "real movement", as the Mother says, one begins to discover the Great Play, so different from the rigidity attributed to it. Behind our phenomena of gravitation, to take one of the rituals, there is what the ancient yogis called *Vayu*, the cause of gravitation and of the magnetic fields (as Sri Aurobindo also pointed out in the conversation of 1926) and it is thus the yogi can eventually defy gravity. Behind the solar or nuclear fire there is the fundamental *Agni*, that spiritual *Agni* which is everywhere, "the child of the waters, the child of the forests, the child of things stable and the child of things that move. Even in the stone he is there", says the Rig Veda (I.70.2); this is the "warm golden dust" of which the Mother speaks, this the cause behind the effect, the initial force behind the material atomic support, "other flames are only branches of thy stock" (I.59). And it is because Sri Aurobindo and the rishis had seen this spiritual *Agni* in Matter, this "sun in the darkness", that they could have the knowledge of its material, atomic effect and of the solar fusions, long before our laboratories. This is also why, knowing the cause, they have dared to speak of transformation.*

---

* If it is true that physical light, the highest speed-immobility, is a remarkable symbol of the supreme Consciousness, it is equally true that the physical sun is another symbol of the supreme Power, as so many traditions, less childish than one believes, have seen. "But the Hindu Yogis," remarked Sri Aurobindo, "who had realised these experiences did not elaborate them and turn them out into scientific knowledge. Other fields of action and sources of knowledge being open before them, they neglected what for them was the most exterior aspect of the manifestation."

For indeed the whole universe from top to bottom is made of a single substance of divine Consciousness-Force and the force or energy aspect of consciousness is *Agni*: "O Son of Energy," says the Rig Veda (VIII. 84.4). This is the Force-Consciousness. This is a heat, a flame, at any level whatever we catch it. When we concentrate in our mind, we discover the subtle heat of the mental energy or mental *Agni*; when we concentrate in our heart or in our emotions, we discover the subtle heat of the Life-Energy or vital *Agni*; when we plunge into our soul we know the subtle heat of the soul or psychic *Agni*. There is but one *Agni* from top to bottom, a single stream of Consciousness-Force or consciousness-energy or consciousness-heat which clothes itself in variable intensities according to the level. And there is the fundamental *Agni* or material *Agni* which is the ultimate stage of the energy of consciousness before its conversion or its condensation in Matter. This is the place of the passage from the one to the other; (let us recall the experience of the Mother: "It is a Movement which exceeds the force or the power that concentrates the cells to make of them an individual form"). Modern science also has finished off well by seeing that Matter and Energy are convertible, the one into the other: $E = mc^2$, this is its great discovery but it has not seen that this Energy is a consciousness, this Matter a consciousness, and that therefore by manipulating the consciousness one can manipulate Energy or Matter. To transform Matter into Energy it knows only of physical processes producing great temperatures, but if one knows the fundamental *Agni* which is the substance of Energy or of Consciousness-Force, one can, in principle, manipulate Matter and come to the same transmutation without reducing one's own body to the state of a living torch.

The conversation of 1926 then puts before us two material facts (and their spiritual basis) which are of the
highest importance from the point of view of transformation: first, that all terrestrial forms whatsoever are
constituted of the same components and that only the
differences of atomic arrangement create different properties (it is the material counterpart of the spiritual fact of
the divine Unity of the world; the world is made of a single
divine substance: "Thou art man and woman, boy and
girl," says the Upanishad,* "old and worn thou walkest
bent over a staff; thou art the blue bird and the green
and the scarlet-eyed"); without this oneness of substance
no transformaion would be possible, for each time one
would need to change a new thing; and secondly, the
fact that this solar fire in Matter is the material counterpart of the fundamental *Agni* which, as Sri Aurobindo
stressed in the very same conversation, is *the builder of
forms*. To handle *Agni* is to be able to modify forms, to
transform Matter: "He tastes not that delight (of the
twice-born) who is unripe and whose body has not suffered
in the heat of the fire," says the Rig Veda; "they alone
are able to bear that and enjoy it who have been prepared
by the flame" (IX.83.1). It is this warm gold dust which
will transmute its material counterpart, the nuclear dust
in our body: *The subtle process will be more powerful than the
gross, so that a subtle action of Agni will be able to do the action
which would now need a physical change such as increased tempe-
rature.*[24] Our atoms, they too are a convenient diagram of
the eternal ritual — nothing is fixed, nothing is ineluctable, there is no end to the possible combinations, no end
to the new Man.

* Swetaswatara Upanishad IV.3.4.

Second Phase (The Body)

It was in 1926 that the second phase began and it continued till 1940. It was a phase of individual working on the body and in the subconscient. So far we have all the clues, all the threads to reach for ourselves the supramental change of consciousness and we know the basic principle of transformation. It is *Agni* "who does the work", says the Rig Veda (I.1.5). But how, in practice, is this *Agni* going to proceed to modify Matter? We cannot yet tell, we know only little bits: *If we knew the process*, says the Mother, *it would already have been done*. All the other realisations have been scrupulously inventoried by the Indian traditions with an extraordinary precision; we know all the methods for attaining Nirvana, realising the cosmic Spirit, finding the soul, conquering gravity, hunger, cold, sleep, illness, going out of the body at will and prolonging life — everybody can attain these, the ways have been known, the stages described by the wise men or the Hindu *shastras* for millenniums. It is a question of discipline and patience — of the "moment" also. But the transformation, nobody has achieved that, it is an entirely unknown way, as though one were going further into a country that yet does not exist. Perhaps it is something similar to what must have happened when the first mental forms began to emerge in the world of Matter and Life — how could the semi-animal organism which received the first mental vibrations have understood and described this strange phenomenon and, above all, how could it have said what had to be done to handle thought? To quote the Mother once more: *We do not know if this or that experience forms part of the way or not, we do not even know if we are progressing or not, for if we knew that we were progressing, it would be that we knew the way — there is no way! nobody has gone there! One will not truly be able to say what it is until this is done.* It is *an adventure into the unknown,* Sri Aurobindo used to say; we are somewhat like a primate before this new creation. We cannot then do more than indicate a few general lines of development, or of difficulty rather, without being sure that this is truly the process. The experience is in the making. When it has succeeded once, just once, in a single human being, the very conditions of the transformation will change because the road will have been hewn, marked out, the primary difficulties cleared away. The day Plato conceived *Phaedrus* he raised all mankind to the possibility of Phaedrus; the day a single human being conquers the difficulties of transformation, he will raise the whole of humanity to the possibility of a luminous, true, immortal life.

One can, however, get an idea of problem No. 1 which challenges the seeker. This *Agni,* when it begins to burn in the mind, in our moments of inspiration, creates, as we well know, a considerable tension, almost a physical heat; when it burns in the heart, in our soulful moments, we know that the breast becomes an intense hearth, so intense that the colour of the skin may change and even an inexperienced eye can notice a sort of radiance, almost a glow around the yogi; when this *Agni* burns in the vital, in moments when we call the force or of our cosmic opening, it is like a compact pulsation, at the level of the navel, almost a tremor of fever throughout the body, for a great deal of force enters a minute channel; but what can be said of that glowing golden dust, *this wine of lightning*[25] in the cells of the body? *This begins to seethe everywhere,* says the Mother in her simple language, *like a boiler ready to burst.* The rishis also said that if one goes too fast one

breaks "like a half-baked jar". Besides, if it were merely
a question of creating something out of nothing, the problem would be relatively simple, but one must do with
what one has, one must *pass* from the present state to another state, from an old organisation to a new one: there is
an old heart still there, old lungs — at what *moment*,
observed the Mother, is one going to stop the heart and
throw the Force into circulation? It is the passage which is
difficult. One requires innumerable repeated experiences,
minute experiences most carefully dosed out, to habituate
the cells so that they do not get frightened in the transition.
The first problem then is to adapt the body and for this
years and years are needed, perhaps centuries. Sri
Aurobindo worked for forty years and the Mother for the
last fifty years has worked at this adaptation. The practical, immediate necessity, then, is to last out; one must
go faster than death. *Fundamentally*, says the Mother,
*the question is to know, in this race towards the transformation,
which of the two will reach first, the one who wants to transform
the body in the image of the divine Truth or the old habit in the body
of gradually decomposing.*

For naturally, the work must be done in one life-time;
one may from one life to another recover the former
progress of the soul and the mind, even of the vital,
which would translate itself in this life through spontaneous
awakening, innate faculties, an already acquired development; it is enough to repeat one's lesson for ten or twenty
years to recapture the thread of former lives — there is
even a fairly striking experience in which one sees exactly
the point where the already accomplished work of past
lives ends and the new progress begins. One knots up the
thread again. But for the body, the progress of the cells,
the progress of the physical consciousness cannot pass

into the next life, that is evident; everything is scattered in the fire or the earth. If one wants a continuity in human evolution, if one wants the supramental being to manifest in our own flesh and not in some new unknown organism which would supplant our mental humanity, it is necessary for *one* human being to accomplish the work in *one* life. If the work succeeds once, it will be able to transmit itself to others (we shall come back to this). Sri Aurobindo used to say it would require three centuries — and he had a clear vision — for a complete supramental being to manifest, luminous, plastic, light, as we have tried to picture it. Consequently we must at least, for want of the complete supramental being (even Plato was not born in a day), prepare in our flesh a transitional being, a link between the human and superhuman types, that is, a being which would have not only realised the supramental consciousness but whose body would have at the same time a sufficient immortality, if one may put it thus, to last through the period of transition and enough power and suppleness to work out its own transmutation or, if not this, to engender by its own energy a supramental being without using the ordinary means of terrestrial birth. For the heavy animal and human heredity which loads our subconscient and which is transmitted automatically by our physical conception is one of the most difficult obstacles in the transformation, at least as difficult as, if not more than, the boilings of *Agni*. This is difficulty No. 2. Perhaps, in fact, it is the real difficulty, much greater than the other spectacular difficulties of the body. We are here before two fundamental problems of the seeker: to give the cells of the body the consciousness of immortality which is already there in our soul and even in our mind, and to sweep clean the subconscient. The progress of *Agni* in the body depends, *it seems*, on these two conditions. The work is then as ever a work of consciousness.

First of all, the duration. In experience one finds that the problem of immortality is always linked with a problem of truth. What is true alone is immortal. If we were completely true, we would be completely immortal, from top to bottom. Up to now, there is scarcely anything else except the soul which is immortal, because it is the truth of the Spirit in us; it is that which passes from life, grows, progresses, becomes more and more conscious. The mind also, as soon as it is sufficiently organised around the central Truth, as soon as it thinks the Truth, wants the Truth, becomes immortal; one finds again very easily one's old formations; there are truths extremely familiar, needs of truth inexplicably imperious. The vital also is capable of immortality as soon as it becomes sufficiently integrated to the central psychic Truth — one emerges into another dimension, familiar as from millenniums; but this is hardly frequent, our life-force is generally much more occupied with all sorts of pastimes than with the will to build a true life. The more one descends the ladder of consciousness, the more does the falsehood thicken and the more all dies, naturally, because falsehood is essentially rotting. If the vital already is sufficiently obscure, the body is full of falsehood. Old age and illness are among its most evident falsehoods — how can that which is True be old, ugly, worn out, ill? the True is radiant, it is beautiful, luminous, eternal. This is evident. The True is invincible. Death and old age catch us only through our lack of Truth.

We should acknowledge that Death is wise as things go today: an immortal Mr. Smith would be a real hash of immortality. Death, everything considered, is a faithful guardian of the Truth. It is strange to see how everywhere, always, things have two faces. If one looks at one side, one needs must struggle, fight, say No; if one looks at the other, one must give thanks and ever more thanks, say Yes and yet again Yes. And one must be capable of both. The hunting down of the "falsehoods of the body", illness, unconsciousness, old age, comes then only in the last place, when the transformation of the higher stages, the mental and the vital, is already over and when the rest of the being lives in the Truth, is established in the Truth. It would be quite wrong to think that one can undertake the supramental yoga before having climbed all the other rungs — one must go to the highest above to be able to touch the lowest, we know.

If silence is the basic condition of mental transformation, if peace is the basic condition of vital transformation, immobility is the basis of physical transformation — not an external immobility but an inner one, in the cellular consciousness. In mental silence and in vital peace we have disentangled the innumerable vibrations of the world, the secret influences which make us act, feel, think; in the immobility of the physical consciousness, in the same way, we begin to disentangle a strange swarming of vibrations and to know of what substance we are made. In the cells we live in a complete chaos; it is a whirlpool of sensations, strong, pleasant, sorrowful, sharp — spear-heads flying up, arrows shooting down and, as soon as the whirling stops, it is like a hole of anguish which must be filled in at any cost by other sensations and always more sensations. One does not feel alive except when in movement. The basis of the work then is to bring a perfect immobility into this chaos — not an equality of soul but an equality of cells. Then the work of truth begins. In this cellular equality our body will be like a transparent pool where the least vibrations will become perceptible, hence seizable and conquerable; all the forces of illness, disintegration, falsehood, all the subconscient deformations and deformities and their horrible little brood will begin to crawl *visibly* in this clarity and we shall be able to grip them. The effervescence of *Agni*, indeed, does not depend so much on an impossibility of cellular adaptation as on the *resistance* of "our" obscurities. This purifying immobility alone can clear the ground and release the overpowering Movement of Agni without the body's beginning to vibrate in unison, getting panicky and entering into rash temperatures.

Once this cellular immobility has been relatively established, we shall make a first discovery; we shall come up against a major obstacle, which is also a major aid in the work of transformation, for always, on all the planes, the opposition is adapted exactly to the force necessary to advance a step farther; it is the dead weight and the lever. Already we have recognised under our thinking mind a "vital mind" which finds marvellous justifications for all our desires, all our impulsions, then a "physical mind" which repeats and repeats a thousand times the same incidents like a persistent tune. But there is a deeper layer yet, a mental bedrock which Sri Aurobindo calls the *cellular mind*. This is indeed a mind of the cells or of groups of cells, which resembles the physical mind largely by its inexhaustible capacity for repeating the same old story but which is not limited to the cerebral region or to the mechanical grinding of crumbs of thought; it is everywhere in the body, *like millions of little voices* one is quick to hear when the other mental layers are cleared, and it stirs up indefatigably not now the refuse of our conscious activities but all our sensorial impressions: it is enough that once a group of cells has been touched by an impression, a fear, a shock, an illness, for them to reproduce indefinitely their fear, their stiffening, their tendency to disorganisation or the memory of their illness. It is a gregarious mind, quite absurd, which spreads farther and farther and vibrates, vibrates everywhere endlessly; which hooks in always the same wave-lengths, the same decomposing suggestions, and reacts imperturbably to the same stimuli as Pavlov's dog to the ringing of the bell. It is the fear of living implanted in Matter. It is the first conscious effort of Matter. And naturally the little bit of initiative at its disposal serves to call in all the disorders through fear and the unconsciousness of death as a repose. But this cellular mind which has a formidable power, if we consider it well, like the ants over the elephant, can put its absurd mechanism at the service of truth as of falsehood; if just once it is hooked on to a vibration of light, it will repeat this with the obstinacy of a mule and, what is most remarkable, it will repeat it day and *night*, unceasingly.* Whatever one may be doing externally, working, discussing or sleeping, it repeats over and over again its one vibration, automatically and altogether independently. Hence its considerable importance for the transformation is easily understood; it can be a unique fixer of the supramental vibration. Here is what Sri Aurobindo says about it: *There is too an obscure mind of the body, of the very cells, molecules, corpuscles. Haeckel, the German materialist, spoke somewhere of the will in the atom, and recent science, dealing with the incalculable individual variation in the activity of the electrons, comes near to perceiving that this is not a figure but the shadow thrown by a secret*

---

* Whence the utility of the mantra which can canalize a vibration of a certain intensity to any point of the body whatsoever or to all points if the cellular mind lays hold of it.

*reality. This body mind is a very tangible truth; owing to its obs-
curity and mechanical clinging to past movements and facile oblivion and rejection of the new, we find in it one of the chief obstacles
to permeation by the supermind Force and the transformation of the
functioning of the body. On the other hand, once effectively converted, it will be one of the most precious instruments of the stabilisation of the supramental Light and Force in material Nature.*[26]

What shall we say of this work? It is infinitesimal. And
the only way of doing it is not to enter into profound meditations which touch but the summit of our being, not to
achieve concentrations or have extraordinary ecstasies but
to be right in the midst of things and work at the level of
the body, down below, every minute of the day and night.
This is why Sri Aurobindo insisted so much on the necessity of outer work and the most ordinary physical exercises,
because this is the only way to try one's strength against
Matter and push into it a little true consciousness or rather
allow *Agni* to emerge freely. It was for this that he used to
walk so many hours every day and work all those hours
of the night. In the midst of this external work and *due to
that*, the seeker will find coming up all the false vibrations,
all the *creases* of the body, as the Mother says. And each
false vibration will have to be rectified. But this is still a
negative way of putting things. In truth there is but one
single great Vibration of divine joy in the world and in all
things — *the* Vibration, for God is Joy; as soon as falsity
is introduced this *very* vibration gets discoloured, it hardens,
stiffens — everything grates. Suffering is the surest sign of
falsity. Sorrow is the falsehood of the world. The whole
work of the seeker then is not so much to struggle against
so-called bad vibrations as to keep the true vibration, the
divine joy in the body, which has the power to set in order
again, relax, harmonise, heal all these small vibrations,

crouched together, wearing, falsifying, in which our cells constantly live. It would be fastidious, as fastidious as the work itself, to describe the innumerable little falsehoods of the body through which there come into it old age, illnesses and death. *To do everything in the true way*, advises the Mother, and there are innumerable false ways of doing the least daily things. As an example we shall stress here only one point of the work among many others: we do everything in a great tension, a hurry, somehow, unconsciously; before the thousand and one calls of the outer life, not to speak of the shocks, we behave physically like the patient in the dentist's chair; everything is cramped, curled up, through haste, through fear, anxiety, avidity — this is the heritage of some millions of years of animality; our substance remembers having struggled for survival, it is all the time hardening itself. This hardening is one of the causes of death and a big obstacle to the establishing of the true vibration. When we stiffen under a shock, we gather all our vital force at a point, like a defence; abruptly an enormous current passes through a minute orifice which turns red and gives pain. If we could learn to enlarge our physical consciousness and absorb the shock, instead of rejecting it, we would not suffer — all suffering is a narrowness of consciousness, at every level. But we understand that if, at one go, that hot supramental gold dust were to precipitate itself in our cells, and the body react by its habitual hardening, everything would blow up. That is, our cellular consciousness, like our mental and vital consciousness, must learn to enlarge and universalise itself. Here too the cosmic consciousness must come in. In mental silence, the mental consciousness universalises itself; in vital peace, the vital consciousness universalises itself; in the immobility of the body, the physical consciousness universalises itself. Immobility, receptivity, cellular wideness would seem to be among the basic conditions for the body-substance to be able to support *Agni* and last out.

But immediately an enormous difficulty arises. Universalisation of the physical consciousness? But then, when there is only *one* body, all other bodies fall upon it, all the falsehoods of the world are there!... It is no longer one man's battle, it is the battle of the whole world. And we approach the real problem. In this physical clearing the seeker makes another discovery that is quite brutal: all his yogic powers crumble. He had already conquered disease, conquered the functionings of the body, perhaps even gravity, he was able to swallow poison without suffering; in short, he was the master of the house, for his consciousness was master. But suddenly from the day he makes up his mind to transform the body, all his powers vanish. Diseases fall upon him as on a beginner, the organs deteriorate, everything functions wrongly. It would seem that the body has to forget its old false decaying functionings so as to learn everything according to a new mode. And death interferes. Between the two functionings, the old and the new which must replace the symbolic organs by the true Vibration, the line which separates life from death is often very thin — perhaps one must even be capable of crossing the line and returning in order truly to triumph? This is what the Mother called *dying to death*, after one of her experiences from which she nearly failed to return. That is, one must face everything, and everything resists. But we know the same phenomenon on higher stages of our consciousness; as soon as the seeker sets out on his path, everything goes wrong; he who believed himself a mind firmly anchored on the truth, he sees file past him the most aggressive suggestions and scepticisms; he believed

himself pure and quite honest and he picks up a series
of vital horrors enough to discourage the worst scoundrels
of this world and a few others as well who do not belong
here. In other words, as Sri Aurobindo has already said,
one cannot resolve a problem on any plane whatever without facing all the oppositions to the Goal. Otherwise it
would not be a victory but an oppression. Nowhere, on
no plane, is it a question of cutting off the evil but of convincing it of its own light. The yogi who by his power had
got rid of illnesses, had not resolved the problem: he had
muzzled the forces of illness, that is all. Now, one knows
well that there cannot be any transformation if the forces
are merely muzzled and if they remain prowling in corners
awaiting their hour. And as nothing can be cut out from
the universe, they needs must be converted. But converted
how? Death, disease are everywhere, they are in the subconscient of our bodies, of all the bodies in the world.
The yogi who had conquered disease, defied death (not for
long, and that is but justice) had conquered these only for
himself and this is why he could not truly conquer. O wisdom of the Law! He had built his protecting shell, enclosed himself inside like a chicken of light, and everything
around swarmed as usual. But if the shell should open,
everything would enter! there is but one body! Ramakrishna lashed by the whip which hurt the bullock beside
him or the Mother struggling against a haemorrhage which
attacked a disciple some hundreds of miles away, without
her knowing anything about it, brings us before the entire
problem — *the body is everywhere*! exclaimed the Mother.
It is everywhere one must conquer, for all the bodies and
for the whole earth. One can transform nothing unless one
transforms everything. Otherwise one is all alone in one's
hole of light. And what is the use of that? What good

would it do if one single man is transformed while the rest die and die? The body of the pioneer of transformation is hence like a battlefield and it is the battle of the whole world which is fought there; everything meets there, resists there. There is a central *point* right below, a knot of life and death, where the destiny of the world is at stake. Everything is gathered in a point.

> *I have been digging deep and long*
> *Mid a horror of filth and mire,*
> *A bed for the golden river's song,*
> *A home for the deathless fire...*
> *My gaping wounds are a thousand and one...*[27]

And he must face all the difficulties, even Death, not to destroy but to change all. One can transform nothing without taking it upon oneself: *Thou shalt bear all things that all things may change.*[28] This is the reason why Sri Aurobindo left his body on the 5th December 1950, clinically due to uraemia, he who could heal others within a few seconds. To die on the cross is moving, certainly, but crucifixions, specially when worshipped, only perpetuate the law of death. *It is not a crucified body which will save the world,* says the Mother, *but a glorified body.*

No, it is not a spectacular work, it is rather a "microscopic work", and it is in the Mire of the world that one must dig.

Second Phase (The Subconscient)

There is then another category of difficulties (but it is the same under another mask), which is not due to the res-

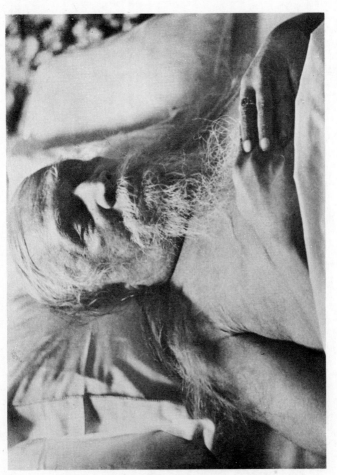

istance of individual, corporal matter but to the subconscient resistance of the whole earth. It is there that Sri Aurobindo met Death. It is there the Mother continues the work. If we want to locate the scene where the whole story — our story — is played out and to follow the course of the work, we must go back to the evolutionary process itself. The emergence of a new grade in the evolution, whether it be of Life in Matter or Mind in Life, is worked out under a double stress: a stress from within or below, of the involved principle which seeks to emerge, and a stress from "outside" or "above", of the same principle as it already exists on its own plane. The conjunction of these two stresses, for example of the mind involved in certain living forms and the Mind as it is formed on its own plane in the course of the descending evolution or devolution, ends up one day by causing a tearing of the vital limits and brusquely the mental emergence in Life. All is involved, all is already there in Matter but the involution cannot undo itself except by the pressure from above which replies to the call from below and breaks the seal as the sun breaks the tegument of the seed. At present, the supermind involved in Matter pushes from within under the form of a spiritual tension, of terrestrial aspirations to Immortality, Truth, Beauty, etc., and, at the same time, it presses from above, from its own eternal plane, under the form of intuitions, revelations, illuminations. This is what the Scriptures express in their own way when they link inseparably the appearance of the "new earth" and the appearance of the "new heavens" ("new heavens and a new earth wherein dwelleth the Truth"), because without the new heavens or rather this new supramental level of consciousness, the emergence of a new earth is not possible. The new earth will be the result of the new "heavens" of the supra-

mental consciousness, even as the present earth is the result of the old mental or overmind "heaven" of the gods
and religions. And thus at all the levels of evolution: the
high and the low hold together. But the emergence of the
new "height" or the new level of consciousness at any
stage of the evolution is not a sudden magic which changes
all the former levels. Between the appearance of the first
amoeba in the field of life and that of the mammals, we
know how many millions of years were necessary to overcome the material inertia and "vitalise" Matter. Similarly,
between the appearance of the Neanderthal man and
that of Plato it took thousands of years to overcome the
resistance of the preceding levels and "mentalise" Life, to
become the complete mental man. Even today how many
men live truly under the mental banner and not under the
sway of the passions of Life? The whole work of the pioneers of evolution, at whatever level, consists precisely in
joining the new height to the former depth; when the high
meets the low, an evolutionary cycle is complete. In the
same way when the pioneer of mental evolution emerges
suddenly into the supramental, his discovery is not a sudden magic which reverses the former laws; he does not
jump to the complete supramental man any more than the
Neanderthal man leaps up to Plato; he must "supramen-
talise" all the preceding levels. Of course, the supreme
Summit and the supreme Depth meet in his consciousness,
Spirit and Matter, the Positive and Negative, and his
powers naturally are considerably developed, but finally
they develop only in proportion to the new resistances he
is going to meet. For the further the evolution progresses,
the closer it touches the deep layers: the principle of Life
colonised only the material crust of the world, the Mind
principle colonises as well as it may its immediate past, the

mental subconscient and the old unruliness of Life; and
the supramental principle confronts not only the mental
and vital subconscient but a yet remoter past, the physical
subconscient and the Inconscient — the higher one rises,
the lower down one is pulled. Evolution does not go higher
and higher up, into an ever heavenlier heaven, but deeper
down, and each cycle or evolutionary circle closes in a
little lower, a little nearer the Centre where the supreme
High and the Low will finally meet, the heaven and the
earth. The pioneer then must clean the intermediate
mental, vital and material ground that the two poles may
meet effectively. When the junction will be complete,
not only mentally and vitally but materially, the Spirit
will emerge in Matter, in a complete supramental being
and in a supramental body — and

... *earth shall be the Spirit's manifest home.*[29]

This clearance of the intermediate ground is the whole
story of Sri Aurobindo and the Mother. The difficulties of
adapting the body to the supramental *Agni* are perhaps,
finally, planned and necessary difficulties. Perhaps it is not
really a material difficulty but a strategic one, if we may
say so. Sri Aurobindo and the Mother were to find, in
fact, in the course of the second phase that transformation
is not only an individual problem but a terrestrial one and
that no individual transformation is possible (or at least
complete) without a minimum collective transformation.
The day the conditions of collective evolution are sufficiently advanced, it is probable that the present material
difficulties of transformation which seem insurmountable
will crumble all at once like a house of cards. There are
never any impossibilities; there are only moments which

come or do not come. All obstacles, of whatever kind, prove to be always in experience precious auxiliaries of a Truth of which we yet do not guess the meaning or the purpose. To our outer superficial seeing the transformation seems to be exclusively a problem of the material kind because we always put the cart before the horse, but in truth all difficulties are inner psychological ones; the spectacular difficulties of adapting the body to this burning *Agni* are perhaps less practical, material difficulties than a difficulty of the whole terrestrial consciousness, as we shall see. But we speak in riddles; the problem Sri Aurobindo and the Mother were soon to come up against would be more easily elucidated by a simple remark of Sri Aurobindo's in his letters to two disciples: *I had been dredging, dredging, dredging the mire of the subconscious....It [the supramental light] was coming down before November* but afterwards all the mud arose and it stopped.*[30] Once again Sri Aurobindo verified, not individually this time but collectively, that if one pulls down a fairly strong light, all the darkness down below groans, violated. It is curious to observe that each time Sri Aurobindo and the Mother have had some new experience marking a progress in the transformation, this progress has automatically been translated in the consciousness of the disciples, without their even knowing anything about it, by a period of increased difficulties, sometimes even of unexpected revolts, of illnesses, as though everything had started grating. Then one begins to understand the mechanism. If we were brusquely to subject a pigmy to the simple mental light of a cultured man, we would probably witness subterranean revolutions which would injure the poor fellow and make him go mad. There is yet much virgin forest down below. The world is

* 1934.

yet full of virgin forests, this is the whole business, in two words; our mental colonisation is a very thin crust over a hardly dry quaternary.

The Vedic rishis, speaking of the subconscient forces or beings, called them "those-who-cover", "those-who-devour", the "robbers of the sun"; one could not describe them better, these are terrible thieves; hardly has one made some progress, drawn down a new light, a slightly more intense vibration, when one is suddenly covered up, pulled down under a suffocating bell-glass where everything disintegrates in a terrible moisture; the harmonious vibration of the day before, so clear, so luminous, so supple, is at one stroke covered over with a gluish thickness, as though it were necessary to wade through miles and miles of sargasso in order to find a bit of light; everything one sees, everything one touches, everything one does, is as though rotten, decomposed by that invasion from below. Nothing has any meaning any more. And yet outwardly the conditions are the same, nothing has changed. *There is a sort of locked struggle,* says Sri Aurobindo, *in which neither side can make a very appreciable advance (somewhat like the trench warfare in Europe), the spiritual force insisting against the resistance of the physical world, that resistance disputing every inch and making more or less effective counter-attacks. ... And if there were not the strength and* Ananda *within, it would be harassing and disgusting work.*[31] And the battle seems endless; one "digs and digs", said the rishis, and the more one digs, the deeper does the bottom seem to sink: "I have been digging, digging... many autumns have I been toiling night and day, the dawns aging me. Age is diminishing the glory of our bodies", thus lamented Lopamudra thousands of years ago, wife of the rishi Agastya, who was also seeking transformation: "Even the men of old who were wise of the Truth and they spoke with the gods... yea, they reached not an end." But Agastya did not let himself be discouraged and his reply is so magnificently characteristic of the conquerors these rishis were: "Not in vain is the labour which the gods protect. Let us have the taste of even all the contesting forces, let us conquer indeed even here, let us run this battle-race of a hundred leadings" (I.179). And truly it is like a hydra. Night after night, in his sleep or with eyes wide open, the seeker discovers very strange worlds. He unearths one by one the places where all the human perversions are born, the human wars, the human concentration-camps — it is down there that what is here is prepared — he catches in their holes all the sordid forces which animate small and cruel men.

> *A lone discoverer in these menacing realms*
> *Guarded like termite cities from the sun.*[32]

And the more Light one has, the more obscurities one discovers; night after night is tracked down the clandestine rot which undermines Life — how can anything be transformed as long as this gangrene is there? And as our mind and our vital are already too well established in the truth, too clear to be attacked by these subterranean forces, it is the body that suffers, for that is the last refuge of Falsehood. One sees very well then by what complicities disease or death comes into the body — each failure down there is a failure here — and one understands tangibly, concretely, in detail, the enormous vanity of those who believe in curing the world by external means and new institutions; hardly has the evil been healed here, exterminated down there, when it revives elsewhere, in other corners, under other forms. The evil is not outside, it is within, below, and as long as that Malady has not been cured the world cannot be cured. Sri Aurobindo has put it well: *The old gods... know how to transmigrate.*[33]

Right at the bottom, beyond the disorders, the fear, the great Fear presiding down below, one finds like an immense Lassitude something that does not want, that says NO to all this labour of living, this rape of light. One feels that if one went down there, to the end of this No, one would be released into a great expanse of stone, as the ecstasy above was a release into a great expanse of Light. Death is not the opposite of Life! it is the inverse — or the door — of the luminous Superconscient; at the very end of the No there is the Yes, and once more the Yes which pushes us again and again into body after body for joy. Death is only the sorrow of that Yes, the great Lassitude right at the bottom, a shadow of that Beatitude. Death is not the opposite of Life! it is the dark relaxation of the body which has not yet found the luminous relaxation of the eternal Joy. When the body finds that ecstasy, that immensity of light and joy in the depths of its own flesh even as above, it will need no longer to die.

Where is the "I", the "me" in all this? where "my" difficulty, "my" death, "my" transformation? The seeker has pierced through the thin crust of the personal subconscient, he comes forth everywhere into the world; and it is the whole world which resists: *It is not we who wage the war, it is everything that wars against us!* We believe ourselves separate, each one in his own little neat skin-jacket, with an "inside" and an "outside", an individual and a collectivity, like the derisive little frontiers of our countries — but everything communicates! there is not a single perversion, not a single shame in the world, which has not some root in us, not a death in which we are not accomplices; we are all culpable and all involved, nobody is saved if everybody is not saved! It is not the difficulty of *a* body, but the difficulty of *the* body, writes the Mother, and yet she does not use a capital B for it. Sri Aurobindo and the Mother uncovered thus, *materially*, experimentally, the unity of substance of the world: no point can be touched without touching all the points, no one can take a step in front or upwards without the rest of the world also taking a step in front or upwards. We were just speaking of a "strategic" difficulty; it could be quite possible that the divine strategy does not want that one point should progress all alone without all the other points. This is why six thousand years ago the Vedic rishis failed. There is no individual transformation possible, complete and lasting, without a minimum world transformation.

Thus was completed the second phase of the work of transformation. After having worked for fourteen years, from 1926 to 1940, in an individual, concentrated way, with a handful of carefully chosen disciples, Sri Aurobindo and the Mother came up against a wall. As soon as the supramental light approached the earth to link up with the same involved light in Matter, torrents of mud came up from the collective subconscient and everything was covered over. *To help humanity out*, remarked Sri Aurobindo, *it was not enough for an individual, however great, to achieve an ultimate solution individually,* [*because*] *even when the Light is ready to descend it cannot come to stay till the lower plane is also ready to bear the pressure of the Descent.*[34] It is significant (perhaps more so than one believes) that the culminating point of the second phase of the work of transformation coincided with the outbreak of the Second World War. When the pressure of Light descends in a single human body among men, the body of the world too begins to glow luridly. What do we know, in truth, about the good of the world, or about its evil?

Before all the collective resistances, Sri Aurobindo and the Mother hesitated a moment; they asked themselves whether it would not be possible to cut themselves off from the rest of the world and progress alone in a straight line with their few disciples, work out the transformation, then come back to a collective work, so that the transformation once accomplished or partially accomplished, spreads through the rest of the earth (it was this idea which had impelled so many spiritual, occult, chivalrous and other groups to choose a secret place away from the world to do their work sheltered from the contamination of collective vibrations); but they saw that this was an illusion and that afterwards the abyss or as Sri Aurobindo calls it the *atmospheric gulf* [35] between the new realisation and the old world would be too vast to be ever bridgeable. And of what use is an individual success if it is not transmissible to the rest of the world? We would be like Anderson's Emperor of whom we were speaking a while ago. If a supramental being appeared suddenly on the earth, nobody would see it! our eyes must first open on another mode of living. *If you go along a road which is ready,* says the Mother, (*for it is with roads as it is with beings, some are ready*) *without having the patience to wait for the rest of the creation, that is, if you realise something very close to the Truth compared with the present state of the world, what will happen? a dislocation of a certain unity, a rupture not only of harmony but of equilibrium, because there will be an entire part of the creation which will not be able to follow. And instead of a complete realisation of the Divine, you will have a small localised realisation, infinitesimal, and nothing will be done of what finally ought to be done.* Moreover, the Mother emphasises, *if one wants to do the work singly, it is absolutely impossible to do it totally, because every physical being, however complete it be, even though it be of an altogether superior kind, even if it be made for an altogether special Work, is never but partial and limited. It represents only one truth, one law in the world—it may be a very complex law but it is always only one law — and the full transformation cannot be realised through it alone, through a single body.... One can attain, alone, one's own perfection; one can become in one's consciousness infinite and perfect. The inner realisation has no limits. But the outer realisation, on the contrary, is necessarily limited, so that if one wants to have a general action, at least a minimum number of physical beings is necessary.*

After fourteen years of individual concentration, in 1940 Sri Aurobindo and the Mother opened wide the doors of their Ashram. Thus began the third phase of the transformation which yet continues, a phase of expansion and terrestrial work.

Third Phase (The Ashram)

An "Ashram" in India is a spiritual or religious community whose members, gathered around a Master, have renounced the world to devote themselves to meditation, concentration, yogic exercises, to attain "liberation". One suspects that Sri Aurobindo's Ashram has nothing to do with this definition, apart from the fact that the disciples are gathered around Sri Aurobindo and the Mother. It is not a sort of exotic convent, still less a place of refuge and of peace; it is rather a forge: *This Ashram has been created... not for the renunciation of the world but as a centre and a field of practice for the evolution of another kind and form of life*.[36] Even before his arrest in Bengal, at a time when he had not even dreamt of founding an Ashram, Sri Aurobindo already used to say: *The spiritual life finds its most potent expression in the man who lives the ordinary life of men in the strength of the Yoga.... It is by such a union of the inner life and the outer that mankind will eventually be lifted up and become mighty and divine*.[37] His Ashram is hence all mingled with the ordinary life, fully in the collective mixture, because it is there that the transformation must be worked out, not on some Himalayan peak. Besides the main building where the Mother lives and where Sri Aurobindo's tomb is found, the 1,400 odd disciples of all nationalities and all social classes, men and women and about four or five hundred children, are scattered all over the town of Pondicherry in more than three hundred different houses. There are no protecting walls, except the inner light; one is immediately next door to the bazaar.

The Westerner who comes with the idea of finding peace and learning "yoga" is hence disillusioned. First of all nobody helps him to learn anything whatsoever (it is unlearning that would be needed rather), there are no classes, no teaching, except the works of Sri Aurobindo and the *Conversations* of the Mother which are at the disposal of everybody (as also the other past teachings, traditional or not). There are no rules either. The disciple must find everything by himself, in himself, in the midst of an extraordinarily active life. He is left to himself. For, how would it be possible to make rules for a work which takes in all the levels of evolution, mental, vital and psychic, all human types, all the traditions (some disciples were brought up in Christianity, others in Taoism, Islam, Buddhism, Atheism, etc.)? Each must find his own truth, which is not his neighbour's. Some believe in the virtue of asceticism in spite of all Sri Aurobindo has said about it and they live in retirement like ascetics; others prefer judo or football; others believe in books and still others do not; some do business, manufacture stainless steel, perfumes or even hundreds of tons of sugar in a new refinery. There is something for every taste. He who likes painting paints; he who likes music has at his disposal all possible instruments, Indian or western; he who likes teaching becomes a teacher at the *International Centre of Education* and covers the whole range from the kindergarten to the university stage. There is also a printing press, laboratories, gardens, ricefields, mechanic workshops for private cars, tractors, trucks; an X-ray department, an operation theatre; all possible professions are represented. It is a microcosm. One may be a baker too or even wash dishes or try carpentry if one believes in the virtue of simple work. There is, besides, no difference between these activities; none is paid for, none is superior to any other. All necessities of life are provided by the Mother, to each according to his needs; there is only one real work, to discover the truth of one's being, for which the outer work is only a means. The strange thing, moreover, is that one witnesses changes of activity as the consciousness awakens; all the values attached to old professions crumble very quickly and, because money has no longer any significance, one who believed himself a doctor finds himself better off as an artisan and the ordinary man finds himself suddenly a poet or painter or plunges into Sanskrit studies or learns Ayurvedic medicine. It is a complete recasting of outer values according to the one inner criterion. When a disciple one day asked the Mother what the best way of collaborating in the supramental transformation was, he was given this answer: *It is always*

the same thing : to realise one's own being under no matter
what form, by no matter *what road — that has no importance —*
*but this is the only means. Each individual carries in himself
a truth and it is with this truth that he must unite himself, it is
this truth he must live ; and in this way the road he follows to join
and realise this truth becomes also the road which will bring him
the nearest possible to the Transformation. That is, the two are
absolutely united : personal realisation and the transformation.
Who knows ? perhaps even this multiplicity of approaches will
give the Secret and open the door.*

There is no common life however, only an inner link.
Some of the disciples have kept the old habit of the days
when the Mother used to have her talks with the Ashram
children, and continue to gather twice a week for a collective meditation; but it is at the sports ground that they
meet (there is of course a common dining room, but many
prefer cooking at home with their families or alone). There
are all kinds of sports, from the traditionl hathayoga to
tennis and boxing; there is scarcely a disciple who does not
devote an hour or two to these each day. The sea is next
door but there is also an Olympic swimming-pool; there
are basket ball and volley ball grounds, a running track,
a gymnasium, a boxing ring, a judo hall, etc. All possible
exercises are practised by all, from the age of five to eighty.
There are also a theatre and a cinema. However, sports
are not an article of faith at all, nothing is an article of
faith except naturally the faith in the divine possibilities
of man and in a truer life on earth. *All you my children here,*
said the Mother to the youngest, *you live in an exceptional
liberty* .... *No social restraints, no moral restraints, no intellectual restraints, no rules ; nothing but a Light which is there.* But
it is a very exacting Light, and it is here that the terrestrial
work begins.

How can one speak of a "terrestrial" work with 1400 disciples or even a hundred thousand? It is that the Ashram is only a point of concentration of the work — in fact, the Ashram is everywhere in the world where men believe in a truer life, whether they know Sri Aurobindo or not, because their inner orientation or their inner will represents a type of concentration or need which puts them automatically in the crucible. The transformation is nobody's prerogative; on the contrary, it needs many people, the most various possible. The Ashram is then a *symbolic* centre somewhat as a laboratory is a symbolic ground of a vaccine which would then operate upon millions of men. *The laboratory*, Sri Aurobindo often called it. This will be better understood if we see that each individual represents a certain aggregate of vibrations and that each one has access to a particular zone of the Subconscient. These worlds, apparently of an extraordinary diversity, are in fact, each of them, constituted of certain typical vibrations; the multitude of forms (or of deformations rather), of beings, of places, events, in a given zone only covers an identical vibration. As soon as one becomes a little conscious and begins to descend into the Subconscient without getting dazed, in order to work there, one finds with some astonishment, almost with amusement, that the physical persons one knows, who are quite different externally when met on the mental or vital planes, are almost invertible and molten in the Subconscient! One wonders whether this is really so-and-so or not. There are thus *types* of people, though altogether separated externally by different religions, different cultures, different social levels and even different ethics, who are all alike in the Subconscient, *as though we saw one through the other*, says the Mother; it is a sort of curious superimposition. And we see only two or three individuals one through the other, for our vision is limited to a close circle, but if we had the total vision we would see that behind them there are hundreds and hundreds of others. And they are agglutinated in well-determined zones. There are beings whom one never meets together in the Subconscient and who are yet very close in external life, and *vice versa*. Then the mechanism of the terrestrial work is clearly seen: *Each one*, says the Mother, *is an instrument for controlling a certain aggregate of vibrations which represent his particular field of work*; each one, by his qualities *and his faults*, has access to a zone of terrestrial consciousness which represents his portion of the collective transformation. And one understands why the transformation cannot be carried out with a single individual, for, however great he be, however vast his inner organisation and his mental, vital and subconscient colonisation, he represents only *one* aggregate of vibrations. He can at the most transform the type of vibration he represents, and even this is not sure, for, finally, everything holds together. And one understands also that the transformation cannot be worked out with little saints. It is not with sanctity that the vaccine is produced but with that part of human disease which one courageously assumes. In any case, the illness is there; but in one instance we close the eyes and go into an ecstasy, in the other, we roll up our sleeves and count our culture test-tubes. An old disciple having complained strongly about the mixture in the Ashram and the "impossible" people found there, Sri Aurobindo observed: *It is necessary or rather inevitable that in an Ashram which is a "laboratory"... for a spiritual and supramental yoga, humanity should be variously represented. For the problem of transformation has to deal with all sorts of elements favourable and unfavourable. The same man indeed carries in him a mixture of these two things.*

If only sattwic [virtuous] and cultured men come for yoga, men without very much of the vital difficulty in them, then, because the difficulty of the vital element in terrestrial nature has not been faced and overcome, it might well be that the endeavour would fail.[38] Another disciple, in the pangs of remorse perhaps, wrote to Sri Aurobindo, "What disciples we are!... I wish you had chosen or called some better stuff — perhaps somebody like Z...." And Sri Aurobindo replied: *As to the disciples, I agree! — Yes, but would the better stuff, supposing it to exist, be typical of humanity? To deal with a few exceptional types would hardly solve the problem. And would they consent to follow my path — that is another question. And if they were put to the test, would not the common humanity suddenly reveal itself — that is still another question.*[39] *I do not want hundreds of thousands of disciples. It will be enough if I can get a hundred complete men, empty of petty egoism, who will be instruments of God.*[40]

Practically, the work gets done through each single psychological difficulty of ours, symbolic of the same difficulty throughout the world — if one touches a certain vibration in an individual, it is the same vibration which is touched in the whole world. *Each one of you,* says the Mother, *represents one of the difficulties which must be conquered for the transformation. And this makes many difficulties! It is even more than a difficulty; I believe I have told you before that each one represents an impossibility to be resolved; and when all these impossibilities are resolved, the Work will be accomplished.* Each individual, as we know, has a shadow which dogs him and seems to contradict the aim of his life. This is the special vibration he must transform, his field of work, his impossible point. It is at once the challenge of his life and its victory. It is his share of progress in the collective evolution of the earth. But something strange happens in our laboratory: in the ordinary life or in an individual yoga, this shadow is more or less latent, more or less troublesome, and it usually dissolves or rather drops into an oubliette; but as soon as one begins a terrestrial yoga, one finds that it does not disappear at all; it comes up again and again with an indefatigable virulence, as though the battle had never been won—as though, indeed, one fought the battle on this particular vibratory point for the entire earth; it would seem that the seeker had become the field of a special keen battle, symbolic of the same battle, more or less masked, on the same point of shadow, in all other men. *You do not any longer do your yoga for yourself alone, you do the yoga for everybody, without wanting to, automatically,* says the Mother. And the seeker verifies *in vivo* the principle of the substantial unity of the world: if one interferes to set straight a single vibration in oneself, myriads of tiny brother-vibrations or sister-vibrations resist throughout the world. This is what Sri Aurobindo calls a "yoga for the earth-consciousness".[41] *Accepting life, he [the seeker of the integral yoga] has to bear not only his own burden, but a great part of the world's burden too along with it, as a continuation of his own sufficiently heavy load. Therefore his Yoga has much more the nature of a battle than others'; but this is not only an individual battle, it is a collective war waged over a considerable country. He has not only to conquer in himself the forces of egoistic falsehood and disorder, but to conquer them as representatives of the same adverse and inexhaustible forces in the world. Their representative character gives them a much more obstinate capacity of resistance, an almost endless right to recurrence. Often he finds that even after he has won persistently his own personal battle, he has still to win it over and over again in a seemingly interminable war, because his inner existence has already been so much enlarged that not only it contains his own being with its well-defined needs and experiences, but is in solida-*

rity with the being of others, because in himself he contains the universe.[42]

Will this task ever come to an end? One would think that the Subconscient is a kind of interminable sewer — "the bottomless pit", the rishis called it — and that to await its cleaning in order to attain a supramental transformation is to risk waiting long. But this is a mere appearance. Each man born does not bring with him a new contingent of the Subconscient and Inconscient: he draws from the same source, he repeats the same vibrations which turn round and round indefinitely in the earth atmosphere. Man cannot create darkness any more than he can create light; he is only the instrument, conscious or unconscious, of the one or the other (and most of the time of both). No new vibrations are brought into the world except those of the superconscient Future which little by little become present and dissolve or transmute the vibrations of our evolutionary past. The Subconscient and Inconscient today are less subconscient and inconscient than they were two thousand years ago, that is evident, we have all paid for this. This precipitation of the Future into the present is the whole key of the transmutation of the world. Yoga is the process of acceleration of the Future, and the pioneer of evolution is the instrument who draws down more and more powerful vibrations. The work of the seeker is not then so much a negative work of scouring the Subconscient as a positive work of calling the light; he precipitates here the vibrations of the Future to accelerate the process of cleansing. This is what Sri Aurobindo calls the "descent", it is the main characteristic of his yoga, as we have said before. *If there is a descent in other Yogas, yet it is only an incident on the way or resulting from the ascent — the ascent is the real thing. Here the ascent is*

*the first step, but it is a means for the descent. It is the descent of
the new consciousness attained by the ascent that is the stamp and
seal of the sadhana [discipline]... here the object is the divine
fulfilment of life.*[43] And when Sri Aurobindo speaks of
"descent" it does not mean only a point above followed by
a point below; it does not mean that one goes on a tire-
some round of duty down below to clean up things a little,
it means that the below ceases to be low. To take an
example, a very prosaic one, and God knows the transformation is prosaic enough, one may go out shopping in
the bazaar in the midst of an opaque and disintegrating
crowd or at night stroll into certain malicious regions of
the Subconscient and do both with the same intensity of
consciousness, of light and peace as one has when seated
alone, eyes closed, in one's room, in deep meditation. This
is "to descend". There is no longer any difference, high
and low are equally luminous and peaceful. And it is thus
that the terrestrial transformation is worked out: the
unity of substance of the world plays *in both ways*; if it is
true that one cannot touch a single shadow without
touching all the shadows of the world, inversely one cannot touch a single light without modifying all the surrounding shadows. All vibrations are contagious, the good
ones also. Each victory won is a victory for all. But indeed
the contrary would be surprising! *It is all the same Being!*
exclaims the Mother, there is but one consciousness, but
one substance, but one force, but one body in the world.
And this is why Sri Aurobindo could say about the Mother
and himself: *If the Supermind comes down into our physical,
it would mean that it has come down into Matter and so there
is no reason why it should not manifest in the sadhaks [disciples].*[44]

The further the seeker progresses towards the height,
the wider will be his access to the lower zones — the Past

he touches is exactly in proportion to the Future he discovers — and the greater too will become his power of collective transformation. Till today, the power brought down has been a mental power or at the best overmental, which could touch only the semi-depths, but now that a supramental or spiritual power has descended into the earth-consciousness through the realisation of Sri Aurobindo and the Mother, it is possible to think that this supreme Future will touch the supreme Depth and hasten the cleansing, that is, finally, the evolution of the whole of humanity. Yoga is a process of concentrated evolution, and the progression is a geometric one: *The first obscure material movement of the evolutionary Force is marked by an aeonic graduality; the movement of Life progress proceeds slowly but still with a quicker step, it is concentrated into the figure of millenniums; mind can still further compress the tardy leisureliness of Time and make long paces of the centuries; but when the conscious spirit intervenes, a supremely concentrated pace of evolutionary swiftness becomes possible.*[45] We have got there. The paroxysms of the present world are no doubt a sign that the descending Pressure is accelerating and that we are reaching a true solution. *It may well be that, once started, the [supramental] endeavour may not advance rapidly even to its first decisive stage; it may be that it will take long centuries of effort to come into some kind of permanent birth. But that is not altogether inevitable, for the principle of such changes in Nature seems to be a long obscure preparation followed by a swift gathering up and precipitation of the elements into the new birth, a rapid conversion, a transformation that in its luminous moment figures like a miracle. Even when the first decisive change is reached, it is certain that all humanity will not be able to rise to that level. There cannot fail to be a division into those who are able to live on the spiritual level and those who are only able to live in the light that* *descends from it into the mental level. And below these too there might still be a great mass influenced from above but not yet ready for the light. But even that would be a transformation and a beginning far beyond anything yet attained. This hierarchy would not mean as in our present vital living an egoistic domination of the undeveloped by the more developed, but a guidance of the younger by the elder brothers of the race and a constant working to lift them up to a greater spiritual level and wider horizons. And for the leaders too this ascent to the first spiritual levels would not be the end of the divine march, a culmination that left nothing more to be achieved on earth. For there would be still yet higher levels within the supramental realm,* as the old Vedic poets knew when they spoke of the spiritual life as a constant ascent, —*[46]

"The priests of the word climb thee like a ladder,
O hundred-powered. As one ascends from peak to peak,
there is made clear the much that has still to be done."†

After all, we have passed all these centuries in preparing the Base: a basis of security and well-being through our science, a basis of charity through our religions and ethics, a basis of beauty and harmony through our arts, a mental basis of scrupulous exactitude — but this is a *basis for something else.* Absorbed in our effort to act rightly, we see only one angle of the great Work — an angle of terrestrial immortality like the rishis, an angle of eternal permanence like the Buddha, an angle of charity, an angle of well-being, all kinds of angles, but we are not going to play forever with toy-blocks like little children! Nothing of all this is an end, it is a negative condition of the Play, nothing

---

* Sri Aurobindo spoke of three grades or planes of consciousness in the Supermind. Their description does not seem to be required at this stage.

† Rig Veda I.10.1.

has yet begun! What has begun? Perhaps only one thing is awaited: that we become aware of the Play for it to begin. We have exhausted all kinds of adventures since Jules Verne, and they have slowly closed before us; what war, what revolution is yet worth our bleeding for it? our Everests are deflowered and the high seas well guarded — everything is foreseen, regulated, even the stratosphere. Perhaps to lead us towards the one single opening in this more and more suffocating world. We have believed ourselves myopic, little moles on the star, and we have corrected the great Eye within and our world-spanning wings by a steely machinery which crushes and crushes us. Perhaps to compel us to believe in ourselves as much as in our machines and that we can do better than they. "They go round and round, battered and stumbling, like blind men led by one who is blind," said the Upanishad long ago.* Is it not time to cast a glance over our constructions and to begin the Play? instead of turning over shovels and pickaxes, gospels and neutrons, to turn over the consciousness and cast this seed on the winds of time that life may begin?

> O Force-compelled, Fate-driven earth-born race,
> O petty adventurers in an infinite world
> And prisoners of a dwarf humanity,
> How long will you tread the circling tracks of mind
> Around your little self and petty things?
> But not for a changeless littleness were you meant,
> Not for vain repetition were you built...
> Almighty powers are shut in Nature's cells.
> A greater destiny awaits you in your front...
> The life you lead conceals the light you are.[47]

* Mundaka Upanishad I.2.8.

And if one glances over the wall, everything is there, already, awaiting only our wanting it:

> *I saw them cross the twilight of an age,*
> *The sun-eyed children of a marvellous dawn...*
> *The massive barrier-breakers of the world...*
> *The architects of immortality...*
> *Bodies made beautiful by the Spirit's light,*
> *Carrying the magic word, the mystic fire,*
> *Carrying the Dionysian cup of joy...*[48]

*   *   *

The Iron Age is Ended[49]

The conditions of the age of Truth may seem severe — this perilous descent into the Inconscient, the battle against the Shadow, the threatening Death; but have we not risked our lives for more futile endeavours? *Man's greatness is not in what he is, but in what he makes possible,*[50] says Sri Aurobindo. The Victory must be gained *once*, in one body. When one single person will have won that Victory, it will be a victory for all men and in all the worlds. For this little earth, apparently so insignificant, is the symbolic ground of a battle which is fought through all the cosmic hierarchies, even as the conscious human being is the symbolic ground of a battle contested in all men — if we conquer here, we conquer everywhere; it is we who deliver the dead and we who deliver life. We are, each of us, through our becoming conscious, the builders of the heavens and the redeemers of the earth. That is why this life on the earth assumes an exceptional importance among all our modes of living, why also the guardians of the

Falsehood persist in preaching to us the beyond. *One must hurry up and do one's work here,* says the Mother, *for it is here that one can really do it. Hope for nothing from death, life is your salvation. It is there the transformation must be achieved; it is on earth that you progress, it is on earth that you realise. It is in the body that the Victory is won.* Then the law of evolution will no longer be that of contraries which pursue us to wrest us from our human childishness, but a law of light and endless progress — a new evolution in the joy of the Truth. The Victory must be gained once. *One* glorious body, one single body must break the iron law for all bodies, this is necessary. And the collaboration of all men to achieve this single Victory. The strategic difficulty of the transformation is fully before us. *If earth calls and the Supreme answers, the hour can be even now.**

---

* Extract from a posthumous collection of Sri Aurobindo's writings: *The Hour of God,* p. 61.

THE END WHICH EVER BEGINS AGAIN*

The realisation of the Vedic rishis has become a collective realisation; the Supermind has entered the earth-consciousness, descended right down into the physical subconscient, at the frontiers of Matter; there remains but one bridge to cross for the final linking up. *A new world is born. At present we are right in the midst of a transitional period in which the two are mingled: the old world persists, yet all-powerful, continuing to dominate the ordinary consciousness, and the new one slips in quietly, yet very shy, unobserved to the extent that externally it changes little for the moment.... And yet it works, it grows, till one day it will be sufficiently strong to impose itself visibly*. All the difficulties are not of a subconscient order.

There is one, very conscious, which puts up a door of bronze before the new world, and this is not our materialism as we would like to think — scientists, if they are sincere, will perhaps be the first to emerge into the Truth — but the enormous spiritual carapace under which we have entombed the Spirit. The real trick of the devil is not to get hold of falsehood or hatred and sow them abroad throughout the world as Attila and the Nazis did — he is much too shrewd for that — but to get hold of a bit of the truth and give it a little twist. Nothing is harder than a perverted truth; falsehood inherits all the power of the truth it encloses. We have been told repeatedly that salvation is in heaven — and it is true, there is no salvation

* *Savitri*, p. 333.

for man as long as his nose is buried in Matter; his salvation is in the superconscient heaven, and probably it was necessary to preach to us the heavens, to begin with, to pull us out from our first evolutionary gangue, animal and economic — but this is only a first stage of evolution which we have made into an ultimate end, hard like stone. And now this end turns upon us. We have denied the Divinity in Matter to shut it up in our holy places and Matter takes its revenge — we have called it brute matter, and brute it is. As long as we accept this Disequilibrium, there is no hope for the earth; we shall oscillate between one pole and the other, both equally false, from material enjoyment to spiritual austerity, without ever finding fulfilment. *The ancient intellectual cultures of Europe ended in disruptive doubt and sceptical impotence, the pieties of Asia in stagnation and decline.*[1]* We need the vigour of Matter, need too the fresh waters of the Spirit, but our materialisms are stupefying and our beliefs only the inverse of our disbeliefs. *The Atheist is God playing at hide-and-seek with Himself; but is the Theist any other? Well, perhaps; for he has seen the shadow of God and clutched at it.*[2]

If we want to heal this Disequilibrium, and all that is in disequilibrium perishes in our bodies, our societies or our cosmic cycles, we must see clearly. We have lost the Password, this is the "balance" sheet of our era, we have replaced the true power by artifices, the true wisdom by dogmas. It is the reign of the gnomes, on all the planes. And it will be more and more the reign of gnomes if we do not put a stop to these mortifying half-truths, from above or below, and plunge into the true source, Within, and find once again the practical secret of the Spirit in Matter.

* This was written in 1914. Perhaps things have improved since then? It is not too evident.

"That which is immortal in mortals...is a god and established inwardly as an energy working out in our divine powers" (Rig Veda IV.2.1). Knowing this Secret, neither the rishis nor the sages of the ancient Mysteries made this terrible division which saps us — "our Father the sky, our Mother the earth"; they did not cut away the difficulty by committing to the beyond our perfection and our plenitude — "Let us conquer even here, let us run this battle-race of a hundred leadings". Having reached the summit of consciousness they did not faint away into a pale ecstasy: "I am a son of Earth, the soil is my mother..." (Atharva Veda XII. 1); having reached the confines of the Infinite they did not find the small things here small: "O Godhead, guard for us the Infinite and lavish the finite" (Rig Veda IV.2.11), "May we speak the beauty of thee, O Earth, that is in thy villages and forests and assemblies and wars and battles" (Atharva Veda XII.44.56). They strove, they were invincible, for they knew that God is in us: "O Son of the body... full of happiness and light, victorious, to whom no hurt can come" (III.4.2,9.1). A conquering truth of upright men for whom death is a falsehood and a defeat. A truth of divine joy upon the earth. No doubt their truth was premature for the hordes of Europe who needed to hear about the heavens before the earth, but the time is perhaps come, at last, to unveil the Mysteries, whether Vedic, Orphic, Alchemical or Catharist, and to find once more the complete truth of the two poles in a *third position* which is neither that of the materialists nor that of the spiritualists: *The ascent of man into heaven is not the key, but rather his ascent here into the spirit and the descent also of the spirit into his normal humanity and the transformation of this earthly nature. For that and not some post mortem salvation is the real new birth for which humanity waits as the crowning movement of its long obscure and painful course.*[3]

It is a message of hope that Sri Aurobindo brings us. Our balance-sheet of the gnomes, finally, is only the sign of a new emergence; always our shadows and declines are the gestation of a greater light which had to descend to break the limits; and there are but two ways of breaking the limits, by excess of light or excess of shadow, but the one precipitates our night into the light and dissolves it, the other precipitates the light into our night and transmutes it. The one sets free some individuals, the other liberates the whole earth. Ten thousand years ago some giants among men had wrenched the Secret of the world, surely, but it was the privilege of a few initiates, and we must all be initiates. Ten thousand years ago we lived in the golden age and all seems now plunged into the night, but in truth it is not night which has descended upon the world as the predictors of the End of Time would have us believe, it is the light which has buried itself in the earth: it was necessary that the Secret be forgotten, it was necessary for humanity to descend the nocturnal curve of the age of reason and the religions and, as a whole, to find again the Secret in all adult men, and the light everywhere, under all the nights, all the miseries, all the pettinesses, instead of a high brazier upon some Vedic or Iranian sanctuary. We are at the beginning of the Times; evolution does not describe an arrow-like path, more and more sublime and dissolving, but a spiral: *It is not a tortuous way to come back — a little battered — to the starting-point; it is there, on the contrary, to bring the whole creation the joy of being, the beauty of being, the grandeur of being, and the perpetual development, perpetually progressive, of this joy, this beauty, this grandeur. Then everything takes on a meaning.* An eternal spiral which does not close in any extreme point — the Extreme is everywhere in the world, in every being, every body, every atom — an ascension step by step which goes ever higher, in order to descend lower, embrace more, reveal more. We are at the beginning of the "Vast" which will be always vaster. The pioneers of evolution have already found other grades in the Supermind, a new curve is taken in the eternal Becoming. At every conquered height everything changes, it is a reversal of consciousness, a new heaven, a new earth; the physical world itself will change soon before our incredulous eyes. And this is not perhaps the first change in history, how many must there have been before ours? how many even can be *with* us, if only we consent to become conscious? — *Successive reversals of consciousness which will bring about a richness of creation always new from stage to stage.* Each time the Mage in us turns over his kaleidoscope and all is unexpected, more true, more beautiful. It depends only upon us to see, the joy of the world is at our doors, if only we would want it.

> *Earth's pains were the ransom of its prisoned delight.*
> *....For joy and not for sorrow earth was made.*[4]

This is the Secret. It is there, everywhere, in the heart of the world; this is the "well of honey under the rock", the "childlike laughter of the Infinite" which we are, this the far depth of the luminous Future which pushes our past. Evolution has not come to an end; it is not an absurd round, not a fall, not a vanity fair, it is

> *...the adventure of consciousness and joy.*[5]

Pondicherry
April 14, 1963

REFERENCES

The quotations from the Mother are extracts from *Conversations* published in the *Bulletin of the Sri Aurobindo International Centre of Education* or from unpublished texts. The quotations from Sri Aurobindo are from the following editions and a few journals.

Collected Poems and Plays 1942
Eight Upanishads 1953
Essays on the Gita 1959
The Future Poetry 1953
The Hour of God 1959
The Human Cycle 1949
Hymns to the Mystic Fire 1952
The Ideal of Human Unity 1950
The Ideal of the Karmayogin 1950
Last Poems 1952
Letters of Sri Aurobindo, 3rd Series (on Poetry and Literature) 1949
The Life Divine 1960
Life, Literature and Yoga 1952
On the Veda 1956
On Yoga II, Tomes One and Two (Letters on Yoga) 1958
Poems Past and Present 1952
The Problem of Rebirth 1952
The Riddle of this World 1951
Savitri 1954
Speeches 1952
Sri Aurobindo on Himself and on the Mother 1953
The Superman 1950
The Supramental Manifestation 1952
The Synthesis of Yoga (On Yoga I) 1955
Thoughts and Aphorisms 1958
Thoughts and Glimpses 1950

D. K. Roy *Sri Aurobindo Came to Me* 1952
G. Monod-Herzen *Shrî Aurobindo* 1954
Nirodbaran *Correspondence with Sri Aurobindo*, Vol. I, 1954; Vol. II, 1959
A. B. Purani *Evening Talks with Sri Aurobindo* 1959
Life of Sri Aurobindo 1958

371

CHRONOLOGY

15 August 1872: Birth of Sri Aurobindo in Calcutta.

1877-9: At English boarding school (Darjeeling).

1879-84: Manchester.

1884-90: St. Paul's School, London.

1890-92: King's College, Cambridge.

1892-93: Return to India. Baroda.

1901: Marriage to Mrinalini Devi.

1902: Revolutionary work in Bengal.

1904: Beginning of Yoga.

1906: Leaves Baroda for Calcutta.

December 1907: First meeting with yogi Lele.

4 May 1908: Arrested by the British government.

1908-9: The Alipore Bomb Case.

February 1910: Left Calcutta for Chandernagore.

4 April 1910: Arrival in Pondicherry.

15 August 1914: Starts the *Arya* (monthly philosophical magazine)

24 April 1920: The Mother settles in Pondicherry.

January 1921: Discontinuation of the *Arya*.

1926: Sri Aurobindo goes into retirement.

15 August 1947: Independence of India on Sri Aurobindo's seventy-fifth birthday.

5 December 1950: The passing of Sri Aurobindo.

1952: Inauguration of the Sri Aurobindo International Centre of Education.

BIBLIOGRAPHY

WORKS OF SRI AUROBINDO*

I — Indian Culture

The Foundations of Indian Culture, "Arya" December
    1918-January 1921 (New York)   1st ed. 1953
On the Veda, "Arya" August 1914-July 1916   1st ed. 1956
Hymns to the Mystic Fire   1st ed. 1946
Isha Upanishad (Sanskrit Text with English
    translations and Notes) "Arya" August 1914-May 1915 1st ed. 1921
Eight Upanishads (Sanskrit Text with English
    translations and Notes)   1st ed. 1953
Kena Upanishad (Sanskrit Text with English
    translations and Notes)   1st ed. 1952
Essays on the Gita, "Arya" August 1916-July 1920   1st ed. 1959
The Renaissance in India, "Arya" August 1918-November 1918   1st ed. 1920
The Significance of Indian Art, "Arya" 1918-1921   1st ed. 1947

II — Philosophy-Sociology

The Life Divine, "Arya" August 1914-January 1919   1st ed. 1939
Ideals and Progress, "Arya" 1915-1916   1st ed. 1920
The Superman, "Arya" March 1915-August 1915   1st ed. 1920
Thoughts and Glimpses, "Arya" 1915-1917   1st ed. 1920
Thoughts and Aphorisms   1st ed. 1958
The Hour of God   1st ed. 1959
Evolution, "Arya" 1915-1918   1st ed. 1921
Heraclitus, "Arya" December 1916-June 1917   1st ed. 1941
The Supramental Manifestation upon Earth, (Bulletin 1949)   1st ed. 1952
The Problem of Rebirth, "Arya" November 1915-January 1921   1st ed. 1952
The Human Cycle, "Arya" August 1916-July 1918   1st ed. 1949
The Ideal of Human Unity, "Arya" September 1915-July 1918   1st ed. 1950
On the War, 1914-1918   1st ed. 1944
War and Self-Determination, 1916-1920   1st ed. 1920
Man — Slave or Free? "Karmayogin" 1909-1910   1st ed. 1966

* All the works mentioned here are published by *Sri Aurobindo Ashram Press,* Pondicherry.

III —Yoga

IV — Literature-Poetry-Plays

V — Nationalism

The Ideal of the Karmayogin, "The Karmayogin", 1909-1910	1st ed.	1918
A System of National Education, "The Karmayogin", 1910	1st ed.	1924
The National Value of Art, "The Karmayogin", 1909	1st ed.	1922
The Speeches, 1908-1909	1st ed.	1922
The Doctrine of Passive Resistance, 1907	1st ed.	1948
Bankim-Tilak-Dayanand, 1907-1916-1918	1st ed.	1940
The Brain of India, 1909	1st ed.	1921

> To commemorate Sri Aurobindo's Birth
> Centenary in 1972 the Complete Works
> of Sri Aurobindo have been issued in 30
> volumes. They appear in two editions:
> De luxe and Popular.

WORKS OF THE MOTHER

(translated from French)

Prayers and Meditations, 1912-1919	1st ed.	1941
On Education	1st ed.	1952
The Four Austerities	1st ed.	1953
The Great Secret	1st ed.	1954
The Supreme Discovery, 1910	1st ed.	1944
Words of the Mother (4 series)	1st ed.	1938-52
Some Answers from the Mother	1st ed.	1964
Words of Long Ago	1st ed.	1947
White Roses (Letters, in English)	1st ed.	1964
Conversations, 1929	1st ed.	1931
Questions and Answers, 1950-1951	1st ed.	1972
Questions and Answers, 1953-1955	(being published in the *Bulletin of the International Centre of Education*)	

SOME WORKS ON SRI AUROBINDO

Amrita and Nolini	Reminiscences (*Ashram Press*, 1969)
Chandrasekharam, V.	Sri Aurobindo's "The Life Divine" (*Ashram Press*, 1941)
Chaudhuri, Haridas and Spiegelberg, F.	The Integral Philosophy of Sri Aurobindo (*Allen & Unwin*, London, 1960)
Chaudhuri, Haridas	The Philosophy of Integralism (*Sri Aurobindo Path Mandir*, 1954)
Das, Manoj	Sri Aurobindo in the First Decade of the Century (*Ashram Press*, 1972)
Dutt, Arun Chandra	Light to Superlight (unpublished letters of Sri Aurobindo) (*Prabartak Publishers*, Calcutta, 1972)
Gandhi, Kishor H.	Social Philosophy of Sri Aurobindo (*Sri Aurobindo Society*, Pondicherry, 1965)
Gupta, Nolini Kanto	The Yoga of Sri Aurobindo, 12 Vols. (*Ashram Press*)
	A Century's Salutation to Sri Aurobindo (*Ashram Press*, 1972)
Iyengar, Srinivasa K. R.	Sri Aurobindo: A biography and a history, 2 Vols. (*Ashram Press*, 1972)
Karan Singh	Prophet of Indian Nationalism, a Study of Political Thought of Sri Aurobindo Ghosh 1893-1910 (*Allen & Unwin*, London, 1967)
Maitra, S. K.	The Meeting of East and West in Aurobindo's Philosophy (*Ashram Press*, 1956)
Mitra, S. K.	The Liberator (*Jaico*, Bombay, 1954)
	India — Vision and Fulfilment (*Taraporevala Sons & Co.* Bombay, 1972)
Narayan Prasad	Life in Sri Aurobindo Ashram (*Ashram Press*, 1968)
Nirodbaran	Talks with Sri Aurobindo, 2 Vols. (*Ashram Press*, 1966, 1971)
	Sri Aurobindo: I am here, I am here! (*Ashram Press*, 1952)
	Twelve Years with Sri Aurobindo (*Ashram Press*, 1972)
Pandit, M. P.	Sadhana in Sri Aurobindo's Yoga (*Ashram Press*, 1962)
	Reminiscences and Anecdotes of Sri Aurobindo (*Ashram Press*, 1966)
Pavitra	Education and the Aim of Human Life (*Ashram Press*, 1961)
	The Future Evolution of Man (*Ashram Press*, 1971)

Purani, A. B.	Life of Sri Aurobindo *(Ashram Press,* 1958)
	Sri Aurobindo in England *(Ashram Press,* 1956)
	Evening Talks with Sri Aurobindo, 2 Vols. *(Ashram Press,* 1959)
Rishabhchand	The Integral Yoga of Sri Aurobindo, 2 Vols. *(Ashram Press,* 1953-1955)
	In the Mother's Light *(Ashram Press,* 1967)
Roy, D. K.	Sri Aurobindo Came to Me *(Ashram Press,* 1959)
Sastri, T. V. Kapali	Sri Aurobindo: Lights on the Teachings *(Sri Aurobindo Library,* Madras, 1948)
Satprem	Sri Aurobindo or The Adventure of Consciousness *(Ashram Press,* 1968)
	On the Way to Supermanhood *(to be published)*
Sethna, K. D.	The Poetic Genius of Sri Aurobindo *(Ashram Press,* 1947)
	Sri Aurobindo, The Poet *(Ashram Press,* 1970)
	Overhead Poetry *(Ashram Press,* 1972)
Tehmi	Sri Aurobindo — The Story of His Life *(Ashram Press,* 1972)
Varma, V. P.	The Political Philosophy of Sri Aurobindo *(Asia,* Bombay, 1960)